D0438007

ALICE

Works by Howard Teichmann

Books

ALICE: The Life and Times of
Alice Roosevelt Longworth

SMART ALECK: The Wit, World and Life
of Alexander Woollcott

GEORGE S. KAUFMAN:
An Intimate Portrait

Plays

A RAINY DAY IN NEWARK

JULIA, JAKE AND UNCLE JOE

THE GIRLS IN 509

MISS LONELYHEARTS

THE SOLID GOLD CADILLAC
(with George S. Kaufman)

PRENTICE-HALL, INC. □ ENGLEWOOD CLIFFS, N.J.

Alice: The Life and Times of Alice Roosevelt Longworth,
by Howard Teichmann

Printed in the United States of America
Prentice-Hall International, Inc., London
Prentice-Hall of Australia, Pty. Ltd., Sydney
Prentice-Hall of Canada, Ltd., Toronto
Prentice-Hall of India Private Ltd., New Delhi
Prentice-Hall of Japan, Inc., Tokyo
Prentice-Hall of Southeast Asia Pte. Ltd., Singapore
Whitehall Books Limited, Wellington, New Zealand
10 9 8 7 6 5 4 3

Library of Congress Cataloging in Publication Data
Teichmann, Howard.
Alice, the life and times of Alice Roosevelt Longworth.
Bibliography: p.
Includes index.
1. Longworth, Alice Roosevelt, 1884-
2. Presidents—United States—Children—Biography.
3. Roosevelt, Theodore, Pres. U.S., 1858-1919—Family.
I. Title. E757.3.T44 973.9'092'4[B] 79-12512
ISBN 0-13-022210-0

CONTENTS

□

To the Memories of
My Mothers,
Kitty and Rose,
who followed Alice's
every adventure
and to
My Fathers,
Jack and Joseph,
whom I disappointed by
not voting the straight
Republican ticket

□ THE INTRODUCTION

lice Longworth was the Jackie Kennedy of her day," Iphigene Ochs Sulzberger, the discerning matriarch of *The New York Times*, observed in 1975. "People like someone who has glamour, and for years, Alice provided the glamour and the style in America."

In 1935, the British writer now known as Dame Rebecca West arrived in this country. Of the New Deal's capital, she wrote in the *Times*, "Physically, the city is dominated by the Washington Monument. One sees it when one least expects it, as one wanders about the wooded and pillared streets, its dark white shaft rising into the blue of high heaven, its shadow falling black over furlongs of sward. Intellectually, spiritually, the city is dominated by the last good thing said by Alice Roosevelt Longworth."

Two generations later, the television journalist, Harry Reasoner, told the audience of *60 Minutes*, "It's nice to be invited to the White House, but the real social coup in Washington is to be invited to tea at Alice Roosevelt Longworth's. She has ... lost none of the wit and high spirits that made her such a popular figure during the Presidency of her father, Theodore Roosevelt. She was the teenager most responsible for the generation gap of 1901. Since then, her candid and sometimes outrageous observations on the American Presidency have livened up otherwise dull Washington dinner parties."

Recently, the eminent editor and historian of the Washington scene, Jonathan Daniels, wrote, "Beside her in our history Dolley Madison was just a manikin. ... Alice was a super pixie between those self-announced battlers for the Lord, her father and Eleanor."

Another Washington based observer, Sally Reston, believes that, "Her house on Massachusetts Avenue is fascinating, but it's Alice herself, so blunt and witty, who's the magnet. She is the true symbol of Washington."

Almost half of this nation's history has been played out during the days of this remarkable woman's life. She is both an institution and a deliciously piquant reparteeist. She is, I believe, worthy of study. Alice Roosevelt Longworth is eternally courageous, provoking, cynical, logical, impossible, incredible, and rebellious to the point of doing just what she pleases. And no more.

She always has viewed life from a front-row seat. Occasionally, she has leaped onto the stage to play a variety of roles: daughter, sister, wife, mother, widow, author, commentator, columnist, wit, critic, and darling of the Washington scene.

Quite often she has been the center of wild controversy, and for eighty of her ninety-five years, more than one whiff of scandal has trailed after her as a heavy perfume might drift in the summer night before a storm.

She has witnessed most of the principals in almost a century of strife, turmoil, war, economic disasters, and social changes with an unperturbed look. Often, as expressionless as a Sphinx, her blue eyes have taken in everything.

Directly related to two American Presidents, her father, Theodore Roosevelt, and her fifth cousin, Franklin Delano Roosevelt, she has had contacts with the

Royal Houses of Great Britain, Germany, Italy, Spain, China, and Japan. Her friendships extend to the nobility of France, the Presidents, Vice-Presidents, and Speakers of the House of Representatives of the United States.

She is a law unto herself. No one in Washington comes close to her by comparison.

She can use her words like weapons. So swift is her attack that her victims frequently never know the daggers have been plunged in and withdrawn before they feel the pain.

Alice Roosevelt Longworth also can be the most charming, fascinating, and amusing person with whom anyone might wish to chat. She is unpredictable—she sometimes snubs the famous for the infamous. Like most of the Roosevelts, in her prime, Alice had the energy of ten active, healthy children.

It isn't exact to call her a school dropout; she only attended school for a couple of months in her entire life. She is self-educated and better read than most college professors. Her interests are intense. She enjoys everything except dull people. June Bingham wrote in the *American Heritage* magazine, "Mrs. L. has a low boring point."

Politics have been nourishment to Mrs. Longworth. She would have starved without them. That's why Washington is her town.

She has a distinct dislike for the title "Princess Alice," a phrase coined by the American press. She also holds a lengthy list of abhorrences and preferences. She is quick to tick them off. Contempt for many high officials is balanced by her devotion to her friends and family.

Almost unbridled is her love for her granddaughter, Joanna Sturm. These two, the ninety-five-year old and the thirty-four-year old, are a matchless pair. One was born in the age of horses and buggies and only fifteen years after the Union Pacific Railroad had met the Central Pacific at Promontory Point, while the other was born in the age of rockets and SSTs that fly the Atlantic in three and a half hours.

Trying to interview people about Alice Roosevelt Longworth was a bit like crossing a minefield. Dangerous. At any time, at any place, any one of the subjects might explode.

"That woman!"

"Never!"

"Are you crazy?"

"Well, I'll tell you one story, but for *God's* sake, don't mention my name."

"But she's a frail, old lady, now," they'd be reminded.

"Maybe her body's frail, but her mind is like a computer, and her verbal alacrity. . . . Well, I'd rather face a loose woman with a loaded gun."

A reassuring factor about the gun and Mrs. Longworth is that with both there are instances when the safety catch is on.

One liberal lady said, "As she grew older, Mrs. Longworth hated crowds. Perhaps, that's the reason she was not infatuated with the masses. The rich and famous always come in smaller groups."

What follows is a collection of the famous, the rich, and those other esteemed persons who were kind enough to help with this project.

In the very beginning, when the task ahead seemed enormous, Iphigene Ochs Sulzberger stood firm in her belief that Alice was an ideal subject for a new biography. Mrs. Sulzberger spoke fondly of her Washington friend, *so* fondly that I was persuaded to go ahead with the project. I thank Iphigene Ochs Sulzberger for her staunch aid and interest.

To the executive editor of *The New York Times*, A. M. Rosenthal, I am indebted for the use of the *Times* morgue, that research and microfilm section which dates back to the year Alice Roosevelt was born.

I am obliged to Richard Hardwood, deputy managing editor, and to William Hifner, librarian of the Washington *Post* for the many photographs and photocopies of material dealing with Mrs. Longworth.

Credit must go to William Ewald, assistant managing editor, features, New York *Daily News*, for his aid and support. To Lee Major, archivist for the Chicago *Tribune*, goes my appreciation for the many articles and photographs she dug up.

I must acknowledge the many contributions made by John Fink, editor of *Chicago*, as well as those of Peter Elkind for the material gathered in the library of the Cincinnati *Enquirer*. Additional thanks must go to Mike Moore of the Milwaukee *Journal* for the material on T.R.'s attempted assassination. And to Andrew Leslie of the Dramatist Play Service for a copy of the Kaufman–Dayton comedy, *First Lady*. Also, to Anne Kaufman Schneider for permission to quote from that play.

I should like to acknowledge the dedicated work and ever-present support of Helen Stark, chief editorial librarian of *The New Yorker*. Thanks should be given to Maureen Torgerson, director of the Washington Office, Associated College of the Midwest, for her successful efforts in obtaining photographs of Mrs. Longworth and her family from the Library of Congress. I am indebted to Dr. William Emerson, of the Franklin Delano Roosevelt Library in Hyde Park, New York, for the correspondence between those first cousins, Alice Longworth and Eleanor Roosevelt, and to Ben Hayes of the Columbus, Ohio, *Citizen-Journal* for his clippings and his recollections of the day Mrs. Longworth was mobbed while unveiling a statue of President McKinley outside the statehouse in Columbus. Thanks, also, to Brigadier General Margaret A. Brewer, director, Division of Information, USMC, for setting in motion the entire resources of the Corps Historical Branch.

At the New York Society Library, Mark Piel, head librarian, and his assistant Rita Atterton were of enormous aid. Also, Robert Palmer, librarian of the Wollman Library of Barnard College receives my appreciation. And to the Butler Library, the Low Library at Columbia University go my thanks. I am also indebted to Rosella Kurkjian, assistant librarian of the Boston *Record-American*, and to Frank Hyatt, of Wide World Photos, Inc., and Carol Fox of the Bettmann Archive. Thanks, also: to Vikki Lovett of Mrs. Jimmy Carter's White House staff. Robert Saudek, president of the Museum of Broadcasting, must be thanked for transcripts of various *60 Minutes* programs as telecast over the Columbia Broadcasting Company's television network, starring Morley Safer, Eric Sevareid, Mike Wallace, and Harry Reasoner. Further gratitude goes to Louise Purslow and Jonathan Aitken of the British Broadcasting Corporation.

In researching a biography such as this, it is necessary to contact by mail, by telephone, by direct personal interview, and when possible, to record on magnetic tape large numbers of relatives and friends of the subject. There can be only one way to list them: alphabetically. It must be noted, however, that for each person whose name appears here, there are at least two who prefer, or, in some cases, demand the discretion of silence with regard to their names.

Since these wishes must be respected, herewith a list of those persons with whom I did communicate: Lucinda Ballard; Simon Michael Bessie; Art Buchwald; Marquis Childs; Richard Coe; Marc Connelly; Daniel Crawford, Researcher Historical Branch, USMC; Charlotte Curtis; Jonathan Daniels; Alfred deLiagre, Jr.; Ethel Roosevelt Derby; Howard Dietz; Eleni Epstein; Dore Freeman; Dr. Martin Gordon, head researcher, Historical Branch, USMC; Ruth Gordon; Melchiorre Grillo; W. Averell Harriman; Helen Hayes; Gunnery Sergeant Robert Hoffman, USMC; Eleanor Howard; Flora Whitney Irving; Jessica Kraft; Joseph Lash; Jack Manning; Flora Whitney Miller; Robert Morgenthau; Mary Perot Nichols; Dr. Remington Patterson; Sally Reston; Archibald Roosevelt, Jr.; Curtiss Roosevelt; Jeanette Roosevelt; Selwa Roosevelt; Ann Safdi; Dr. Stuart A. Safdi; Madalyn Schlezinger; Silas Seadler; Christine Stevens; Roger Stevens; Howard Strickling; Joanna Sturm; Joseph Viola; Thornton Wilder; Roger Wilkins; other friends, acquaintances, and those who depend upon Mrs. Longworth's patronage and choose to remain anonymous.

It is difficult to give ample credit to Dr. Henry Graff, former chairman of the History Department of Columbia University for his knowledge, scholarship, and aid in the final preparation of this book.

I am in the debt of my editor, Robert Sussman Stewart, for his suggestions. To my literary representative, Candida Donadio, goes my thanks for her patience and advice. I will always be obligated to my dear friend, Constance Ernst Bessie, who, with her usual enthusiasm, called frequently with the much-needed and hard-to-find names, addresses, and telephone numbers that were necessary for the completion of this book.

David T. Steckler, whose detailed research on the American Presidents from McKinley through Ford has proved so valuable that he must, without question, receive my gratitude. Lynn R. Steckler, for her ability to provide diversions from the monotony of work, has my everlasting thanks. Eileen Kelly has listened to and transcribed hours of magnetic tape, changing the recorded voices into words legible on paper, I am profoundly grateful.

Finally, Judith T. Steckler, deserves her own private medal. Mrs. Steckler raises two children, works for two surgeons, does her own housework and cooking, and still managed to read and research most of the books, newspapers, and magazines that were of help to me. And then, over and beyond the call of duty, she typed this manuscript, all eight drafts, and in her spare time gave me sympathy, encouragement, and love.

It would be completely impossible to end this introduction without the words that follow. As she has for years, one woman has worked tirelessly and unselfishly beside me. This is not a thank-you—she doesn't want that—it is an acknowledgment to my wife who in reality co-authored this book. In case there are some who do not know her name, it is Evelyn Teichmann.

H.T. □

ALICE

I □ THE DEBUT

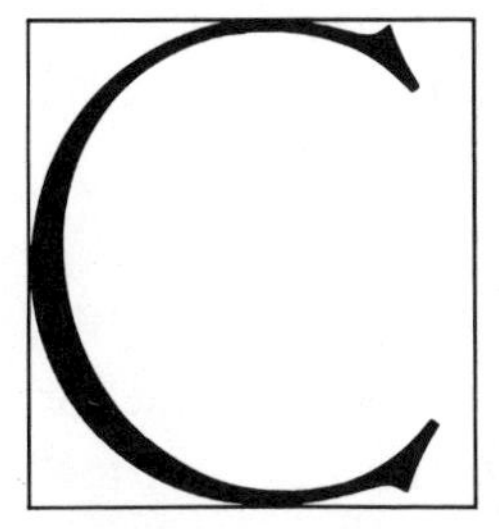

onsider Cinderella. Only the circumstances are slightly altered. Yes, the stepmother is present, but she isn't mean. Nor is the stepsister or the stepbrothers. They are younger than Cinderella and terribly enthusiastic and supportive. But the hearth is there. And so is the fireplace. It's blazing merrily. In Maine, Vermont, Upper Michigan, Minnesota, Nebraska, and Wyoming the temperature on the night of the ball may be considered mild; in Washington, D.C., 15 degrees above zero is crisp and cold.[1]

No need for a fairy godmother. No need for the pumpkin and the white mice. The dance is being held, not in the King's palace but in the White House, and Cinderella's father is the twenty-sixth President of the United States. The Executive Mansion blazes with light. Six hundred guests[2] have been invited, but since this is not a state function, Cinderella's father is not at the head of the receiving line. Instead, rather like the father of the bride at a wedding reception, he mingles with the guests, smiling and pumping their hands. And the cards which summoned the lucky ones are engraved:

Mrs. Theodore Roosevelt[3]
invites you
to
the debut
of
her daughter
Alice
at
The White House on January 3, 1902

Alice Roosevelt, the only child of her father's marriage to Alice Hathaway Lee of Boston, is seventeen years old.

On the outside, she is dashing and beautiful, imperious and independent. She stands five feet seven inches tall and with her upswept hairdo, she has the bearing of a young empress.[4] Her fair skin is flawless, her features strong. She is afraid of nothing except sentimentality. She rides, hikes, swims, shoots as well as her father. On his side, she traces her lineage back to the earliest days of New Amsterdam. On her mother's side she goes back to the *Mayflower*.

Secretly, she is frightened, jealous of her position in the family, loves and resents her mother's successor, Edith Carow, and the children born to that second marriage.[5] She covers this, however, with a mask of grandeur and wit that is already as sharp as the unbuttoned foils with which her father fences.

There will be no Prince Charming on this night. No glass slipper, either. Both the Prince and the slipper will come forth in later years. The Prince will be a bald-headed bachelor from Cincinnati, and eventually he will rise to be Speaker of the House of Representatives. Both he and Alice will set their sights higher, but Herbert Hoover, not Nicholas Longworth, will receive the Republican nomination and the Presidency.

As for the glass slipper, so much a part of the Cinderella story? Wait. It will appear. Right now, the United States Marine Corps Band, resplendant in their special full dress uniforms of sky-blue tunics with scarlet stripes running down their trouser legs, waits for the signal.[6] The bandmaster, whose three chevrons denote the rank of sergeant, finally raises his baton and the band strikes up the first tune. One of the biggest bashes since Dolley Madison danced in the East Room is about to begin.

From the alcove near the Red Room the band plays light, martial airs, while Mrs. Roosevelt, standing before the East Room entrance, presents her daughter to her guests.[7] For the most part, it is a gathering of young people. Young Army and Navy officers turn out in their dress uniforms and decorations. So do the younger members of the diplomatic corps. Although the gowns of the girls are beautiful, there is a marked absence of the lavish display of jewels usually seen at White House functions. Flowers, ribbons, and costly lace take their place. Alice wears virginal white organdy and carries a bouquet of white roses, and when she acknowledges the last of her invited guests, there is a slight pause, the rustle of sheet music is heard, and then the Marine Corps Band changes from 4/4 time into the rhythm of a waltz. It is called "Debutante."[8]

A pause, and then the crowded guests stop chattering to look. Who will claim the first dance with the girl who, in slightly over a year, has become known to the nation as "Princess Alice"? With controlled indifference that borders on the sublime, she slowly hands her flowers to an attendant and waits for her partner. Who will it be?

One of the verses of the "U.S. Marine Hymn" ends with:

> If the Army and the Navy
> Ever look on Heaven's scenes,
> They will find the streets are guarded by
> The United States Marines.

Out from the crush of the crowd steps Major Charles L. McCawley, USMC.[9] He inclines his head slightly, offers his arm to Alice, and sweeps her out onto the dance floor. Hundreds of couples follow them.

McCawley, born in Boston, son of the eighth commandant of the Corps, is her father's military aide.[10] He has seen Alice and the other Roosevelt children on an almost daily basis. Erect and correct, he waltzes her gracefully, knowing full well that the waxed linen crash beneath their feet will soon be replaced by a hardwood floor. It will be a tribute to Alice's charm and persuasiveness.

At her first state dinner, she had been seated next to the Speaker of the House, autocratic, crusty old "Uncle Joe" Cannon. Knowing of her coming-out party, Alice laughed and teased and persuaded the Speaker to have the House appropriate enough money for a dance floor in the East Room. It was only the first of her many personal triumphs and political frustrations, for while the bill for the money passed both House and Senate, thanks to the procrastinations of the Congress, there was not enough time before the coming-out party to install the floor.

Alice smiles this night, but Major McCawley knows that she steams underneath. The White House debutante and her guests are dancing upon a waxed-linen floor.[11]

When the waltz gives way to a two-step, Major McCawley thanks his partner and surrenders her to another young man. Twenty dances are scheduled to be played by the band this night. They range from polkas composed by John Philip Sousa to lancers by Reginald deKoven to Strauss waltzes.[12]

The young men who whirl her about are not unknown to her: Kenneth Robinson, related to her on her father's side; Payne Whitney, a Manhattan cousin; and then there's that very distant relative from upstate

New York.[13] For two years now at family gatherings, at Oyster Bay socials, people have been saying he and Alice would make the ideal couple. She is so beautiful and aristocratic in her carriage, he is so handsome and patrician. He dances with her twice this night, and people speak of it. But they will not marry. He will wed her first cousin Anna Eleanor within two years. And Alice will be Anna Eleanor's maid of honor. And when Alice marries Nick Longworth a year later, Eleanor's husband (she has dropped the Anna), Franklin Delano Roosevelt, will be in the first carriage in line at the White House gate.[14]

Now it is midnight! But Cinderella does not race for home. This *is* home. Instead, she leads her guests through the greenery-festooned East Room, Red Room, and Blue Room to the State Dining Room where tables almost sag under the weight of buffet suppers.

When appetites are satisfied, older guests make their farewells and offer their thanks to the President and Mrs. Roosevelt. But for Alice custom goes by the board. If there is no champagne to drink, just New York State cider ("A humiliation!" she tells her intimates; "And no cotillion, either," she complains),[15] then there *will* be more dancing. A word of entreaty to the band-master, and the waltzing begins anew. Her father is opposed to this, but his strong-willed daughter wishes it in no uncertain terms. And so it is.

A few weeks earlier, Owen Wister, the Philadelphia society author who wrote *The Virginian*,[16] from which almost every cowboy story may be dated, visited the President.

Alice rushed in, said how d'ye do, and raced out. Talk between the two men resumed when suddenly Alice burst in, flung a few words in their direction, and vanished again. The third time she dashed in, her father said, "Alice, the next time you come in, I'll throw you out the window!"

"Why don't you look after Alice more?" Mr. Wister asked after her departure.

"Listen," her father said, "I can be President of the United States—or—I can attend to Alice. I can't do both!"[17]

Shortly after 2 A.M., a truly shocking hour for entertaining in official Washington, the last of the guests depart. This is considered by old timers from the Hill, the cave dwellers, and those-in-the-know on the newspapers, to be the most completely successful affair they can remember.

When she is asked how she likes her coming-out party, Cinderella responds. "I enjoyed it," she says, "moderately."[18]

2 □ THE IDES OF FEBRUARY

The years following the American Civil War were tumultuous. The opening of the West followed the subjugation of the South. The Southerners faced the agony of Reconstruction, carpetbaggers, and the stationing of Federal troops in the former Confederate states. In song, literature, and drama the frontier blazed with guns, cattle drives, and gold strikes. Except for occasional dips in the economy called panics, Americans prospered as never before.

Theodore Roosevelt, born on East 20th Street[1] in New York City in 1858, grew up hearing of the bitter but embellished stories of the Civil War. As time passed, hard feelings gave ground to tales of the gallantry in combat. This proved to be good listening and even better reading for the small, sickly boy who early in life developed poor eyesight and asthma. His father, a well-to-do glass importer, expected little of young Ted, but within the boy himself burned an unknown, unsuspected ambition. Even deeper was his determination to make his body hard and tough.[2]

Although he'd been taken to Europe twice, his real interest lay in the Western part of the United States, in the hard-riding, hard-roping, crack-shooting men who pitted themselves against one another, the elements, and the natural obstacles of endless plains and sky-high mountains.

When he went to Harvard College in 1876, as a science major, young Roosevelt forced himself into the most rugged sports. Baseball, he felt, seemed too easy. He didn't weigh enough for varsity football. Boxing, in his mind, was manly, and he went out for the squad as a lightweight.[3]

At the start of his junior year at Harvard, in 1878, thoughts of the West, of grizzlies and wolves and campfires, left him. He met Alice Hathaway Lee and fell in love, almost at first sight. The place was "the home of Richard Saltonstall, a member of the Dining Club and of Porcellian, and one of Theodore's classmates."[4]

"See that girl?" he demanded of friends some weeks later. "I am going to marry her. She won't marry me but I am going to have *her*!"

Alice Lee, related to the Cabots, the Saltonstalls, and the Higginsons, came from what must have been considered the grandees of Boston society. Ted pursued her the way he did everything in his life: relentlessly. Within the year they became engaged. Within two, they married. Theodore Roosevelt was twenty-two, Alice Lee nineteen.

She had grace, beauty, and a sense of quiet. He had a degree from Harvard.

The skyscraper had yet to appear in New York. The city contained low buildings three to five stories high. Many people still used fireplaces and coal-burning stoves. The chimney sweep remained as important to Manhattan as he had been to Dickens' London. By and large, the streets were paved with cobblestones brought to New York as ballast by the ships that would return to Europe, their holds filled with American farm produce or industrial ware. The poor suffered, the rich grew richer, and the middle class tried as always to "make do."

"A man and his wife rolling cigars seventeen hours a day in a sweatshop," wrote John Kouwenhoven, a historian of New York, "could earn a maximum of fifteen or sixteen dollars in a seven-day week."[5]

With the exception of the old Dutch colony that occupied a small section of the southern tip of the island, all of Manhattan is laid out in a gridiron pattern. Generally speaking, most avenues run north and south, all streets run east and west. Certain streets, by design, are major arteries and are wider than the others: Canal Street, Houston Street, 14th Street, 34th Street, 42nd Street, 57th Street are among them.

The doyens of society occupied the land in the neighborhood of Fifth Avenue and 34th Street. Fifty-seventh Street—near what was then known as The Central Park—fast became a fashionable address. Forsaking East 20th Street with its Dutch stoop, the Roosevelts moved to number 6 West 57th Street.[6]

A man of moderate wealth, Theodore Roosevelt, Sr., lived only until his forty-sixth year, but in that short time, among other things, he founded the Orthopedic Hospital of New York and the Children's Aid Society. His high sense of morality was the most important legacy he left Ted, Jr. He died in 1878, in the house on 57th Street, without ever meeting his son's "sweet Alice Lee."[7]

T.R.'s mother, Martha, *had* met Alice Lee and approved of her. His mother was pleased that after their two-week honeymoon in Oyster Bay, Theodore brought his gentle wife home to live with his family. They were given their own rooms on the third floor, but they took their meals with Ted's mother and sisters. Alice Lee's favorite in-law, T.R.'s sister Anna, nicknamed Bye, was a warm outgoing woman who had the capacity to make the persons she liked feel cuddled and secure.

T.R. recorded in his diary, "Our intense happiness is too sacred to be written about. My cup is almost running over."[8]

Martha (Middie) Roosevelt had hoped that her son would give up his intense interest in nature and his peculiar penchant for writing and choose a solid profession. Roosevelt obliged by entering the Law School at Columbia University.

To the surprise of everyone, he entered politics, too. Long considered a place out of bounds to gentlemen, the political arena—in Manhattan, at least—was occupied by the Democrats who sacked and plundered the city's treasury from their headquarters, Tammany Hall, while at the same time they met the needs of millions of immigrants.

Although his father-in-law and his uncle always voted the straight Democratic ticket, Theodore joined the Republican Party and dropped out of law school. In 1881, he ran for the Assembly, the Lower House of the Legislature in Albany. That a young man of good blood should seek such an office confused his family and amused his friends.[9]

On the first Tuesday after the first Monday in November, Theodore Roosevelt won his first election. He and Alice moved to Albany in January. After poking about through the lazy Hudson River town, T.R. proceeded to the legislature. In pince-nez eyeglasses and evening clothes, he attended the Republican caucus. He found conditions there a bit discouraging.

"The Republicans are bad. But at least they have numbers of lawyers and farmers among them," his diary revealed, "The Democrats include six liquor sellers, two bricklayers, a butcher, a tobacconist, a pawn broker, and a typesetter.... Worse yet, twenty-five are Irish."

He laughed about that last observation, because, as his biographer William Henry Harbaugh wrote, "Before the end of the five month session he was to form strong friendships with several Irish Democrats...."[10]

In 1883, Alice Lee told T.R. what he had been waiting to hear. She was pregnant. No more Albany. Not for Alice. Back into the big townhouse on West 57th Street she went—up into the third-floor bedroom she shared with her husband when he was in town.

In the state capital, Democrats and Republicans listened with interest to freshman Assemblyman Roosevelt. Publicly, he circulated and legislated successfully. Privately, he fretted over the health of his wife and the forthcoming birth of his child. Each week he took the train from Albany to Manhattan to be with his family. Alice appeared to be well. She became closer to Theodore's sister Corinne, Mrs. Douglas Robinson, who had recently given birth to a small son. There was no hint of impending tragedy, merely a touch of discomfort most women experience in the ninth month of their pregnancies.[11]

On Tuesday evening, February 12, 1884, a girl was born. Alice survived the ordeal and seemed to be in good health. In Albany, his fellow legislators gathered around Theodore Roosevelt and offered their congratulations. "On Abraham Lincoln's birthday. A fine sign," said the Speaker.[12] But a second telegram arrived shortly after the congratulations saying that Alice had taken a "sudden turn." A worried Roosevelt caught the last train for a New York engulfed in heavy fog. At 10:30 P.M. he arrived at 6 West 57th Street. His stunned brother Elliott blocked the doorway, greeting him with the words, "There is a curse on this house! Mother is dying, and Alice is dying, too."[13]

Hurrying up to her room on the third floor, Theodore Roosevelt found a young wife, in a mahogany four-poster bed, who was barely able to recognize him. He held her in his arms. Later in the hall he questioned the doctor.

"Bright's Disease," he was told. Alice suffered from an acute inflammation of the kidneys.

He walked down the stairs to his mother's room. There, her illness had been diagnosed as typhoid fever. Dazed, bewildered, he wandered from his mother's bedside to his wife's. At three o'clock, early on the morning of the fourteenth, Roosevelt stood at the foot of his mother's bed and watched her die. Helplessly, he repeated his brother's words, "There *is* a curse on this house."[14] An upstairs maid turned down the flickering blue gas jet until it merely glowed in the dark.

The next afternoon at two, Alice Lee Roosevelt died, leaving behind a tiny infant and a bereft husband.

Twin horse-drawn hearses arrived in front of 6 West 57th Street on Saturday, February 16. Two rosewood coffins were carried out and driven to the Fifth Avenue Presbyterian Church. The Reverend Dr. John Hall conducted a brief service. He prayed for the husband and the three-day-old infant. At the end, Dr. Hall himself broke down and wept.

Later, Roosevelt entered the following in his diary, "For joy or for sorrow, my life has now been lived out."[15]

In memory of her mother, the child was named Alice. Her father, somehow, returned to Albany, leaving his daughter in the hands of nurses who were supervised by his female relatives. He was a man broken in spirit and heart, and when the legislative session concluded, he fled West into the Badlands of the Dakota Territory to try to regain a reason for living.

When he sat alone those nights and looked into the inky sky that hung over the Dakotas, the autumn after Alice Lee's death, Theodore put on paper the anguish he felt.

"She was beautiful in face and form, and lovelier still in spirit: as a flower she grew, and as a fair young flower she died. . . ."[16]

In his grief, Theodore Roosevelt couldn't see the clearing ahead. And he couldn't possibly have envisioned that the baby far away in New York would grow up to be one of the fairest and heartiest flowers in all of American womanhood.

3 □ THE BELLE ON THE BICYCLE

Baby Alice was cherished by Auntie Bye and visited now and then by Theodore. Infrequently, she looked into his sad intense eyes—mostly she stared at his broad back after he said good-bye to her. Sometimes, Alice saw a wave of his large hand. He *never* mentioned her mother. She did not understand why. "The only rational explanation that I have heard," wrote Nicholas Roosevelt, "is that T.R.'s determination to regard his first marriage and his life with Alice Lee as a chapter never to be reread was so great that he deliberately buried it in the recesses of his memory forever."[1]

Theodore Roosevelt had escorted a particular girl to social affairs and outings since he was a young man. The family assumed that the couple would announce their engagement after his graduation from college. Her name was Edith Kermit Carow. Roosevelt referred to Edith as "Her Ladyship" and he agreed with his sisters who said that, "Edith has good days and bad days."[2]

Her moods were as changeable as the colors of a Western sky: kind and considerate at times, irritable and irrational at others. Nevertheless, T.R. thought her intelligent, cultured, and "up-to-date on current events."

When Alice Lee died in 1884, Edith Carow suddenly started to pay more calls on T.R.'s sisters. Corinne now lived in not-too-easy-to-get-to New Jersey with her husband.[3] The maiden lady, the other sister, kindly Bye, resided in a more convenient place—a townhouse on Manhattan's upper Madison Avenue in the same block with the now famous Clarence Day family.[4]

The despondent Theodore did not at first want to look at other young women or share their company. Pleasure during the months following Alice Lee's death made him feel guilty. Avoidance of females became the order of T.R.'s life.

One afternoon, however, in the Madison Avenue townhouse, the windows open and the curtains billowing gently, Theodore stomped across his sister's threshold. To his surprise and annoyance, he found his former childhood playmate, Edith Carow.[5]

The annoyance had no lasting effect, for within three weeks, the couple became secretly engaged. In the late winter of 1886 they sailed for London. Staying at separate hotels, they readied themselves for the nuptials in a registry office. "Theodore Roosevelt, Gentleman," as he was listed on the books of that Office, and "Edith Kermit Carow, Spinster," as she was listed, prepared for their union. On December 2, 1886, Edith Carow and Theodore Roosevelt were married in London.[6]

In January 1887 as the winter sun brightened Auntie Bye's comfortable home on Madison Avenue in New York, Alice was introduced to her new mother.[7]

The three-year-old Alice wore high-buttoned shoes, a party dress with a silk sash and carried a bouquet of pink roses which she presented—as she had been instructed—to Edith Roosevelt.[8] Both adult and child were on their best behavior.

To protect Alice and her beloved aunt from the trauma of good-byes, Teddy sent his daughter to her maternal grandparents at Chestnut Hill, Massachusetts, for a few weeks. When she returned to the Roosevelt country home in Oyster Bay in July, it was to a stricter, more formal household. Her stepmother was already pregnant with the first of her five children. More was made of Edith's condition than of Alice's.[9]

But the daughter of Alice Hathaway Lee, while she accepted her new mother and later her brothers and sister, would always feel slightly different. Not better, but special. She was, after all, the child of the *first* marriage, and as the years when on, certain privileges accrued to her. A trust fund had been set up for Alice, and the interest allowed her to buy extra clothes and gifts for herself and those about her.

The Boston Lees even sent a pony, which she named General Grant after a pony her father had once owned. T.R. insisted that when Auntie Bye was nine years old, she found it a strange coincidence that there had been a man who had been named after her brother's pony.[10]

Alice visited her grandparents each spring and fall of her childhood. In Massachusetts, the round-faced child with a ribbon in her hair, and blue wonder in her eyes, was pampered and catered to as tangible evidence of her late mother having walked upon this earth.

"I was spoiled and made much of to my heart's content," Alice said, and she admitted that the first few nights back home she always could, "... taste the tears with my bread and butter."[11]

Until Alice reached her tenth year, she suffered from the feeling of not belonging, and certain apprehensions of being unloved. She didn't identify completely with either the Lee or the Roosevelt family. The resulting effects were twofold: Alice had to fight shyness for many of her days, and she attacked people sharply as a defense against being rejected. The positive side of Alice's betwixt and between life showed itself in her early independence and rebellion.

The years 1886 and 1887 had been emotionally rewarding but financially ruinous to Roosevelt. When he went out West originally, besides hunting and studying nature, he had invested over $50,000 in land, cattle, a ranch house and other buildings. In '86 a drought dried up his acreage, killed much of his livestock, and a fire burned down his ranch buildings.

The winter of '87 was as severe as any Westerner could remember. That was the end. T.R. sold his holdings and warned Edith, "Be nice to Alice. We might have to borrow money from her one day."[12]

By the time her father celebrated his thirtieth birthday, he was a dedicated politician. Early in her life he had run for the office of mayor of New York. In a three-way race, he came in third. Henry George, the "Single Taxer," came in second. Elected was Abram S. Hewitt, a Regular Party Democrat.[13] In politics, as happens so frequently, the loser doesn't lose. President Benjamin Harrison appointed Roosevelt a member of the Civil Service Commission, and off he and his family went to Washington, D.C. Harrison, the twenty-third President, was the first Chief Executive Alice ever met.

This was Alice's first encounter with the city she would love and which, in turn, would love her. Alice thought of Washington as a delightful village—very different from New York. There was none of the hustle and bustle and overcrowding of Manhattan. Instead, fewer people, less noise, the pace of pedestrians and horse-drawn carriages were considerably slowed down, much like that of a small Southern city. The smell of salt from the tidal marshes on which Washington had been built was almost always in the air. Great flocks of birds whirled and turned in the sky, apparently ignoring the presence of life below.

The major problem for Alice, in those days, was the brittleness of the Roosevelt bones. Her first cousin, Anna Eleanor, had to wear an iron back brace, brother Kermit an ankle brace. Regularly before bedtime, Alice's mother stretched her legs in a steel mechanism attached to her lower extremities.[14] Until thirteen, which seemed forever to Alice, she was ordered by the physician to wear leg braces from the knees down to the ankles. To her humiliation, while running or even walking, the braces frequently locked and threw Alice to the hard ground.[15] They accomplished their purpose. Alice became one of the Capital's most tireless walkers. Her strides were long, her steps were fast.

After six years with the Civil Service, the Roosevelt family was uprooted once again and returned to New York, where Alice's father joined the board of police commissioners, and became its head. Although he was known as a reformer, Theodore Roosevelt was able to work within the establishment.[16] He made the best police commissioner New York has ever had. To this day, a portrait of him hangs in the office of the police commissioner of New York City.

Alice Lee and Theodore had worked on plans for a country home. Edith and Theodore finished them.[17] Summers, weekends, and holidays were spent at Sagamore Hill, a large wooden house atop a knoll overlooking Long Island Sound. It was a rambling place that eventually would be filled with four boys, two girls, and countless trophies of their father's skill as a hunter. The smallest room on the second floor was reserved for Alice.[18] It was Spartan with a narrow bed, a bureau, a small desk, and racks of books. What appealed to Alice was the secret door that opened into the boys' room. The slightly slanted roof outside the boys' window supported a wooden ladder that Alice used whenever she wished to escape at night.

Hermann Hagedorn wrote about the childhood happenings at Sagamore Hill in a particularly engaging way. Obviously, the stories he related about the Roosevelt children were the often-repeated tales that the family enjoyed handing down over the years.

There was the day of Kermit's christening. Mame Ledwith, the number-one children's nurse, assigned Alice the task of keeping Ted, Jr., quiet. It could not be done. The three-year-old boy was overcome by excitement. During the ceremony, he pointed to the Reverend Mr. Washburn's white surplice and blurted out, "Why is that man wearing Mame's dress?" After Alice calmed her young brother, the "baby in the blanket" started to cry. Ted, Jr., yanked himself free of his sister, and happily and loudly announced to the assemblage, "Baby bruvver Kermit meows!" The solemnity of the occasion evaporated.[19]

Then came the evening when Ted, Jr., felt overcome by his own physical shortcomings in comparison to his father. After looking in a mirror, he wailed, "Ted got no mufstache. Ted got nothin' but a mouf!"[20]

Following Ethel's birth in August 1891, Alice felt she had been patient with her parents long enough. "How do little babies come?" she demanded of Edith. "God sends them. No one knows exactly how," her mother replied automatically in the usual way for 1891.[21]

Alice decided that, being the eldest child, she owned the apple orchard. Her siblings accepted her terms completely. Each one rented a tree from her and paid for it annually by climbing up at Alice's bidding and picking the fruit for their older sister. This form of indentured servitude continued until they were well into their teens, and apparently no one complained, neither Alice, the landlord, nor her brothers and sister, the happy tenants.[22]

A flood of newspaper reporters poured onto the grounds of Sagamore Hill to question T.R. after his overwhelming victory in the Spanish-American War. A man from the *Herald* grabbed little Archie and asked, "Where's the Colonel?" The confused young man replied honestly. "I don't know where the Colonel is, but Father is taking a bath."[23]

Colonel Roosevelt believed in strict discipline in the Army and at home. Kermit and Ethel played together often and fought with each other frequently. Ethel liked to bite—hard—any bare spot she could find on her brother. One afternoon, Kermit—in desperation—kicked Ethel with the iron brace he wore on his ankle. Father appeared with the punishment. First, a lecture, then T.R. picked up the sinner and shook him vigorously. Tears streamed down Ethel's anguished face. "Shake *me*, Father," she implored. "*Please*, shake *me*."[24]

Once when twelve-year-old Alice and seven-year-old Kermit visited Auntie Bye in Farmingdale, Long Island, they ventured far away, became confused about their directions, and wound up in a swamp. Their aunt sent out a search party for the children, but no one thought to look in the swamp because they had been warned never to go there. After a few hours of anxiety and fright, Kermit whimpered his main concern, "What will Father say when he hears that two of his children have drowned?"[25] Alice told her brother, "Father will be furious, so we *have* to survive."

Alice's father supported William McKinley for President in 1896. After McKinley's election came another appointment: Theodore Roosevelt, Assistant Secretary of the Navy. It was back to Washington.

There, talk of tantrums emerged from the children's quarters. The other Roosevelt daughter was easy to manage, and so were the boys; the cries came from Alice.

The child, whose mother dies shortly after giving birth, feels guilt—as though in some inexplicable way, the newly born babe is responsible for the death. The infant, and later the child, feels irrational hate at being deserted. How could a loving mother deliberately die and absent herself from her parental obligations? And then, there are mixed attitudes toward the survivor—some days, jealous affection mixed with concern that the lone parent also might suddenly disappear. Other days, antagonism aimed at the father, so stern and demanding at times, it's *his* fault that the mother is not there to fuss over and fondle her. Thus, a child grows up, bitter, suspicious, hostile. The fact that no one, including T.R., ever mentioned her own mother to her, wrote cousin Nicholas Roosevelt, "subtly warped the development of this brilliant but basically unhappy person."[26]

Her brothers taunted her that she did not have the same mother as they. She saw herself as a "chunky" girl, "heavy, awkward" to use her own words.

During the second stay in Washington, Roosevelt presented her with a surprise that helped release her tensions and overcome her timidity. She regained confidence in her once wobbly legs. The gift of a bicycle from her father gave Alice the chance to start atop the hill on Connecticut Avenue and coast clear down to Dupont Circle with her feet on the handlebars. This afforded her the opportunity to join a boys' club; she was the solitary girl member.

Her childhood included more than the recently discovered fun and games. At five years of age, Alice had begun to experiment with various forms of enchantment, witchcraft, and sorcery.

She had heard the tales of superstition from a black-haired, dark-eyed Irish nurse who had helped care for her. Alice stored away the information as a squirrel stores nuts—there would be a time when both could pull out the fruits and use them.

The following is what a man born within a generation of Alice had to say about those persons who have an intense interest in the occult. The founder of psychoanalysis, Sigmund Freud, as interpreted by Dr. Ernest Jones, wrote,

> ... amulets, mascots and talismen ... few people are completely free of superstitious beliefs.... Such beliefs come about through the projection into the outer world of thoughts, fears and wishes, which have undergone repression, not recognizing their presence in his unconscious, and yet feeling signs of their presence, the subject concludes that they are operative in the outer world. It is highly significant that the majority of them can be traced to repressed death wishes, originally against some loved person. Such beliefs operate in the

> most primitive level of the mind, that of animistic magic and belief in the omnipotence of thoughts.[27]

Spells, or "murrains" as Alice referred to them, were called upon to help her in her moments of travail. Belief in little idols, crossed fingers, and similar feats of making "magicks" exist within her to this day. "I was half savage, half civilized. Aren't all children?"[28]

After Edith gave birth to Quentin, the last of her five children, in 1897, family life at the Roosevelts deteriorated. Everyone except T.R. started having symptoms. Ted suffered migraine headaches and then a nervous breakdown. His mother had pain from neuralgia, such pain that she could no longer run the house or manage the children. Alice was "running wild with those boys," and doing poorly in public school. She liked the boys and hated the schooling. Her father finally called in doctors for consultations and conferences and one of the decisions made was that Alice would be better off in New York with Auntie Bye and her husband, Lt. Commander William Cowles of the United States Navy.

It was a sudden decision, with no warning to Alice, but instead of feeling rejection, she took to the plan at once. That is when they promised her she wouldn't have to attend a regular school as her peers did.

Entire vistas opened for Alice—her education came out of books and plays and newspapers and from meeting people in Auntie Bye's front parlor. She turned from tomboy to sophisticate, and like the Count of Monte Cristo, she was ready and the world was hers.

As adolescence bloomed within Alice, an explosion took place in Havana harbor. The United States battleship *Maine* blew up, and America, with some prodding, went to war with Spain.[29]

Hurriedly, her father resigned his post with the Navy Department and, with Leonard Wood, an Army surgeon with the permanent rank of colonel, organized the first United States Volunteer Cavalry. First, as a lieutenant colonel, then when Wood received his general's star, T.R. moved up to colonel. Roosevelt's leadership of the regiment proved spectacular. Cowpunchers and polo players, Western hunters and those who rode to the hounds in red jackets and black caps were united by Alice's father into a regiment known as the Rough Riders.

When the Riders were based in Florida, Alice and the family visited the troop. Immediately, the fourteen-year-old girl, who could sit a horse as well as anyone in camp, became the regiment's favorite. Her father, meanwhile, cut through Army red tape and arranged for his men to move to Cuba. There, in the Battle for San Juan, he ordered his regiment to dismount and impetuously led them up what was called Kettle Hill to victory. The tales of gallantry and glory read by the asthmatic young Roosevelt had come to life.[30]

He returned home an authenticated military hero. Promptly the people of New York State elected him their governor, and Alice rejoined the family.[31]

The Executive Mansion in Albany was notoriously ill-heated and sensationally ugly. Had it not been for her mother's trust fund, Alice might have disappeared into the drabness of that small upstate city.[32] As it turned out, she did not remain there long.

Thomas C. Platt, the Republican boss of New York State, created a new phrase on the American political scene by declaring her father "a perfect bull in a china shop."[33] Theodore Roosevelt's reform measures proved unpopular with politicians of both parties. In the Republican Convention of 1900, the question was not whom to renominate—the incumbent McKinley was the obvious choice—it was who should get the number-two spot on the ticket?[34]

William McKinley's Vice-President, Garrett A. Hobart of New Jersey, had died during the previous year. New York State Republicans saw an excellent chance to "kick upstairs" their obstreperous governor. An appeal to the King Maker of the party, Mark Hanna of Ohio, met with disapproval, and a warning, "To make Roosevelt Vice-President would place but a single life between this madman and the Presidency."[35] Not an unqualified endorsement. The convention ignored Hanna's advice. That fall, McKinley and Roosevelt swept into office.

For Alice, that third trip to Washington was the charm: for the rest of her life, she considered the nation's capital her home.

By tradition, the Vice-Presidency is a passive post. Prestige, perhaps. But power? Never. "Cactus Jack" Garner, himself a Vice-President once, declared, "The office ain't worth a bucket of warm spit."

Circumstances, however, often overrule the words of even the wisest of men. By 1900, American intelligence sources uncovered a group of anarchists based in Paterson, New Jersey. Reports circulated that the anarchists planned to assassinate world rulers in the following order: Austria, England, Italy, Russia, and the United States. A former silk weaver of Paterson, New Jersey, killed King Humbert of Italy.

On September 6, 1901, the Chief Executive of the United States visited the Temple of Music at the Pan-American Exposition in Buffalo, New York. McKinley shook hands with multitudes of admiring Americans. As he reached out to greet one Leon Czolgosz, the crazed man fired two shots from a revolver concealed in his scarf-wrapped right hand. Both shots entered the body of the President.[36]

Alice, who had been crossing fingers and pointing at dates on the calendar, did a victory dance and then promptly pretended indifference.

From the outset, doctors doubted the seriousness of the President's condition. Roosevelt appeared in Buffalo at once but was told to return to his holiday camp, high in New York's Adirondack Mountains, where he was roughing it with his family. Advice from physicians and surgeons attending the President included the suggestion that the Vice-President continue his vacation.

Less than a week later, on September 14, 1901, William McKinley died.[37]

"He's always wanted to be President," Alice admitted with candor. "Now he *is* President. Hurrah, for Daddy!"

Years later she was asked to express her emotion at learning her father was to be Chief Executive of the United States—Alice did not pause. Her answer was "Utter rapture."[38]

4 □ THE WITCH IN THE WHITE HOUSE

Everything came to pass as she decreed. Her father was sworn in as the twenty-sixth President of the United States. The "magicks" had worked. The anarchist had taken care of McKinley, and she felt now that her sorcery could be taken seriously. To the seventeen-year-old Alice it was inevitable that her father should be President.

The Roosevelt family took the train to Washington and waited patiently for the sickly, solitary old Mrs. McKinley to move out of the Executive Mansion and back to Ohio.

Then they charged!* The President, his wife, and the six children. To the new First Family, the Executive Mansion was a great disappointment—Albany on a larger scale. The interior contained furnishings that Alice tartly called "Late Grant and Early Pullman."[1] The outside walls ranged from a dullish buff to an uninspired gray.

At the new President's request, the exterior was painted white and from that time on, official stationery bore the engraved words, "The White House."

When Congress appropriated the funds, architect Stanford White began refurbishing the front of the building.[2] From Salemi, in the province of Trapani near the Sicilian city of Palermo, he imported the master sculptor, Vincenzo Grillo, to carve in marble the capitals

*At that point, Theodore Roosevelt, six weeks before his forty-third birthday, was the youngest President in American history, and possibly the most energetic.

of the pillars around the Executive Mansion. The Sicilian became enraptured with T.R. and even more with his oldest child. "Elegante, bellissima," he would exclaim about Alice.[3]

Concerning the interior of the residence, after the removal of potted palms, stained glass windows, and fading silk[4] screens, the state rooms downstairs were given coats of fresh paint, yards and yards of new wallpaper, and the sense of prominence they deserved. Upstairs, there were bedrooms for all the family, but extensive remodeling had to be done.

With the coming of the Roosevelts, the White House took on an air that it never had before or since. While Theodore infused it with political action, his children shook the building with countless pets, pillow fights, and pranks.[5] When Quentin became ill and confined to his bed, Ethel Roosevelt Derby recalled, his brothers and sisters managed to smuggle his pony, Algonquin, into the White House, and utilizing the elevator, bring the animal into the sick lad's room. This cheered up the ailing brother immensely, but caused consternation among members of the White House staff.[6]

"Ike" Hoover, who gave forty-two years of service as the chief usher of the White House and maintained daily contact with ten Presidents and their families, never saw anything to equal the Roosevelts. Teddy's children "took delight in roller skating, bike-riding and walking on stilts," all over the polished floors of the house.[7]

Ethel Roosevelt Derby confessed in later years that Alice urged them to crawl under the tables at state dinners, "pinching the knees of friends and begging them for food."[8] Consider the effect these below-the-table visits had on official dinner guests. But then, all of her life Alice preferred startling people to boring them.

As the eldest child, as well as the natural leader of the Roosevelt children, Alice brought to Washington—in addition to the idols, amulets, and charms that went with a young witch—a blue macaw named Eli Yale, which rated a room of its own. And for good reason. The bird had a bill that could crack a whiskey glass. Another of her creatures was a snake named Emily Spinach; the Emily was after a thin aunt, the Spinach was because the snake was green.[9] Other Roosevelt pets included an eagle, a cougar, a bear, and a badger. When Emperor Menelik, of Abyssinia, sent them a lion and a zebra, the President ordered the animals delivered at once to the Washington Zoo. His children protested frantically. T.R. remained firm.

The President and Edith arranged for Alice to have the large chamber and dressing room directly across from their own. Alice didn't care for the unattractive old walnut furniture and brass beds, but the ten-year-old Ethel, who had the adjoining room, eyed her older sister's quarters with envy—particularly the bulky dressing table with all the mirrors. She sometimes stole in and used Alice's comb and brush. In the last few months of her life, Ethel recalled that she could still "close my eyes and smell the enchanting scents of that room: powder, soap, lilac sachets, and rose water."[10]

Early in Roosevelt's Administration, Adolph Ochs, publisher of *The New York Times*, journeyed to the capital for a visit with the new President. Shortly after he returned, his daughter received a photograph of the Chief Executive. In the lower right-hand corner, he wrote, "To Miss Iphigene Ochs, a nine year old, Regards, Theodore Roosevelt."[11]

When she was twelve, Miss Ochs and her cousin from Cincinnati, Iphigene Molony Bettman, went to Washington with Jim Molony, who had been an assistant district attorney in Ohio's Queen City and a Republican of unquestioned loyalty to the Party. The young girls were in the Capital to see the sights:

> And somehow—I don't know how it was arranged—but [we] had an interview with the President in his office [the New York Iphigene recalled]. "And we went in there and I remember Uncle Jim talking to the President about Lord knows what, and my cousin and I sat listening.[12]
>
> And then, a secretary came in and said, "Mr. President, I don't like to interrupt you but there are a line of handshakers to see you." And the President said to Uncle Jim, "Just sit down over there and wait. This won't take long." And so we sat on the side near his desk. And these people came in and one man had a little girl about seven or eight. As they came along, the President said, "Wait a moment." And he leaned over and took a rose out of the vase and presented it to the child. As he came back, I remember his saying to Uncle Jim, "Only half a minute, only half a minute to get them for life."

Years later, Iphigene Ochs Sulzberger told this to Alice Roosevelt Longworth. The President's daughter said, "Absolutely typical of my father. The politician every minute."[13]

T.R. was not only a good politician, he was a good parent. Alice still remained under his authority for the moment, and T.R., realizing she possessed a keen mind, " ... made his daughter Alice learn something new out of a book every night before she went to bed, and tell him what it was at breakfast every morning, no matter how late she was out the night before," James Reston, then Washington bureau chief of *The New York Times,* wrote in 1966. "The device worked..."[14] In a relatively short time, she became a mistress of the English language and a master of the art of political banter.

"Little Miss Roosevelt," the press had dubbed her. But "Little Miss Roosevelt" dissolved on the photographers' "wet plates" after her coming-out party. Gone were the white dresses with their pink ribbons. In their place, Alice wore dashing black gowns, sweeping white hats, feathers and plumes and finery that bedazzled Washington.

Alice, Edith, and Edith's secretary shared a secret that amused the three of them. The newspapermen constantly telephoned to inquire about the clothes the female members of the First Family intended to wear. Since the President's salary was then only $50,000 a year, and he conscientiously paid the bills for the debut, the trips, and most other expenses, Alice and her mother did not have large wardrobes in their closets. Alice, as usual, concocted a devilish plan—they designed outfits they didn't own and had the secretary describe them, in detail, to the callers.[15]

"Oh," the secretary would say, "tomorrow night Alice is wearing her beige velvet gown trimmed with orange lace. The satin shoes have been dyed to match the lace. Her mother will probably choose the brown taffeta, low neck and billowing skirt. The slippers will match the moire belt—both will be russet."

Even the yellow-press "Town Topics," which once accused Alice of stripping down to her chemise at a party, never caught on to their secret.

The Gay Nineties generation had grown weary of American girls being packed off to Europe to marry British, French, German, Austrian, Russian, and Italian titles. Americans wanted a title for one of their own, and the rank they settled on was no less than Princess.

The Kaiser sent over his brother, Prince Henry of Prussia, with a request that Alice christen the royal yacht, the *Meteor.* Alice was flattered and thought it sounded like fun. "My major preoccupation was to have a good time." Roosevelt, not being a particular admirer of the Germans, was irked and refused to allow her to make a speech, but grudgingly gave permission for the christening. The public read the papers and decided the Prince from Germany had come to the United States to propose marriage to "Our Alice." That's when it started. From then on, she became Princess Alice.

Large enough to contain much of the world's maritime shipping and all of its naval vessels, the natural harbor in New York's upper bay berthed the American-built royal German yacht. On Shooter's Island, tucked away hard by the New Jersey shore, in a pouring rainstorm, Alice Roosevelt hurled a bottle of French champagne at the Kaiser's pleasure boat.

After luncheon, her parents returned to Washington, and Alice, with her royal escort, stopped in New York.[16]

If the Prince *did* ask for her hand, she must have said no. The only engagement the Roosevelts announced was that the Prince had taken Alice to the Metropolitan Opera that same night.

Alice had amber-colored hair, remarkably gray-blue eyes (postman color, she called them),[17] and an imperious lift to her chin. For the cameras, she smiled infrequently in her early days as a Princess. Behind her cool facade lay more than a trace of sensitivity, and when countless newspaper cartoons depicted her father's face dominated by a sparkling if large-toothed smile, young Alice decided the artists of the tabloid press should not capture her likeness in that manner. The result was that, while she posed for countless photographs, she rarely beamed, and almost never laughed in front of the shutters.

Her moods swung between impetuous gaiety and sullen withdrawal. In the theater, it would have been called type casting. Alice not only *looked* the part, she *was* the daughter of an immensely popular President. Her energies matched his and when certain advantages came her way, despite her father's wish, she accepted them—regally.

Alice made the transition from gamine to great lady with remarkable ease. Her father's personality included boldness. His daughter had it, too. But the quality that greased the skids for Alice was not birth or position but charm. She became both mischievous and formidable at the same time. With a sharp mind and a quick tongue she took sass from nobody and feared no man. And men clustered about Alice, seven deep at parties, her Aunt Corinne said.

Within four years, Princess Alice became the most photographed person in the world. She was considered wild, "fast," uncontrollable. She smoked, supposedly used powder and rouge on her face, bet on horse races, and sat on grand pianos. She broke old and set new social customs in Washington. She even traveled without a chaperone. Nothing that Alice actually did was in poor taste. Everything proved she was a responsible Roosevelt from the former Dutch colony of Nieuw Amsterdam. Although he may have been at times enraged by his daughter's behavior, the President of the United States never was ashamed.

She stood five feet seven inches in her stocking feet and weighed, it was estimated in the public prints, 150 pounds, although how this may have been possible is a tribute to the corsets of the day. Her appetite was enormous; in the afternoon: steaks and chops, potatoes, vegetables of all kinds. No desserts, however, at any meal.[18] Obviously, she needed that much food for the energy she expended. She could ride a horse astride or sidesaddle, she hiked with her father and his staff through the roughest parts of Rock Creek Park in Washington, and then danced continuously throughout the evenings.

Alice burst upon the American people, and soon after the rest of the world, like a rocket at night on the Fourth of July; she zoomed high, she was clearly seen, but unlike a rocket, the sparks she left behind never completely disappeared.

"Alice!" her father thundered when he learned that Alice used cigarettes, "you shall not smoke under my roof!"

"Very well, Father," she replied calmly, and thereafter hied herself to the top of the White House, puffed her cigarettes, and neatly kept her promise by smoking *above* his roof not *under* it.[19]

Following her own debut in Washington, five Misses Roosevelt "came out" at the New York Assembly: Dorothy, Christine, Alfreda, Anna Eleanor, and Alice. Nicknamed by Knickerbocker society the Magic Five, the most prominent and certainly the most popular proved to be Alice.[20]

Rumors of her engagement flashed across three thousand miles of telegraph lines and onto the pages of newspapers and other periodicals. Printed stories of her forthcoming marriage to Prince Eitel Fritz Adalbert of Prussia, Prince George of Greece, or any one of the Czar's many brothers abounded.[21] Alice never took time to deny them. She simply had nothing to do with the aforementioned royal personages. If it helped circulation, she would not hinder American enterprise.

Other industries benefited from her actions. Songwriters, dressmakers, milliners, glovemakers, wallpaper makers, manufacturers of ribbons, dyers, cloth makers—entire portions of American economy were given over to production of Alice-aligned goods. "Alice, Where Art Thou?" became one of the most popular songs of the day. "Alice Blue Gown" followed it with far greater popular success. A dressmaker came up with a fabric the color of which matched the radiant blue of her eyes. Alice had the dress made, wore it once, heard the song, and put the gown in the back of her closet, but couldn't resist taking it out again after a few months.

Generations of young American women wore Alice Blue gowns. More infant girls born then were named Alice than at any other time in our history. "Alice" spread like a happy infection across the land. To the people, at that point, she could do no wrong. One evening, a group of literary notables and politicos, including Booth Tarkington, author of *Penrod, Seventeen, Alice Adams,* and *The Magnificent Ambersons,* gathered in the White House. After dinner, Alice entered the dining room and immediately was asked, "Is it true that you stood on your head at a tea to show the fat Congressional women how to reduce?"

Without a word, Alice led the group to the gymnasium. Explaining that she was wearing a tightly fitted evening gown and couldn't participate in the gymnastics, Alice brought up the matter of "girth control." Within a moment, an internationally known novelist found himself on the floor doing push-ups. To outdo him, a pompous but powerful United States Senator did six successive handsprings. The President looked on. He held the power, but Alice cracked the whip!

She forsook the carriage when the automobile came into being. Alice's idea of a car was not one of those little two-cylinder runabouts that caused horses to rear on Washington streets. She ordered a four-cylinder, bright-red touring car, as it was known, that could be used in town and driven in the country at the high speed of thirty miles per hour.[22]

Her father, however, forbade her to accept delivery of the machine. Tears and entreaties, even the hope that her indulgent grandparents in Boston might be cajoled into buying the auto for her, did not succeed. Her father was firm. "Wedded to horse flesh," the Washington *Post* reported, "the President refuses to allow Alice to take possession of a motor car".[23]

The result was that she borrowed the automobile and chauffeur of the daughter of the Russian ambassador. As the most enthusiastic autoist in the capital, she soon dispensed with the hired chauffeur and took the wheel herself. Accompanied by her maid, she zipped about at a rate that brought her at least one summons from the Washington police.

In 1903, together with the machine's owner, Countess Margarite Cassini, she drove to New York, and then, by stages to the playground of American society, Newport, Rhode Island.

Highways in that year existed primarily for horse-drawn vehicles. The roads were marked by deep ruts that the wheels of heavy wagons made deeper. During the rains these lengthy canals caused traffic to sink axle-deep into the mud. No signs were posted to indicate a city or a town, a curve or a hill. Automobilists wore goggles, gauntlets, canvas coats known as dusters, and atop the ladies heads were hats held on with chiffon scarves tied under their chins. They felt as daring as the men and women who first crossed the mountain peaks of North America and descended into that vast and endless plain that is today the heartland of America.[24]

That summer, Alice's engagement book listed the various balls, dances, luncheons, dinners, suppers, and other social events that the aristocratic city offered. No intruder she, her lineage went back before the others'. Society was enchanted to have Alice within their midst. What jarred them was that Alice drove her automobile from Newport back to Washington by herself.

1904 was an excellent year, not for wine but for Roosevelts. Her father, who had sought election as President for the first time, trounced the Democratic candidate, Judge Alton B. Parker, in a landslide of 2.5 million votes. Even her first cousin, Anna Eleanor, and her fifth cousin, Franklin Delano Roosevelt, had crossed over and voted for T.R.

"At last," an ebullient T.R. told his wife after the returns were in, "I am no longer a political accident!"

Alice had been in the upstairs room at the White House on election night, 1904, when the jubilant President Roosevelt answered the press' question: would he seek another term? With his usual boldness he wrote, "Under no circumstances will I be a candidate for or accept another nomination."[25]

One of T.R.'s biographers, William Henry Harbaugh, observed, "That was the worst political blunder of Theodore Roosevelt's career."[26]

Secure that the American people wanted him as their Chief Executive, Alice's father struck courageously into the political actions that characterized his Presidency: "Trust busting," the Panama Canal, the circumnavigation of the globe by the great White Fleet, the settling of the Russo-Japanese War, for which he received the Nobel Peace Prize for 1906.[27]

While he remained in the capital, Alice traveled to Cuba, where she visited the sights and scenes of her father's military triumphs; to Puerto Rico, where Governor General and Mrs. Wood made her their house guest; to New Orleans, for the Mardi Gras, and a trip to the racetrack at the fairgrounds. Her presence at the track drew record crowds, and when they learned a horse was running in the George Washington Handicap named Sweet Alice, almost everyone in the clubhouse compartment of the grandstand got down a bet on the filly. The best Sweet Alice could do was to come in third. In all other respects, the social visit turned out to be a howling success.[28]

On the front page of the May 28, 1905, New York *Sun*, the headline read:[29]

> MISS ROOSEVELT HITS BULLS EYE.
> TRIES HER HAND AT RIFLE RANGE
> ON CONEY ISLAND
>
> The accompanying copy went as follows:
>
> Miss Alice Roosevelt and a party of friends rode to Coney Island last evening in automobiles and made the rounds of the shows in Luna Park and Dreamland. Miss Roosevelt tried her skill at the rifle range and scored three bulls' eyes out of five. "Wild Burt," the ex-cowpuncher who is in charge of the rifle range, told

> Miss Roosevelt that he had known her father in the West. Miss Roosevelt seemed much interested and asked him with a smile: "Can he shoot any better than I can?"
>
> "Wild Burt" looked at the recently made score and shook his head, being much too gallant to make comparisons. Miss Roosevelt was accompanied by Mrs. Harry Payne Whitney, J. M. Waterberry, J. J. Blair, and Lawrence Waterberry.
>
> During the party's visit to the park, all the electric lights went out and the grounds were in darkness for twenty minutes. The trouble was caused by the burning out of a transformer in the lighting plant.[30]

Vastly overweight, twinkly eyed, heavily mustachioed William Howard Taft served as Secretary of War in her father's Cabinet. His wife secretly nursed higher ambitions for her husband, but for the moment the post he held suited her very well.

In the summer of 1905, Secretary Taft decided upon a junket to the Orient. His first invitation went to Alice Roosevelt. The large party, composed of politicians, newspapermen, assorted friends, and the President's daughter and her personal maid, left Washington by special railroad cars. Her luggage included three flat trunks, two steamer trunks, many suitcases, bags, hatboxes, and a special container for her sidesaddle.

Riding along the westbound tracks, Alice greeted Independence Day by rising early, having breakfast, and going out to a car on the rear of the train and taking potshots at receding telegraph poles with her own revolver.[31] Why a young woman, especially the daughter of the President, should possess a handgun never arose as a question in anyone's mind. That she shot well seemed important.

In San Francisco, they toured the town and enjoyed everything from the Barbary Coast to the Embarcadero. But sightseeing was not enough. With so prestigious a group in their midst, San Francisco society demanded and received many receptions. And "how the crowds gathered, how they stared, and how they queued[32] up to be introduced!"

"You must be tired to death shaking hands with so many people!" exclaimed a pretty young girl at Alice's side at one of the San Francisco receptions.

Hermann Hagedorn wrote that Miss Roosevelt "seemed less to smile, as she replied, than to radiate. 'Tired?' she cried. 'Why I could throw my arms around their necks and kiss them! Everyone has been so nice to me!.'"[33]

After winning over the better part of northern California, Alice, along with Secretary Taft's party, sailed aboard the S. S. *Manchuria,* bound for the Hawaiian Islands.

The island of Oahu enchanted Alice. Crystal clear air, heavy with the scent of gardenias, met her as she disembarked. Young Hawaiians showed her how to dance the hula, and she did it well and often.[34] The party made excursions to plantations, volcanoes, and beaches. Secretary Taft spent hours begging photographers not to take pictures of Alice in her bathing suit, which consisted of a silk or mohair dress, high-necked, with long sleeves and long black stockings, plus bathing shoes. "Mr. Taft thought that there was too much skin showing," Alice chided him. The man hosting the trip acknowledged that the "outfit looked unladylike."[35]

After leaving Hawaii, the crew of the *Manchuria* rigged a canvas swimming pool up on deck for Alice. Instead of going below and changing into her bathing costume, Alice kicked off her shoes, unclasped her watch from her blouse, and plunged fully clothed into the pool, anticipating the Kennedy pool antics by some fifty-five years!

Reporters had a field day with that story. Copy was filed from the *Manchuria*'s radio that had Alice coaxing everyone from Congressman Nicholas Longworth of Cincinnati to fat old Secretary Taft into the pool.[36] The truth is that the sorceress charmed Bourke Cochran, a friend from New York, into the water. And that was all, but it set tongues wagging throughout the world.

In Yokohama, the Japanese called out, "Banzai!" to Alice and she called, "Banzai!" right back to them. In Tokyo, Alice met the Emperor and the Crown Prince. "There was also a rather grand garden party for us at the American Legation," she told Michael Teague of *Vogue* magazine years later. "All the Japanese ladies wore big floppy hats and carried parasols. I have some photographs of that. We look like a slightly stoned version of the Ascot scene from *My Fair Lady*."[37]

She banqueted with the royalty, received bows reserved for Japanese Princesses, and began to collect what she and her family called her loot. Lacquered boxes, silk screens, fans, and royal Japanese costumes were some of the items included in the booty brought back by Alice. Potentates all over the Orient contributed to it. The party left Japan at night to the sounds of wild cheers and the lights from thousands of paper lanterns.

In the Philippines, where Taft had once served as governor, the gifts and ceremonies continued. Alice reviewed the troops, danced the local steps in native costume, received a pearl ring from one sultan, and a proposal of marriage from another.[38] The Sultan of Sulu believed his people were so devoted to Alice that if she would remain, he would make her Sultana of the Sulu Archipelago.

"In a harem? As his seventh wife?" she inquired. Then, in more definite tones, "No, thank you!"[39]

Alice watched with horror one afternoon as Fredrick O'Brien, editor of the Cable News, seized by a cramp while swimming in the Pacific, was being swept out to sea by the undertow. Realizing O'Brien's peril, Congressman Longworth, at the risk of his own life, rescued him.[40] After that, Alice's attention toward the Representative of the First Ohio District became pronounced.

She had flirted with Congressman Longworth back in Washington, where his excellent wine cellar complemented the expertise of his own cooking for the younger people within the inner circle of the capital's social wheel. His membership in the proper clubs—The Alibi, for example—marked him, along with his bachelorhood, as a future partner.[41]

Hong Kong awaited them, then Canton, Shanghai, and Peking. "We were met by a posse of Court officials. Most of them had been at Harvard or Oxford and spoke impeccable English. One had even been the cox of the Cambridge rowing crew. Quite extraordinary!" The Dowager Empress of China, the cruel, ancient but wise ruler, Tz'u Hsi, had a huge dinner the first night at her summer palace. Alice described the evening to Michael Teague: "I'm not surprised Henry [Kissinger] puts on weight every time he goes there. The courses alternated between 'European' food, which was served with champagne, and Chinese dishes with which we had a delicious local rosé wine, like a brandy and *very* strong. I didn't like the champagne but loved the other. The result was I got quite drunk."[42] (Quite possibly, this was the only time in her life that Alice Roosevelt drank to excess. She has a lifelong distaste for strong spirits.) She enunciated her words as carefully as she could and wondered if she would be able to walk the line back to her quarters without swaying. "I wove my way off to bed. I didn't even notice my hard Chinese pillow that night, and must have fallen asleep in my evening clothes because I can remember getting up in the early hours of the morning and hurriedly putting on my nightgown before being roused by my maid, Anna, who would have been absolutely horrified if she had found me fully clothed in a stupor."[43]

It was in Japan that Alice turned to the American Minister, Lloyd Griscom, and tapped him on the shoulder.

"Do you see that old, bald-headed man scratching his ear over there?" she asked the diplomat.

"Do you mean Nick Longworth?" he inquired.

"Yes. Can you imagine any young girl marrying a fellow like that?"

"Why, Alice, you couldn't find anybody nicer," Griscom responded.

"I know, I know." she murmured thoughtfully, "But this is a question of marriage."[44]

The Longworth matter evidently didn't arise again until the travelers returned to American shores. Meanwhile, the battleship, U.S.S. *Ohio* took the Taft party to Korea where they were greeted with buglers and troops, and taken by special train to Seoul to meet the Emperor and his Empress.[45]

Then, back to Japan and home to the West Coast. Alice landed at Oakland where her father paid duty on twenty-seven boxes of her collectibles.[46]

Waiting to carry them across the continent in a record three days was a special train provided by the railroad magnate, E. H. Harriman, whose "trust" T.R. was about to "bust." Before anyone could board the train, eager waves of reporters questioned them. Had there been a shipboard romance? Was Princess Alice engaged?

When questioned by the press, Alice turned away all inquiries by replying that it was the express wish of her father that she say nothing.

When questioned by the press, Congressman Longworth merely said that Miss Roosevelt had been an excellent sailor.

When questioned by William Howard Taft if she was engaged to Nick Longworth, Alice replied, "More or less, Mr. Secretary. More or less." Of course she had her fingers crossed behind her to make the proper "magick."

"Is Alice Roosevelt engaged to Nick Longworth?" the editor of the Chicago *Tribune* telegraphed his Washington bureau chief. The reply came immediately. "She and Nick Longworth went out driving alone this afternoon. If they are not engaged, they ought to be."[47]

5 □ THE MAID OF HONOR

Among Alice followers there existed the very real question of whether she ever would marry. In 1905, her outspokenness, her lack of predictability caused concern that any man would want such an independent wife. It was a day of women's being confined to the kitchen and the kids.

About the only outside activity women in the early 1900s could find to occupy their time, if they had time to spare, was in the church and charitable organizations. The women's club movement pushed through centuries of secondary status for females; and among the educated and/or wealthy many reform movements took root, not to the degree they exist today, but the beginnings were there. Alice saw life not through the reform movements, not through the ladies clubs, but through the social whirl. Even there, her lack of inhibitions revealed her to be more of a madcap than the staid daughter of a President of the United States.

A friend of hers was a girl named Martha McCook whose parents did not believe in drinking. Theirs was a "dry" house before "dry" was the law,[1] although prohibition was in effect in many places beginning in 1851 in Maine.

En route, by train, to stay with the McCooks for a weekend, Alice bought miniature bottles of liquor from the porter in the dining car. That next night, she placed one in each glove and during dinner presented them to the attractive men on either side of her. The other guests at the table looked away but, as usual, there was whispering about the President's daughter. Her refusal to conform stamped her as one not easily placed in a conventional mold.

A desire to indulge in her own pleasure, a lack of care and affection for her family singled out Alice from other Roosevelt children. "Speak softly and carry a big stick," a cardinal principle of Theodore Roosevelt's foreign policy, worked well with the nations of the world but he was forced to employ different measures with his daughter Alice. Threaten her he did, but to little avail.

Teddy fumed at the reports of her escapades. He wrote a "scorching" letter to her in Newport, reprimanding Alice for not writing the family and only thinking of herself and the friends she had made in the "400."

"The only Newporter my father liked was Grace Vanderbilt," Alice Longworth told Henry Brandon. "She was a dear. She collected kings. Her yacht was called *Kingfisher*."[2]

Samuel Ward McAllister, Arbiter of New York and Newport Society, had introduced the term "The Four Hundred" for the crème de la crème of New York's Social Register. The term originated in 1888, when McAllister gave a condescending interview to the *Tribune*.[3] Mrs. William Astor's ballroom had space only for that number and, thereafter, the group was considered the elite. But *not* to President Roosevelt—he considered the display of their wealth "vulgar."

Even though Alice pretended remorse and wrote her father an apology, the scolding letter from the President ended up in ashes as Alice, in a typical temper, set fire to it.

"A hellion, that's what she was," her sister said, "capable of doing almost anything to anyone at any time. While she may have been a joy to behold, what wickedry she might commit next was felt almost constantly by almost all the family."[4]

While some of her friends feared she would never find a man to put up with her idiosyncrasies, others had speculated for years that the beautiful Alice might marry the handsome Franklin Delano Roosevelt. At dances, they appeared to be the ideal couple. In her late teens Alice looked like a sleek swan, the very essence of American womanhood.

They called Franklin "the Gibson Man," a matching male for the stylistic drawings of women by Charles Dana Gibson.[5]

Eleanor was as far away from the Gibson Girl look as any young woman in America. "Plain," was the most flattering word Eleanor's mother could find for her.

From the time she was five years old, Alice discovered she had a distinct talent for mimicry. She could imitate Eddie Foy and Joseph Jefferson, the actors.[6] She could capture the voices and features of statesmen and rulers, but most of all, she liked to imitate, from childhood on, her first cousin and playmate, Eleanor Roosevelt. Anna Eleanor's father was Elliott, T.R.'s brother, who had stood in the doorway on 57th Street, and hurled that frightening statement to Roosevelt, "There is a curse on this house." By the time Eleanor reached her twelfth year, both her parents had died. All of her life, sometimes with great cruelty, Alice would mimic Eleanor. And when his turn came to be imitated, she would do Franklin.

Cruelty toward Eleanor wasn't her major occupation as a teenager. At a Christmas dance their Aunt Corinne gave in New York, Alice, her long bronze hair whipping from side to side each time she tossed her head, danced gaily with Franklin until she saw Eleanor, hidden in the shadows of a distant wall.[7] The poor lonely girl cringed and tugged at the short hem of her dress. Although her legs were already too long, Eleanor's grandmother had insisted she squeeze into a dress that had ruffles ending at the knee. The other young girls wore gowns that swept the floor. If this wasn't enough, Eleanor's mousy hair and buck teeth gave evidence she would never be a beauty. Alice waited until the end of the dance, and then, as she and Franklin were applauding, she whispered in his ear. He turned, looked back at Alice. Then, obediently, he put on his best smile and marched across the floor. The duckling squirmed and hoped he might walk past her. But, no. He stopped squarely in front of her.

"Eleanor," he asked dutifully, "would you like to dance this one with me?"

"Oh, Franklin," she sighed gratefully, "I'd love to!"[8]

In the arms of another man, Alice smiled as she danced: no cousin of hers was ever going to be a wallflower for an entire evening.

An act of kindness, most onlookers thought, a gesture. Still, the girl for Franklin would naturally be Alice. Not so. Franklin never impressed Alice.

"He was the kind of boy whom you invited to the dance but not the dinner," Alice told Pulitzer Prize winning author Joseph Lash. "A good little mother's boy whose friends were dull. Who belonged to the minor clubs and who never was at the really good parties."[9]

While Alice flitted and flirted from Newport to Bar Harbor, while she was toasted in Boston and Philadelphia, while she dined and met the rulers of Japan and China and Korea, Eleanor stayed close to home, and eventually, to her own surprise, heard the young man from Hyde Park propose to her. She accepted immediately.

Their engagement announced, Eleanor wrote her Uncle Theodore to inquire if he would give her away at her wedding.

"Tell dear Eleanor," the President answered, "that I *can* attend the wedding."[10]

Never one to let an occasion pass without a word of comment, Alice said, "She'd better be careful. Father always wants to be the corpse at every funeral, the bride at every wedding, and the baby at every christening."[11]

The nuptials were scheduled for the seventeenth of March, 1905.

Alice received an invitation to serve as the maid of honor.

"You angel," she wrote Eleanor, "I should love to above anything. It will be too much fun. Let me know where I'm to hat and clothe myself so that I can arrange about fittings. Really you are a saint to ask me."[12]

At the ceremony, Alice stood on the altar and received the wedding bouquet from the bride.

Following the service, Theodore's high-pitched voice was heard to say something about "keeping the name in the family," and the celebrating began—without Uncle Ted.[13] Although he was President and a statesman, he was still a politician and, as every politician in New York City knows, March 17 is St. Patrick's Day, so to the cheering of small boys at the curb, Alice's father left early to address two of the dinners that night, one given by the Friendly Sons of St. Patrick at Delmonico's, the other for the Sons of the American Revolution at the Astor.[14]

Catching the bouquet must have worked its own form of "magick." Almost a year later, eleven months to be exact, Alice herself became the bride.

6 □ THE BRIDE

The freshman Congressman was the fourth generation to come out of Cincinnati. His great-grandfather had gone west and staked a claim to several hundred acres of land, many of which eventually became the heart of downtown Queen City across the river from Kentucky.[1]

His sister had married the Comte de Chambrun. Nicholas had attended Harvard and had joined the same club to which Alice's father had belonged, the Porcellian.

Nick Longworth was tall, bald, sported a luxurious mustache; he had never married, although he had attracted the ladies, and, of no small importance, he belonged to the Republican Party.

That was enough for Theodore Roosevelt, who lived in fear that his daughter might take the "Princess Alice" foolishness seriously, and marry a title. The American President was violently opposed to those marriages. While Nicholas Longworth stood in the White House study asking for Alice's hand, T.R.'s daughter stood in his wife's bathroom, as Edith brushed her teeth, and told her of Nick's proposal. The notion of telling her mother while she had a toothbrush in her mouth was to give Edith time to think. Good tactics, both upstairs and downstairs.

An elated Alice, after she and Nick received parental consent, telegraphed her Aunts Bye and Corinne:

"I always told you that Old Nick would get me and he has."[2]

On December 13, 1905, when President and Mrs. Roosevelt made the official announcement of the engagement of Alice and Nicholas, "Young women all over Washington blanched," the bride-to-be's sister-in-law claimed, "and some not so young in Cincinnati, Philadelphia, and New York."[3] Nick not only did well at the polls, he did well with the ladies.

There were differences, of course. Alice's idea of a good time was a day at the races; Nick's idea was an evening in a concert hall. Alice thought a good tune was the unofficial anthem of the Rough Riders, "There'll Be a Hot Time in the Old Town Tonight." Nick preferred Bach, Beethoven, and Brahms. She played first fiddle. He played the violin. She was twenty-two. He was thirty-six.

February had been the fateful month for Alice. She had been born in February, her mother and grandmother had died in that month. Her wedding would take place on February 17, 1906.

Long before that eventful day, newspaper stories poured out of Washington and New York. Alice's wedding gown would be blue. It would be white. It would be cream-colored. It would be eggshell.

On January 22, 1906, the Hearst paper, the New York *American* broke the story:[4]

> MISS ALICE'S WEDDING GOWN, TROUSSEAU MARVELS OF ART
>
> New York Modiste Making Dresses for Bride and Mrs. Roosevelt
>
> For the first time the *American* is able today to present an accurate picture of the marvelous trousseau including

> the details of the wedding gown Miss Roosevelt, who will be the sixth bride to go forth from the White House, will wear when she is wedded to Congressman Nicholas Longworth next month.

In its early afternoon edition, the New York *Sun* gave further information:[5]

> The rarity of White House weddings has put everyone on tip-toe with interest in the coming event. They have been equally interested in the wedding gown and other dresses in the trousseau. The marked individuality of Miss Roosevelt makes it certain that she could by no means leave either the material or the style of making or the garniture of the wedding trousseau to her dressmaker.
>
> There are twenty-six yards of material in the wedding gown, over which will fall a full court train to consist of a like number of yards of brocade and satin in a graceful lily design, exquisite in texture and one of the many sumptuous pieces of brocaded and embroidered satin presented to Miss Roosevelt during her trip to the Philippines.
>
> The white wedding gown will fit closely to the waist, then sweep away in a long train.
>
> It is said that the bride's bouquet will consist of lilies and white orchids, but Mr. Longworth has not taken anybody into his confidence in this respect.[6]

The stories printed about the Roosevelt-Longworth wedding went on and on, run not in the so-called society sections but on the front page of almost every newspaper in the country.

At the time, President Roosevelt pressed Congress for the passage of a Pure Food and Drug Act, and debate in the two chambers of that august body raged. Nothing equaled the public's interest or the press's play of Alice's wedding.

Following detailed discussion of her wardrobe, newspapers fixed their stories on the gifts being received at the White House.

To quote Alice's own understated words: "I had about the sort of presents that any girl gets from her relatives and friends and friends of the family ... with the exception of a few from foreign potentates."

They placed all gifts in the White House attic and Secret Service men guarded the rooms twenty-four hours a day.[7]

For Alice and Nicholas, the government of France, on behalf of the French people, sent a Gobelin tapestry.

King Edward of Great Britain forwarded a snuffbox with a miniature of his imperial head done in gold and blue enamel.

Kaiser Wilhelm of Germany contributed a gold and diamond miniature of himself.

The King of Italy came through with a mosaic table that was so large the happy couple could never find room for it.

Emperor Franz Joseph of Austria-Hungary[8] impressed everyone with a pearl and diamond pendant.

King Alfonso of Spain, through his diplomatic pouch, sent antique jewelry.

The Pope had an emissary deliver a gift of religious jewelry.

The Emperor of Japan shipped a pair of silver vases to the bride-to-be and her future groom.

The Dowager Empress of China put all royalty to shame. She sent:

8 rolls of brocaded gold cloth
2 rings
1 pair of earrings
1 lot of white jade
1 white fox coat
1 ermine coat

Alice's favorite gift came from the recently liberated people of Cuba.[9] Originally, their government had decided to send Alice and Nick a handmade bedroom suite of Cuban woods, inlaid with semiprecious stones native to the Caribbean island. The prospect of such an unattractive gift caused Massachusetts' Senator Henry Cabot Lodge to move rapidly through diplomatic channels. As an influential member of the Senate's Foreign Relations Committee, his suggestions carried more than an ordinary amount of weight. His first idea included the scrapping of the proposed bedroom furniture. This was done without any uproar. His next notion meant the acquisition of a necklace fitting for the first child of the President of the United States. Thanks to the intervention of Senator Lodge, the people of Cuba, through their government, presented Miss Roosevelt with a wedding gift of sixty-three matching pearls. In 1906 it was valued at $30,000!

As the date for the wedding grew closer the American people seemed to take on a frenetic quality. It became a national event. Individuals who had never set eyes upon Alice, let alone Nick, began organizing to send gifts to them.

One group sought to raise a fund of $800,000 in cash as a wedding present. To Alice's consternation, her father put a stop to that movement.

Other donors were more fortunate. Accepted at the White House were two turtle doves named appropriately Alice and Nick. Also, the couple received a Boston terrier with his pedigree engraved in silver, several sewing machines, washing machines, irons, andirons, twelve cords of seasoned wood from Wisconsin lumbering interests, even a carload of coal from Local 8 of the Pennsylvania United Mineworkers.

"I'll accept anything," Alice said, "except a red hot stove."

"And she'll take that, too," her father added, "if it doesn't take too long to cool off!"[10,11]

Gifts from the New York Congressional Delegation and Nick's colleagues on the House Foreign Affairs Committee appeared to be in excellent taste.

The Ohio Congressional Delegation, however, committed the political gaff of presenting the couple with a large sterling-silver punch bowl, only to incur the national wrath of the Women's Christian Temperance Union. Quickly, the punch bowl was exchanged for a loving cup.[12]

Her father's old regiment and Nick's club at Harvard sent gifts, as did members of the Cabinet, assorted governors, Senators, and other members of Congress.

Nick's mother, forsaking the romantic for the practical, settled $5,000 a year for life on the couple.

Nick gave Alice a diamond necklace.

Alice's father, President or not, had no other alternative than to pick up the tab for the entire wedding.

Saturday, February 17, 1906, came up sunny and remained so throughout the entire day. "Roosevelt weather" it was called.[13]

The House of Representatives, after inviting Nick to occupy the Speaker's chair for a short time, moved to adjourn and take the day off—although officially it was not a national holiday.[14]

In the capital one wouldn't have suspected it. Church bells began ringing early in the morning. By 9 A.M. every florist shop in Washington had been sold out.

A notoriously late sleeper, Alice arose at eleven and peeked out of her bedroom window. There, she saw Capitol police trying desperately to control the ever-swelling crowd of onlookers. Feigning a return to her bed, the bride-to-be was dissuaded by her sister and her mother into preparing herself for the occasion of the day.

Newspapers reported the first carriage in line at the White House South Gate held Mr. and Mrs. Franklin Roosevelt. Wrong. Mistake. Eleanor Roosevelt, pregnant with her first child, remained up in New York. The Mrs. Roosevelt who sat on the carriage seat beside Franklin was his mother.

Inside the White House, Nick arrived in a frock coat. It reached his knees and was charcoal gray. His trousers, necktie, and gloves were gray, his shoes black. Only his shirt and the flower pinned onto his left lapel showed white. His eight ushers wore identical clothes.[15]

Upstairs, Alice who chose to have no maid of honor and no bridesmaids, preferring to be the single star of the day, slipped into her wedding gown with ease. The "something old" was the lace from Alice Lee's bridal dress. Her hair gave her trouble. What with orange blossoms and heavy white veils, the pompadour slipped from side to side, or at times, collapsed completely.

The thousand guests, headed by the Episcopal Bishop of Washington, the Right Reverend Henry Yates Satterlee, who waited to perform the ceremony, shifted from one foot to the other, as the heat in the festooned East Room grew more intense. The Marine Corps Band played softly.

Twelve o'clock had been sounded by the city bells. The guests looked out along the corridor toward its farthest end. But the big mahagony doors that gave entrance to the State Dining Room were closed. A minute passed, and still no sign of opening the doors where the ushers were waiting the signal to form the procession. Another minute went by. The band had ceased playing.

Then at four minutes past noon, the doors flew apart, and the ushers appeared and took their positions.

A signal to the band. *Click*! went the conductor's baton.[16] A bugle call broke the silence, and every military man present recognized the ruffles and flourishes that are reserved for "The President." As the few sounding notes died away, click went the conductor's baton again, and then, his musicians burst out into the strains of the wedding march.

From their place at the far end of the corridor, the ushers started forward, their step in unison to the music. They were two by two, and young Theodore Roosevelt led one of the files. Behind them came the President, with his daughter on his left arm.

The bride was slightly pale, but showed no sign of nervousness. Everyone agreed that she had never looked more beautiful. As she passed those lined at the end of the corridor nearest the East Room, some of whom she knew, she turned toward them, but while looking into their eyes she gave no token of recognition other than a brightening of her smile.

The President was smiling, too, as he delivered her to her prospective groom. The Marine Corps Band stopped.

The bishop intoned the proper words, the couple spoke the accepted answers,Nick slipped a ring onto the third finger of Alice's left hand, and they were married.

With the conclusion of the ceremony, a great kissing and congratulating began. Her father, at last released from his formal responsibilities, shook all hands, his large teeth sparkling with the famous T.R. grin.

When the time arrived for Alice to cut her own wedding cake, the knife proved to be too dull. Once again, it was the Marines to the rescue! Charles McCawley, no longer a major but Colonel Charles McCawley, USMC, senior military aide to the President, drew his dress sword and handed it to Alice. Without hesitation, she plunged it into the cake, and the cake cut easily. Five other military aides drew swords from scabbards for the use by the new Mrs. Longworth. One of the aides was a young Army lieutenant named Douglas MacArthur. He would return one day, not only to the Philippines but later to Washington.

Meanwhile, her elated father nodded in approval. "Alice has behaved mighty well under trying circumstances," he said.[17]

Before the photographer's flash powder exploded for the wedding portrait, Franklin arranged Alice's formal train.[18]

Her mother sighed, her sister held her breath, her brothers gritted their teeth. The afternoon drew to a close, and Alice still remained in the White House. The opportunity for one of her totally unpredictable actions existed. Well after four, Alice came downstairs wearing her beige traveling suit, collected her husband, and quite calmly left through the side door for her honeymoon.[19]

The joyous couple went by carriage to a plantation in Virginia, called Friendship. It was owned by the McLean family. The next day a train took them to Key West, Florida, and finally a steamship to Cuba.[20]

Connubial bliss was the order of the day until they reached Santiago. There they went by mule train to San Juan Hill, where her father and his troops had fought so valiantly. Someone had laid on a plentiful store of daiquiris made with a local rum. By the time the happy couple returned to Santiago, they were ready for their first big quarrel.

Significantly, it was held under the Peace Tree, and while neither bride nor groom could recall how it began nor what it concerned, Nick, a politician, and Alice, the daughter of a politician, compromised before dinner, and their marriage continued.

"I do remember," Alice said later, "feeling that I held my own and was successfully obnoxious."[21]

7 □ THE MARRIED WOMAN

Alice and Nick returned to the capital. Washingtonians watched to see how the most famous young woman in America, and the most eligible ex-bachelor, would carry on their lives.[1]

Nick's mother had discreetly retired to Cincinnati and left the house to the newlyweds and their servants. On March 4, 1906, the day of their return, the Longworths lunched with the Roosevelt family, and had dinner alone in their place on 18th Street. It was the first time the two had dined together without being the honored guests of someone or other, since they had been married.[2]

In the following weeks, they were entertained at so many parties that a local cleaner and dyer advertised, with pride and without shame, that his establishment had already cleaned, "fifteen hundred pair of Alice Longworth's gloves." Some of their spare time, if any was to be had, went into planning Nick's fall campaign for reelection to Congress from the First Ohio District. Alice was ready. She had her father's confidence.

"And besides, we always won in those days," she recalled.[3]

But the election would be held in autumn, and this was spring, and now she was a wife, and not a daughter. Alice faced obligations, both political and social, that she never had before. The rituals and traditions of society in Washington were burdens she felt no inclination to carry. "Days at home," the insanity of dropping calling cards at other people's houses, so they could stop by and leave their calling cards, seemed bothersome and Alice quickly put an end to the practice.[4]

The days she was obligated "to receive" proved particularly irritating to the young bride. Not only did acquaintances intrude, but strangers off the street felt free to come in. Sightseeing carriages unloaded their passengers, and out-of-towners trooped into her home, hoping to see Alice Longworth. Sometimes, they picked up a spoon or a small trinket for a souvenir. After a couple of weeks of this, Alice bristled. She let it be known that she was keeping her home "off limits" to all except those who had been invited.

By May, they left the humidity of Washington for the dry heat of Cincinnati. Rookwood, where the older Mrs. Longworth held unquestioned authority, had considerable acreage, well-kept formal gardens, but the house itself was in a slight state of disrepair. To Alice's chagrin, she found herself in much the same condition as her cousin Eleanor. How she had scoffed that Eleanor had married a Mama's boy. Now, there was Eleanor, a virtual prisoner on that tract of land above the Hudson River Franklin called a farm, in Hyde Park, New York, and here she was, baking on a bluff overlooking the Ohio River. But being Alice proved a decided advantage. Like the daughter of a good military commander, she surveyed the field, did what had to be done—in this case it meant attendance at the Biannual Cincinnati Music Festival—and beat a tactical retreat to Washington.

By June, she and Nick sailed for Europe aboard the S.S. *St. Louis*. She would have preferred to cross on the *Kaiser Wilhelm der Grosse*, then the most fashionable steamer plying the North Atlantic route.[5] The President of the United States made it clear: if his daughter went to Europe, it would be aboard an American Line ship.

Seaworthy, clean, and comfortable with a good larder, a fine wine list, the *St. Louis* took the Longworths to Southampton in regulation time, eight days, eight nights. Every courtesy was extended to Mr. Roosevelt's daughter and her husband. By the time they arrived in London, Nick grew testy at the frequency he heard himself called Mr. Alice Roosevelt. It made him remember what his uncle-in-law had said to him during his engagement. Douglas Robinson, husband of T.R.'s sister Corinne, had taken him aside and said, "Nick, when I married a Roosevelt I did so in ignorance. It never occurred to me that I was marrying into a Presidential family, but with you it is different, and when you find yourself bullied and ignored or hung on the family like a tail to a kite, you will not be able to plead ignorance for you are doing this thing with your eyes open."[6] Advice or not, Nick blew up once or twice, but Alice, being a persuasive young woman, managed to calm her husband.

In London, they stayed with the ambassador to the Court of St. James's, Whitelaw Reid, and his wife, at Dorchester House.[7] King Edward VII invited them to lunch at the royal box at Ascot. They sojourned in France, where the President of the Republic entertained them. The President sat on Alice's right, M. Georges Clemenceau, who would serve as the French wartime Premier, sat on her left. They went to Germany. The Kaiser took them aboard an imperial yacht, where he received them in imperial fashion.

Two months passed that way, and then they returned to the United States. The national press had been running stories about the Longworths constantly; many of the articles were unflattering. In London, Alice had urged

Nick to appear before King Edward and Queen Alexandra in black silk knee breeches and black silk stockings. American editorial writers thought that Nick had gone too far, that his costume was undemocratic. Alice assured them that he had only followed English protocol.

At the New York pier, the couple avoided interviews, and hurried to join the President at Sagamore Hill. In her home town, the local papers fawned.[8]

> Oyster Bay, New York, August 12th. All Oyster Bay was alert yesterday and today for a sight of "Miss Alice" as they still call Mrs. Nicholas Longworth. They were rewarded yesterday when she drove into town with her brother Theodore. She held the reins in the dog cart. She drove off to the news store, bought some magazines, talked with an old acquaintance or two, and then crossed over to the drug store. Afterwards, Doc Schneider who keeps the store said, "I tell you, she hasn't changed a bit from when she was seven years old. There's nothing stuck-up about her. She likes soda just like she did when she was a little girl." Mr. & Mrs. Longworth attended church with the President this morning. Most of the village gathered around the door to see Mrs. Longworth as she came out. "It's really a pleasure to be back here," she told her neighbors, "If I see one more King I'll have him stuffed."[9]

After a needed rest, and after everyone had heard most of the stories about their second honeymoon, Alice and Nick headed for Cincinnati and the campaign.

The wild, unrepressed young woman seemed to have grown into a sedate adult. She even showed humility, a trait not displayed before. Her maiden name was mentioned often, and she finally said, "I'm Mrs. Longworth now—not Alice Roosevelt."[10]

Since it was 1906, Alice's quote to the newspaper reporters was very proper and unlike Alice. She said, "I would be very glad to try to assist my husband to return to Congress if he would permit me."[11]

Nick permitted her.

Cincinnati was awed. So was the rest of the country. The girl who had arrived the previous year surrounded by thirty Secret Service men, now stood alone or, at the most, alongside her husband and shook hands by the hour. Crowds gathered to hear Nick. The slightest reference to the President or his policies drew joyous shouts of "What's the matter with Alice?" and equally vigorous shrieks of "She's all right."

That Alice Roosevelt Longworth should appear in Marion, Xenia, Findlay, Toledo, and Columbus brought out crowds of monumental size.

"The Daughter of the Nation and the dearly beloved stepdaughter of the Queen City," is what the press and the public called her.

ALICE MAKES POLITICS FASHIONABLE IN CINCINNATI, the headlines read.

Nick who remained politically far to the conservative right of his father-in-law, accepted all this as a good politician would. Ohio loved Nick's wife. Ben Hayes of the Columbus *Citizen* wrote, "On the eve of Alice's arrival, the life of Columbus hairdressers was frantic. All the ladies demanded Empress Eugenie coifs with coronet braids and marcel waves" and the next day they rioted trying to get near her in front of the statehouse in Columbus when she dedicated a statue to William McKinley.[12]

In November 1906 Nick won reelection with ease. "It certainly doesn't hurt to be married to Alice," an Ohio editor wrote.

Alice was pleased with Washington life in 1907. She began to appreciate her family and to spend more time with them. Late every afternoon, all the Roosevelts who were in town gathered in her stepmother's bedroom at the White House. They gossiped about public and private happenings. Alice almost hated to leave them to rush home to dress for dinner.[13]

The press started to report that Carry Nation did not approve of Mrs. Longworth's unconventional behavior. Loose talk had it that Alice smoked her own monogrammed cigarettes, danced the hula, and allowed liquor to be served in her house.[14] Some of the reporters agreed with Mrs. Nation. "After all, she is the President's daughter," they wrote.

"The trouble with reporters," Alice said in her own defense, "is that they expect me to wear a halo and I only wear a hat."[15]

Nothing bothered her. The Panic of 1907 started with a run on the Knickerbocker Trust Company, a New York bank, and spread along Wall Street like flames through a wooden tenement. It was over just as fast. Nick and his mother suffered some losses, but Alice's income was not affected.[16]

The twenty-three-year-old Mrs. Longworth insisted upon learning to play poker. She enjoyed the company of men more than women, and she figured, rightly, that she would not be excluded if she mastered their favorite card game. A regular player in Nick's group was "Uncle Joe" Cannon, Speaker of the House. When the President warned her that "Uncle Joe" was a tobacco chewer and would require a spittoon, she thought the men were trying to discourage her from becoming a member of their game.[17] Not at all. Speaker Cannon showed every sign of needing a spittoon the minute he walked in the door. His cheek bulged. There was no spittoon. A substitute was found immediately—

an empty umbrella stand which he used throughout the evening—to Alice's discomfort.

Nick taught her well, and even led her gently to the point where she grew to appreciate or at least tolerate classical music and Nick's violin—a Cremona.

"It still sounds like the name of a cigar to me," she teased him.[18]

The only off-key string in all this harmony came when Alice realized that her father was sincere in his determination to give up the Presidency. T.R., without much warning to his family, started to talk loudly in favor of Mr. Taft. When he spoke to Republican groups, he threatened, "Vote for Taft—or you'll get me again."[19]

Alice, who saw humor in practically every situation, did not find anything amusing in that statement. She suspected the Party leaders of trying to unseat "that damn cowboy" as they called their President. She ballooned into a rage. Part with the prosperity of the nation? The peace of the entire world? For what? For a scrap of paper he had dashed off on a bustling election night?

"I would gladly sacrifice my right arm not to have written that," her father told her later. But it *was* written, and people *did* remember it, and he *must* stand by his word.[20]

"Who on earth can take your place?" Alice demanded.

The list was long: Charles W. Fairbanks, T.R.'s Vice-President. A drone. J. B. Foraker, senior Senator from Ohio. Shifty. "Uncle Joe" Cannon, Speaker of the House. Uncouth. Charles Evans Hughes, governor of New York. Arrogant. Elihu Root, Secretary of State. Good but unelectable.[21]

There remained one man, fat, jolly, his blond mustache bobbing over his smiling lips. Teddy chose Will.

Alice and Nick split the summer of 1908 between riding in the Yellowstone National Park and surfing off Waikiki in the Hawaiian Islands. After five weeks, they were ready for home and politics.

When they returned to Cincinnati, there was little doubt that the members of the coming convention would hop onto the Taft bandwagon. There would be polite gestures toward other candidates, but that's all they would be—gestures. Alice admitted in later years that she had wished "something would happen to Taft," and her father would be renominated.[22]

"Not surprising," a family friend of the Tafts said. "Everyone knew that Alice wanted a ninety-nine-year lease on the White House."[23]

The Windy City is the ideal place for windy political conventions. Alice's initial attendance at a Republican convention was in that crescent scar on the Illinois prairie called Chicago. A new city, compared with those that had been long settled in the Eastern watershed of the United States, Chicago had been freshly rebuilt following the fire of 1871, when the better part of the wooden city had burned to the ground.

Construction since the Chicago fire was of brick or stone. The waters of Lake Michigan, always tranquil during the early summer, barely kissed the shoreline. A few grains of sand, a few blades of grass, and then came Michigan Avenue along which the mansions of the mighty were ranged as fortresses running north and south. On what Chicagoans called the near North Side were avenues lined with homes, meat markets, grocery stores, fruiters, vegetable stalls, fresh fish markets, and hardware stores. After that, the houses grew progressively shabbier as they went westward to meet the Illinois sod.

To the southwest lay the stockyards, citadels of the Armours, the Swifts, the Morrises, and the other barons of beef, sheep, and hogs. For meat, the railroads of America made Chicago the hub of all transportation. From the West came the live animals. From Chicago to the rest of the nation went the steaks and chops and hams for the world. A shift in the wind at any time would cover large parts of the city with a stench that everyone knew came from "back of the yards." It was the odor of steaming hot animals' blood as it poured out onto the killing floor. The slaughter went on relentlessly. Six days each week. On the seventh, while men ate and women cooked, animals trembled in their pens, waiting for the Judas goats to lead them to their end the next morning.

East of Chicago lay the steel towns, Gary and Hammond. Iron ore from Minnesota and Wisconsin would be shipped by steamers through Lake Superior and Lake Michigan to meet the coal wrested from the earth in southern Illinois, Kentucky, Ohio, and West Virginia. In Gary and Hammond, they mixed the ore and the coal, and made steel. Poles and Hungarians manufactured the steel and shipped it to Chicago. To the north, a scarce hundred miles away, lay the city of Milwaukee, filled with good Germans making better beer. Still farther north, were the forests of Wisconsin and Minnesota, where Swedes and Norwegians toppled the timber, and, like their cousins in the steel mills, sent the lumber to Chicago. From the West came the grains: corn from Iowa, wheat from Kansas. Alfalfa and soy beans had not been planted as yet but in time they would be, and the Commodities Exchange on LaSalle Street would become second to none in the world.

Bursting with energy and pride, Chicago *was* the ideal place for a national political convention. In 1908, Alice joined her husband and their friends, Ruth and

Medill McCormick, to watch the Republicans nominate a candidate for the Presidency. Medill McCormick published the Chicago *Tribune*, and he had a fair idea of what would take place. Another newspaper editor joined them. He was William Allen White of the Emporia, Kansas, *Gazette*. He knew too.

Alice secretly hoped that the convention would draft her father, but on the first ballot, Theodore's personal choice, William Howard Taft, received the Party's nod.

The last day, Alice gave William Allen White a scoop. She knew ahead of time that "Sunny Jim" Sherman would be selected as the Vice-Presidential candidate.[24] White had the exclusive story, and the Republicans had a reactionary to balance their ticket.

Alice's main pleasures came from the enthusiasm generated outside the hall and away from the delegates. Big crowds, large parties, much intrigue, pictures in the newspapers—Alice loved it all. She didn't want to wait four years for another Republican Convention. Alice, Nick, and a group of friends hired two private railroad cars and attended the Democratic Convention in Denver.

The temperature that summer was hotter than the political speeches. Everyone waited for breezes that never came, and at one point, in desperation, they had the McCormick butler hose down the roofs of the cars to give them some relief.[25]

"William Jennings Bryan won the Democratic nomination, but that butler with the hose was the luckiest man in Denver," Mrs. Longworth said.[26]

Alice and Nick spent election night in Cincinnati—as did Taft. The candidate went home to vote and be slapped on the back, and Alice watched and resented all the pampering and petting the local folks gave him. After the one-sided returns came in, Nick's female relatives "cooed over Taft." The Ohioans apparently took satisfaction in owing nothing to Roosevelt. It was torture for Alice on election night. The Buckeyes applauded as Taft beat William Jennings Bryan. Everyone took credit for Taft's victory. Alice would have liked to banish them all. A victory for Taft? But the name Roosevelt was never mentioned. In Rookwood, where they waited for the returns, it came out Taft, Taft, Taft all evening long.

"They called Taft great," Alice sniffed rapaciously. "Great in girth, perhaps, but great in nothing else." Before the night of "gloating" ended, her attitude had gradually changed from annoyance to animosity.

She aimed most of her arrows at the new President-elect. Alice wrote in her reminiscences that "as far as I was concerned, the stage was set for the steps that led to the breakup of a beautiful friendship."[27]

To intensify her resentment, as soon as she and Nick set foot in Washington, they heard that her father's appointees were going to be replaced (Taft had promised T.R. that his men would remain with the new Administration), and that Mr. Taft's ambitious wife had disapproved of Edith Roosevelt's housekeeping habits in the Executive Mansion.[28] Helen Taft intended to put the front doormen into livery, and discharge the policemen and elderly government employees. Mary Randolph, secretary to six First Ladies, said, "Mrs. Taft replaced the ancient ushers who wore frocked coats and looked like characters out of a Dickens story."[29]

Mrs. Taft—Nellie to her husband and friends—also interviewed housekeepers and cooks.

The lowest blow to Mrs. Longworth came a few days before the Inauguration. Mrs. Taft met Alice at a mutual friend's home, and offered to send her a ticket so that she could get into the White House reception.

"I," cried the incensed Alice, "I, who had wandered in and out for eight happy years!"[30]

The night before the inauguration, the Roosevelts invited the Tafts to dinner and to spend the night. The White House glistened, and there was a faint odor of furniture polish and the scent of fresh flowers and burning logs.[31] The building was ready for the new tenants, but Alice and her family felt a heavy shadow of sadness and regret at giving up what had been theirs.

At the table, President Roosevelt dominated the conversation. A master of all matters, he skipped with ease from one subject to another. Mrs. Roosevelt was radiant. Like the men, she wore black. The Tafts, who had arrived just before dinner, sat at the table and controlled their apparent eagerness to get on with the workings of tomorrow.[32] Also at the table were Admiral and Mrs. Cowles (Auntie Bye and her seafaring husband), Secretary Elihu Root who was going from the State Department into the Senate, and his wife, Edith. Nick and Alice remained quiet for the better part of the meal. Only Captain Archibald Butt, who that night escorted the Tafts' close friend from Cleveland, Miss Mabel Boardman, laughed at the outgoing President's anecdotes. Captain Butt had reason to be lighthearted. As one of T.R.'s military aides he had been singularly honored to be invited to the farewell dinner. Moreover, he knew he would continue as President Taft's aide.

Captain Butt considered the conversation at the meal to be "first rate," while Alice recalled that it was "lugubrious."

At the conclusion of the dinner, President Roosevelt and President-elect Taft led the gentlemen into the study. Five of the ladies went into the library. Alice threw a shawl over her head and shoulders, and eased her way out onto the White House grounds.[33] She walked to the garden, reached through the railing, and scooped up a few handfuls of cold, hard soil. Alice, "the wicked witch," drew a small box from her purse and buried it in the hole. She covered it with a sweep of her hand. In the box lay a "bad little idol," who could be counted on to bring ill fortune in the future to the occupants of 1600 Pennsylvania Avenue.[34]

Changing her gloves, Alice rejoined the ladies.

Looking up at the leaden skies over Washington, through the library window, Alice murmured, "It's going to snow." Her voice failed to indicate any regret at the prospect of a damp and dreary Inauguration Day.[35]

The evil idol was never found, but in the following months he did his work.

8 □ THE PARTY'S OVER

For Alice, the weather on Inauguration Day couldn't have been more pleasing: rain and sleet mixed with heavy snow. Her father, the outgoing President, left the White House in a phaeton drawn by a team of horses. Beside him sat his wife. On the jump seat across the aisle from him sat his son-in-law, Nicholas Longworth. Alice rode up on the box beside the coachman. As the carriage rolled out of the White House grounds and headed for the railroad station, waiting crowds cheered. Alice made as ugly a face as she could manage and called to them, "This, darlings, is what you're going to get after we're gone."[1]

The surrey deposited Colonel and Mrs. Roosevelt at Union Station. Good-byes made, the former President and his wife were applauded as they boarded the train for New York and Oyster Bay. Alice and Nick had the coachman drive them to their Washington home.

By now, the weather had become so inclement that the ceremonies had to be moved indoors. The largest storm Washingtonians could recollect drove the Presidential party into the warmth of the Senate chamber.

"I was ecstatic!" Alice remembered. The white stuff refused to come down fast enough to suit her.

At noon, William Howard Taft, baking in the heat of the crowded Senate floor and its packed galleries, took the oath of office and became the twenty-seventh President of the United States.

"His inaugural address," Alice commented, "was noted for an abundance of lack and shortage of luster." The gray and white slush along Pennsylvania Avenue matched the heavy clouds that hovered over the ten square miles of the District of Columbia. Tradition was broken only by the presence of Nellie Taft riding in the open horse-drawn carriage alongside the new President.[2] A President's wife had never ridden in the parade from the steps of the Capitol to the doors of the White House, but Nellie had new ideas. After getting "Will" to pressure Congress to appropriate money for four autos, she felt she had earned a place on the seat next to him.[3] That night, she and Will would be driven to the Inaugural Ball in a motorcar. Trumpets seemed muted by the falling snow. Mouthpieces on the brass instruments froze, valves closed, reeds split—only the snare drums competed with the heavens. Once inside the White House, Taft quickly divested himself of his silk hat, his greatcoat, and gloves. Throwing himself upon a sofa, he waited for the springs to absorb his 350 pounds. Then he spoke.

"I'm President now and I'm tired of being kicked around!"[4]

Chief Usher Ike Hoover recalled the incident with clarity. Until that moment, Mr. Taft had been the jolliest, friendliest visitor the Roosevelts ever had entertained. With that statement, his speech and his attitude toward the servants and staff members changed radically. He snapped, he scowled, he snarled. After being wedged in several times by the sides of the bathtub used regularly by his predecessors, the President ordered and had delivered a new convenience, large enough, claimed the men who built it and installed it, to accommodate four men of normal stature.

Alice's mother, Sweet Alice Hathaway Lee. When she died, Theodore Roosevelt thought his life was finished.

Library of Congress Collection

Culver Pictures, Inc.

Sweet Alice's daughter, Alice Roosevelt, sets styles early. The toddler is with her Auntie Bye, circa 1885.

The Bettmann Archive, Inc.

Alice's second mother,
Edith Carow, the woman behind
the successful politician.

Library of Congress Collection

The President
and the First Lady.

The gang's almost all here; T.R. holding baby Kermit. Ted, Jr., stands beside Alice while Edith provides an ample lap for Archie and Ethel.

Now, the gang's *all* here. Quentin, T.R. in his riding boots, Ted, Jr., in his glasses, Archie, Alice already wearing one of those broad brimmed hats, Kermit, Edith, and Ethel.

Library of Congress Collection

Innocence.

Library of Congress Collection

Sophistication.

Exterior. Sagamore Hill, Oyster Bay, Long Island. Sunny and cheerful. Today, the trees have grown to such heights as to put the old house in the shade.

The Bettmann Archive, Inc.

Interior. Sagamore Hill. The living room is cluttered with mementos of T.R. On the table is a Remington bronze; on the wall, a buffalo head shot by the twenty-sixth President; on the far wall, a painting of T.R. as Colonel of the Rough Riders, the regiment he commanded in the Spanish-American War. Not showing are a set of moose antlers from which hang his campaign hat and field glasses.

The Bettmann Archive, Inc.

Auntie Bye's house on Madison Avenue in what is now midtown New York. Alice went here instead of to school. The Clarence Day family of *Life With Father* fame lived nearby.

Library of Congress Collection

Soon after Alice's debut, 1902.

The Bettmann Archive, Inc.

Miss Alice Roosevelt, 1905.

The Bettmann Archive, Inc.

Christening the Kaiser's yacht. Alice still has in her sitting room the broken champagne bottle encased in glass.

Culver Pictures, Inc.

Representative Nicholas Longworth of the First Ohio District and Miss Alice Roosevelt of the First Family aboard the S.S. *Manchuria* bound for the Orient and eventual matrimony.

That was the new chief's most significant personal demand. That, and raising the Presidential salary to $70,000 a year, and, for good measure, a traveling fund of $20,000.[5] He assigned more political responsibility to his wife than any President had before him. Taft respected Helen Herron Taft's opinions and constantly took pride in the judgments of the woman whom he married in 1886, and whose ambitions for her husband were a thousand times higher than the Kentucky cliffs that ran along the south bank of the Ohio River. Nellie, as her husband and their friends called her, was thoughtful, Nellie was kind, Nellie could even be understanding, provided it was understood that Will's political career be furthered.

William Howard Taft, whose dancing feet were as light as a butterfly flitting over a flower, had skipped from Yale to the Cincinnati Law School to Cincinnati's prosecuting attorney's office to the Superior Court Bench, and then Federal service as solicitor general to circuit judge, to governor-general of the Philippines, and finally Secretary of War. How much credit for his election to the Presidency was due to Theodore Roosevelt, Nellie Taft never conceded.

Nellie Taft had ideas for the old "President's House." Most of the rooms on the ground floor were closed to the public. She hired a housekeeper and almost all new servants. With the exception of Charles McCawley and Archibald Willingham Butt, who was promoted from captain to major, the President's staff went, too.

Nellie attended the top-level political meetings. No appointments could be made without her presence.[6] A chef appeared, entertainment grew lavish, and then the murrain took effect. Two and a half months after the

Tafts moved into the White House, Nellie Taft had an incapacitating stroke. Will spent the rest of the days of his Presidency teaching his wife to speak and walk again. Taft's political progress met with limited success. It tickled Alice to quote her father. "Taft meant well," T.R. said, "but he meant well feebly."[7]

One afternoon, a weary President Taft sat nibbling his favorite fruit, a McIntosh apple, while going over a stack of official papers. An aide knocked on the door of his office. The aide, with apologies, explained that an unusual circumstance had arisen. A kitchen servant, shaken and dismayed, at that very moment was packing her few belongings into a suitcase. She was leaving without giving her notice. Many of the other White House backstairs staff were considering the same action.

"Why?" demanded the President.

They agreed the White House had an inhabitant about whom they hadn't been warned—a ghost.

The apple flew into the wastebasket, and Mr. Taft pulled himself majestically to his feet. It was as if a large mountain had slowly emerged from a tranquil sea.

"What do you mean?"

"Well," the aide reported, "more than one maid and houseman has seen a gossamer figure or felt a frigid hand on their shoulders. A couple of the maids couldn't keep from screaming. Sometimes, they left their tasks, burst into sobs, and ran for more populated areas such as the kitchen."

"I won't have it!" the President said in a stern, loud voice. "I won't have these stories spread. The newspapers will snap them up and print them. I forbid anyone who works in this house ever to mention the subject to me or anyone else again."

"Yes, sir."

With a bit of Taft's anger spent, he lowered himself back into his chair and asked, "Who the devil's the ghost supposed to be?"

The aide swallowed air, and bravely but quietly announced, "Abraham Lincoln's youngest son."

All the fury returned.

"Tell them it's nonsense, and never again do I want that story repeated."

Apparently, a Presidential order on ghosts didn't carry much authority. The tale *was* repeated, and Alice heard it.

"There are worse things than ghosts," she said. "Bad Presidents in the White House are worse than apparitions."[8]

"When they say, 'Mister President,'" Taft admitted, "I always look around and expect to see Roosevelt."[9] But Teddy was not anywhere near Will.

While Colonel Roosevelt, as he preferred to call himself, outfitted an African safari from Madison Avenue's Abercrombie & Fitch, Alice remained in Washington. She spent afternoon upon afternoon watching Wilbur and Orville Wright pilot their flying machine over Fort Myer in Virginia. Alice set the fashion, as usual. Her society friends could hardly wait to join her each day. They considered it an honor to visit the Longworth motorcar and to have Mrs. Longworth serve them lemonade, tea, or sometimes a surprise gin fizz.[10] One day, Alice tried to persuade Glenn Curtiss, the aviator, to make a cross-country trip in his plane with her aboard. Mr. Curtiss said he would only agree to fly her from one end of the field to the other.

"Fifteen minutes in the air?" Alice tossed her head. "Too tame for me!"[11]

"Apart from the Monument," Major Butt wrote to his mother early in 1909, "Alice Longworth is still the greatest attraction in the Capital."[12]

In June of the same year, after a short trip to Paris during May, Alice was told by Ambassador Reid that he did not see how she had much of a time as she spent only two days in the French capital.

"Ah," replied Alice, "but I was there three nights and it's the nights that count in Paris."[13] The Bishop of London, seated near her, was greatly amused.

Alice was amused when she learned that President Taft had taken to riding. There came that afternoon when the President could not make the ride and urged Mrs. Taft's secretary to exercise his horse.[14]

"I felt like a fly on the back of an elephant," Mary Randolph told Alice. "As for the horse, he didn't even know I was there!"[15]

The Tafts started a few social customs which Alice approved. They gave a series of garden parties; the ladies carried parasols and wandered about—the men dabbed their damp foreheads with linen handkerchiefs and stood in the shade under the striped awnings. The chosen were asked to ride along in their carriages down by the Potomac River to listen as John Philip Sousa led the band.

"There are days when I like Nellie Taft so much, I feel sorry that she doesn't have a more attractive husband. He has so much brain and so little beauty," Alice said.[16]

When the President's oversensitive reaction to this statement was reported back to Mrs. Longworth, she considered the matter gravely and replied, "A gentleman—or a lady—is a person who is never *un*intentionally rude to anyone."[17]

Will Taft often spoke wistfully of the "Roosevelt luck." He had missed it on his own Inaugural Day. Knowing nothing of the little idol buried in the White House grounds near the garden fence, he cursed the day his Nellie had taken ill.[18]

The "Roosevelt luck" had followed Theodore to Africa.[19] The blacks adored him. So did the European colonials. Entire regiments of animals fell before his rifle. Ostensibly, all of this shooting was done for the benefit of the Smithsonian Institution of Washington, D.C.

During the eighteen months her father absented himself from American shores, Alice took a sniping attack with her usual aplomb. She had been smoking cigarettes during most of her years in the White House. Suddenly, the issue flared up on a national scale.

The Christian Endeavor Societies, the Daughters of the American Revolution, the Epworth League, the Women's Christian Temperance Union, the Daughters of the Pioneers, the American Playground Association—all vigorously attacked Mrs. Longworth for her use of the tobacco weed.[20]

"Tell them not to forget that many of their grandmothers and great-grandmothers smoked corncob pipes," Alice retorted.

While her friends tried to defend Mrs. Longworth, Mrs. J. H. Armstrong, of Pittsburgh, provoked a storm by announcing, "I look upon a woman who smokes as on a woman who bleaches her hair—with suspicion."[21] This proved too much. Alice, upon hearing the story, took off her hat and showed reporters a head of hair with no dark roots.

Thousands of letters poured into Congressman Longworth's office in the Capitol.

"Until she starts chewing tobacco, I have little to say." The Representative from Ohio added, "When my wife gets into trouble, which isn't rare, I run down into my cyclone cellar and wait for the storms to pass."[22]

Society matrons felt Mrs. Longworth should bring suit against one of her major critics, Carry Nation.[23] Alice remained aloof. Not everyone did. In Wollaston, Massachusetts, the girl who one day would grow up to be the leading lady of stage and screen, Ruth Gordon Jones, watched in horror when her mother threw down her copy of the Boston *Globe.*

"Oh, *poor* President Roosevelt!" Mrs. Jones cried.

"What happened?" Ruth wanted to know.

"His daughter Alice was asked to leave the lobby of the Copley Plaza because she was smoking a cigarette."

Ruth wished somebody would ask *her* to leave the Copley Plaza.

Years later, when she had dropped the Jones and become Ruth Gordon, leading lady, she inquired of Alice Roosevelt Longworth how she felt at being asked to leave the hotel lobby because she'd smoked a cigarette.

"*Dee*-lighted," Alice replied promptly.[24]

At a French embassy dinner which Mr. Taft attended Alice arrived *after* the President, "An unpardonable offense in official Washington," as Archie Butt put it.[25] But, making a star's entrance, she threw the assembled company into a delightful mood. Taft took her hands between his and said, "Alice, if you will only stop trying to be respectful to me, I believe you would become so."[26]

Alice waved her hand toward the guests. "Then I would bore you to death as the other women do!"

Hostesses in Boston, New York, and Washington complained that Alice danced the popular but scandalous Turkey Trot.[27]

"I don't care," Alice mimicked Eva Tanguay's famous song. "I never care what people say."

Mrs. Longworth continued to startle her countrymen and women. In January 1912, she appeared at a Washington ball wearing a blue tulle dress with a train that parted to show a pair of slippers with cut-glass heels.[28] She'd been married to the Prince for four years now, and since she had no fairy godmother to warn her to depart at midnight, Alice danced until dawn. Flashing crystal slippers could be seen, and there were those who even imagined they saw her ankles.

The memory of Mrs. Longworth still causes the First Lady of the American theater to bubble with animation. "I grew up on the legend of Alice Roosevelt," Helen Hayes remembered excitedly. "I can still see my family gathered around the kitchen table reading about her exploits. I was lost in admiration of her."[29]

On the night of April 14, 1912, the Royal Mail Ship *Titanic* ripped her starboard side along a great iceberg in the dark and freezing North Atlantic. Within a matter of hours, this newest and most luxurious steamer of the White Star Line sank into the icy waters—bow first. Among the hundreds of lives lost was Alice's dear friend, Major Archie Butt.

Close to Roosevelt, close to Taft, Butt had known of the simmering feud that existed between the two men. His nerves frayed by the conflict, he required peace and rest. President Taft had ordered him to seek the quiet of a European holiday. He went, but with many misgivings. Alice was not surprised when she learned of his presentiments. Butt had written his sister-in-law Clara, "Don't forget that all my papers are in the storage warehouse, and if the old ship goes down, you will find my affairs in ship-shape condition."[30]

The break between Roosevelt and Taft, which had driven Major Butt to Europe, began over the Steel Trust. The Payne-Aldrich Tariff Act, which favored American Big Business, infuriated supporters of T.R. Taft's failure to veto the Tariff Act placed him in direct opposition to his former mentor.

Progressive Republicans grew even more disenchanted with Taft as a result of the Ballinger-Pinchot Affair. Roosevelt's lieutenant on conservation had been James R. Garfield. Taft removed Garfield in favor of Richard A. Ballinger. Ballinger was accused by Chief Forester Gifford Pinchot of allowing a Morgan-Guggenheim syndicate to grab Alaskan coal reserves. Taft fired Pinchot. Roosevelt raged, Taft wept, and then Teddy announced, "My hat is in the ring!"[31] The rift was final. Alice Longworth realized her husband had three options: Nick could side with her father, he could remain steadfast beside Taft, or he could drop out of politics.

"Never," she confided to friends, "have I seen anyone suffer like Nick. His loyalty toward my father is pitted against his Ohio obligations toward Mr. Taft. Father recommends he remain with Mr. Taft to protect his future in his home state. I have never been so sorry for anyone."[32]

Alice, who had been too young to see any of the battles of the Spanish-American War, realized she was watching a first-class political struggle between her father and President Taft.

Taft surrounded himself with lawyers. If a loophole could be found, everyone from his Secretary of State on down could be counted on to find it. Teddy repudiated the "Regular" Party machinery.[33] His supporters told him that if he would stay away from the convention, the nomination would be his. But Roosevelt enjoyed hand-to-hand combat.

Questioned by the Chicago *Press* as to the state of his health, upon his arrival in that city, T.R. replied, "I'm as strong as a bull moose."[34] Those last two words proved to be the popular name of his soon-to-be-formed Progressive Party.

Alice and Nick rolled into Chicago and were driven to the ultra-fashionable Blackstone Hotel by their friends, the McCormicks. After a desultory glance at their corner suite, Alice and Nick hurried to the sprawling Congress Hotel where her parents had taken apartments. At dinner that evening, her father once again warned Nick to stay out of the fight. This admonition did not apply to Alice. She waved an airy good-bye to her husband and followed her father's people to the Auditorium.

The second day, T.R. stood before the convention for fifty-two minutes, the delegates shook red bandannas and shouted their welcomes. From the rostrum, Roosevelt—his shrill voice piercing up to the highest seat in the far galleries—warned of the consequences of selecting a conservative and admonished the crowd for its deceitful practice of hiding Progressive delegate credentials. He knew not only how to inform an audience, but how to stir it. As he finished each sentence, the crowd roared, "Thou shalt not steal!" Sitting in a box next to her mother, Alice watched the impassioned faces of his devoted followers; she heard their cries; she felt the vibrations they set up.

"The cause of our opponents has now become naked," T.R. called out, "the cause of the special privilege in the business world!"[35]

"Thou shalt not steal!" his earnest audience chanted.

"We fight in honest fashion for the good of mankind." Finally, he reached the climax. Throwing aside his notes, he pulled back the lapels of his frock coat.

"We stand at Armageddon," he proclaimed, "and we battle for the Lord!"[36]

Pandemonium rocked the hall.

The next day, in Chicago's Coliseum just below the southern boundary of the Loop, Senator Warren G. Harding, of Ohio, in a flurry of "flowery words and empty sentences," placed in nomination the name of William Howard Taft.[37] "Will" never had captured the imagination of the American people. He was a colorless man, and Roosevelt knew and understood it only too well. By contrast, T.R. always drew crowds. Dynamic, attractive, and imaginative, the Rough Rider was loved by the people. His successor was merely respected as the temporary holder of the nation's highest office.

Cheers and jeers floated up through the smoke at the Coliseum. Delegates threw down their placards and fought with their fists. Political bosses made certain the name Roosevelt was not heard. The "Bull Moosers," as they had become known overnight, trekked from the hall into the sunshine of Wabash Avenue. Inside, the roll was called. Taft received the Republican nomination on the first ballot. No surprise there.

The shocker came when the "Bull Moosers" rented Orchestra Hall on Michigan Avenue facing Grant Park, and that evening, in convention, the Progressive Party nominated Theodore Roosevelt as their candidate for President of the United States. Amazement, indignation, and fear. How had the Republican Party been splintered? One of Roosevelt's relatives expressed it well, "Trying to keep Teddy out of politics was harder than trying to stop the 'World's Oldest Profession'—*Im*possible."[38]

In Baltimore, Maryland, the last part of June, the "out party" opened *their* convention. After a series of verbal battles—certainly as bitter as had engulfed the Republican Convention—the Democrats nominated Governor Woodrow Wilson of New Jersey on the forty-sixth ballot.

Alice, who had been staying with her friends the McLeans, close by, observed, "There was no sweet harmony there, either."[39]

Mrs. Longworth had disliked Woodrow Wilson since he gave out an interview in 1907:

> I have not seen much of Mr. Roosevelt since he became President, but I am told that he no sooner thinks than he talks, which is a miracle not wholly in accord with the educational theory of forming an opinion.[40]

Alice, her father, and Nick went to Sagamore Hill for a weekend prior to the big political push. They sat on the piazza, which is what Colonel Roosevelt called his front porch, and were almost unaware of the sunset. The peacefulness of their surroundings did not soothe them. They rocked violently in the white wicker rocking chairs, and decided that Alice should take no part in the coming proceedings.[41]

After that uncomfortable weekend, both her husband and her father took to the political trails. Since both men had asked her to remain out of the strife, the young woman did as she was bidden—staying for the most part in Rookwood and consuming a diet that consisted only of eggs, fruit, and Vichy water.

On a warm evening, October 14, 1912, Alice about to partake of her meager meal, was interrupted by a telephone call from a night editor on the Cincinnati *Enquirer*. He told her precisely what had just come over the Associated Press wire.

It read MILWAUKEE, WISC. ROOSEVELT SHOT BY FANATIC. MORE TO FOLLOW.[42]

Alice refused to believe the AP flash, but it was true.

9 □ THE SWEET REVENGE

Having been a victim of crank calls for many years, Alice would not put any credence in the news that her father had been shot. Not until her friend Ruth Hanna McCormick telephoned from Chicago, did she accept it as a fact.

John Schrank, fanatic, opened fire upon Theodore Roosevelt[1] as the former President stepped into his automobile in Milwaukee. The bullet tore through his overcoat, his spectacle case, and folded manuscript, fracturing his fourth rib, and lodging a little short of his right lung. Stunned, T.R. fell backward, coughed, and stood up again.

"Stop that!" he commanded as the crowds reached out to seize Schrank. "Don't allow anyone to hurt that man."

Police removed the would-be assassin while physicians examined Roosevelt. Although the doctors objected, T.R. demanded to be driven to the auditorium. "I will make this speech or die,"[2] he said. "It is one thing or the other."

"Friends," he called out in a hoarse voice from the platform, "I have to ask you to be as quiet as possible. I have just been shot." His audience gasped, but Roosevelt waved them back into silence.

"It takes more than that to kill a Bull Moose."[3]

He proceeded to speak for just under an hour, denouncing Wilson, calling down shame upon his old friend Taft, and urging his listeners to vote for the new Progressive ticket.

Upon his conclusion, a team of surgeons raced him from the platform to a specially outfitted railway car and headed for Chicago.

"I'll never forget those little green rooms in Mercy Hospital," Alice said. She arrived there and spent a precious few moments listening to her father's astonishment at the entire experience.

"The doctors have decided to leave the bullet where it is," he whispered. Relieved that he would be spared the scalpel, Alice nodded understandingly.[4]

Two weeks later, her father spoke to 16,000 people jammed into New York's Madison Square Garden. One of America's best journalists, Richard Harding Davis, wrote, "Tonight's demonstration carried the sound of congratulations and thanksgiving."[5] Alice appreciated the sentiment but she knew that words tapped out on a typewriter could not be translated into votes at the ballot boxes across the United States.

The authorities placed Mr. Schrank in a mental hospital, where he died in 1942.[6]

The weather on Election Day, 1912, in Cincinnati reflected coming events. The skies were dark and the air muggy. In the evening, Nick and Alice went to the club, "Where everyone was my enemy," and then to the newspaper office.[7] No question. Wilson would win.

Alice came by her antipathy toward Woodrow Wilson quite naturally. She had, from childhood on, cradled a healthy dislike for teachers of the formal sort, the exception being Henry Cabot Lodge, who taught economics at Harvard while her father attended that college. T.R. wouldn't take a course from Lodge, because the other students told Roosevelt Lodge was "too strict in his grading."[8] Wilson had taught in many institutions of higher learning, emerging as the president of Princeton. He gave up that lofty seat only when the voters of New Jersey propelled him into the governor's chair in Trenton.[9]

Born in Staunton, Virginia, Wilson's grim visage looked dour and sour to Alice. There was none of the heartiness—assumed though it may have been—of Will Taft. Certainly, he had none of the excitement of her father.

Wilson had a wife and three daughters, and no one knew better than Alice that, should they move into the White House, the cameramen and reporters would quickly forget about Mrs. Longworth, and concentrate on the young Wilson women.

For this campaign, Wilson adopted the motto "The Great Freedom." Alice heard it, and remarked, "It's a nice slogan. What does it mean?"[10]

The election results, hastily chalked up on the blackboard in the newspaper office, confirmed her fears. Wilson had won by a large amount.[11] Not a majority, but large enough to defeat his two Republican opponents. Colonel Roosevelt took second place, almost a million votes more than Taft had received, but the Longworth family did not find a great deal of consolation from those figures.[12]

A Democrat was going to be the next President—a repugnant thought to Alice. Even more disturbing was the unexpected discovery that Nick lost his seat in the House of Representatives by a dubious 97 votes. At one point, they took hope in the false information that he was leading by some 1,800 ballots. They waited six days for a recount, and *still* the questionable 97 votes kept him out in the cold.[13]

The Longworth family, pessimistic beyond belief, felt sure that Nick's political future was nonexistent.

Alice was more optimistic. She believed that one term back in his own district would make Nick even stronger with his constituents.

The last few months in Washington were filled for the "lame duck" Longworths with farewells. Alice tried to adjust to their departure from her favorite city. "Oh, how much I do hate to leave," she told her friends.[14] Time ran out. She consoled Nick by recalling Tim Sullivan's comment regarding members of the House. The old chief of New York City's Tammany Hall said, "Congressmen? In Washington they hitch horses to them."

Nick took off for Cincinnati, but Alice stayed on in Washington to close their home and attend a formal tea with the new President's wife, Ellen, and their three daughters, Margaret, Jessie, and Eleanor. Closing the Longworth residence turned out to be more enjoyable than the visit to the White House. Quite obviously, the new First Lady was ailing, and she and her daughters spoke to Alice in polite but cool tones. The female members of the Wilson family were not as forgiving as politicians.

Suddenly, Rookwood, that gray, dismal, old mansion inspired Alice to make plans for travel.

Shortly after their honeymoon in 1906, Alice and Nick had visited Panama. Cut away from the northern neck of Colombia, the new republic existed because of her father's determination and the possibility of the firepower of his gunboats anchored off shore. With Colonel Goethals, who was in charge of construction of the Panama Canal, they had ridden through the jungle in his private car, the *Yellow Peril*. It had been called that because of the disease that had felled workers and because many of those laborers, who had dug beside Americans from both hemispheres, had been of Oriental parentage.

Returning to Panama in 1913, Nick and Alice rode on the first ship that crossed the Isthmus from the Pacific to the Atlantic.[15] Colonel Goethals—now General Goethals—showed them the famed Culebra Cut, and the various locks that raised or lowered the ship with singular ease.

"Where is the *Yellow Peril*?" Alice asked.

"Where she belongs," General Goethals replied. "Somewhere on the bottom of the Miraflores Locks."[16]

Life in Rookwood consisted largely of picnics, musicales, and limited conversations with a provincial mother-in-law who never quite understood Alice and her hunger for Washington and politics.

Mrs. Longworth had learned to "play act" at a young age. Like the majority of children, she enjoyed pretending and she never stopped. If she had come from a different background, she could have been an excellent actress. One person well acquainted with Alice *and* the theater, said, "Her imitations weren't those of an amateur. She polished her roles until they glowed. I was reminded of Alice when I saw Jane Alexander do Eleanor Roosevelt in the television adaptation of Joe Lash's book. Ms. Alexander gave a brilliant performance—I tell you—Alice Longworth was even better. She was perfect!"[17]

Perfect—and that's the way she played most of the roles in her life. One of her best turned out to be that of Wife. By 1913, no matter how well she had tried, there were over-the-back-fence reports that the Longworths had reached "an arrangement."

Nick, at forty, seemed to have caught the "seven year itch," an urge for the company of other women.

Acquaintances stated that Alice became aware of the situation early, and outwardly, at least, reacted with her usual aristocratic calm.

If Alice was unhappy with her "open" marriage, she did not complain. If she confided to a close friend, possibly Ruth Hanna McCormick, her confidences remained secret. She must have suffered some hurt, though. One of the most desirable and sought-after women in the world, at twenty-nine she was apparently shown that unquestioned loyalty from Nick went to the Republican Party but not necessarily to his wife.

When "Fishbait" Miller, former sergeant at arms of the House of Representatives, published his memoirs, he wrote that Nick Longworth was "the greatest womanizer on the Hill."[18] In Cincinnati circles, the local people circulated a story that Alice, once walking in a park near town, almost stumbled over her husband as he lay in the summer grass, caressing an attractive girl. One version of the story, had the young woman on the ground saying, "Hello, Mrs. Longworth." Another version had Alice turning her head and pretending not to see. The speed of her steps and her heartbeats must have quickened.

While Nick went to parties escorting a girl on each arm, Alice attended different affairs—frequently political, and very often with Senator William E. Borah of Idaho. Much was made of this, but very little fact can be uncovered. A few years later, John L. Lewis, founder of the Congress of Industrial Organizations, entered her private picture. Both men were dynamic, eloquent, and extremely taken with Mrs. Longworth.

Alice's family, particularly her father, took "Till death do us part" literally. They considered divorce unacceptable—not for religious reasons or political. T.R. believed in strength in all aspects of life.[19] Divorce would show a weakness of choice or perseverance. Alice abided by the same rules. It took many years for Mrs. Longworth to divulge the truth about her twenty-six-year marriage to Nick.

"I didn't exactly revel in it," she confessed.[20]

Wilson's inaugural address was, as Alice expected, "stuffy." On the other hand, she was glad to see that the Democrat's new Vice-President, Thomas Marshall, of neighboring Indiana, showed some humor in his speech.

"I believe I'm entitled to make a few remarks," the Vice-President stated at the beginning of his talk, "because I'm about to enter a four-year period of silence."[21]

Alice visited Washington only once during their two-year absence from the capital, "and that was just to look things over." She was dismayed to find the city crawling with those "odd beings" called Democrats.[22]

Through the salons of Massachusetts and Connecticut Avenues, the homes in Georgetown, Alexandria, Virginia, and adjoining Maryland, through the corridors and cloakrooms of the Capitol itself, a story circulated dealing with the new President. According to the tale, Wilson started to consider the possibilities of the White House when he was still a graduate student at nearby Johns Hopkins University. When, after many years, the electorate voted him into the Presidency, he visited an old and very deaf aunt.

"How are you employed these days?" the elderly lady asked.

"I've been elected President," he responded.

"Of what?" demanded his deaf aunt.

"Of the United States!" he shouted into her ear trumpet.

"Don't be silly," she said, and put down her trumpet in disgust.

Mrs. Longworth sided with Mr. Wilson's aunt.[23]

Even Alice's foes considered her a social asset. When they heard she was in town for a short time in the winter of 1914, she received an invitation to a party in the White House. She accepted and spent most of the evening sitting in the East Room on those "uncomfortable little gold chairs," whispering unflattering comments about the Administration to the people who gathered around her.[24]

"Mostly father's sympathizers."

She was never invited back.

"Someone must have been a spy," she told her sister.[25]

The new President made peculiar decisions—at least, so it seemed to Alice. One of the strangest was the appointment of her cousin Eleanor's husband as Assistant Secretary of the Navy, the same post Alice's father had held before he resigned and left to fight the Spanish.

She found him seated behind her father's old desk, smiling broadly and looking not at all uncomfortable. Alice congratulated Franklin and gave him one of her extra-long cigarette holders.[26]

In the fall and winter of 1913-1914, Alice's father and young Kermit went on an expedition up the Amazon River to explore the uncharted "River of Doubt." "One disaster after another," he confessed upon his return.[27]

> We had an uneventful trip into the interior of Brazil. Then we tried to come back. Insects ate away at us, two boats were lost when the river rose suddenly one night. Hostile Indians killed one of our dogs. Kermit's boat capsized, and one of the natives was lost. Food ran low. One of the party went insane and killed another explorer. Finally, the fever got to me. I had malaria, dysentery, and my fever went up to 105. I thought about suicide but decided against it because I was afraid Kermit would insist on bringing my body out.[28]

On April 30, 1914, Colonel Roosevelt, and what remained of his party, emerged from the seething green jungle. They had traveled 1,500 miles. Roosevelt himself had lost seventy-five pounds. He would never recover from all that beset him. Physical deterioration would continue until the very end of his life.

In June of that same year, Kermit, his father, and Alice went to Madrid, where Kermit married Belle Willard, the daughter of the American ambassador.

Then Alice went on to Paris for the Grand Prix horse races. On June 28, 1914, the Austro-Hungarian Archduke, Franz Ferdinand, was fatally shot by a Serbian nationalist, "None of the people there," Alice wrote of her Parisian friends at the Grand Prix, "who talked about it gave any sign of realizing that it was the match that touched off the fuse."[29]

The Russians felt duty-bound to declare war on Austria. The French were part of the Entente Cordiale which linked them with Britain. Before anyone realized it, Kaiser Wilhelm's infantry goose-stepped into Belgium.

Nick had no trouble in gaining reelection in 1914. It was just as Alice had predicted. They returned to the

Capital, and Alice, with much elation said, "It's great to have our exile behind us."[30]

Back in Washington, Alice did more than "settle in." She made certain to keep up the image of unconventionality.No more corsets—Alice needed breath for what she had to say. Flesh-colored stockings with her Alice Blue dresses—flesh colored when all proper ladies wore black. "What *will* she do next?" her peers asked. It didn't take long to find out. Mrs. Longworth answered her door to guests wearing pants! Plunder from her trip to the Orient in 1905 continued to make fashion. In this case, she brought out silk Chinese pajamas.[31] And while her husband played his violin and famous friends buzzed about the latest news, Alice Longworth sat on the floor in front of the fireplace, puffing away on her monogrammed cigarettes. Ellen Maury Slayden, a Congressman's wife, wrote in her diary that Alice, "moved her body like a leopard cat," and Jonathan Daniels added, " ... a feline figure and (against Wilson) one ready with talons..."[32]

Wilson had other reasons for worry. The Mexican guerrilla Pancho Villa frequently raided the Texas border. When at last Wilson committed American cavalry to the punitive expedition against the Villistas, the soil of Mexico swallowed up almost every rebel in sight.[33]

In 1915, Alice drew criticism for wearing pantalettes in public. As usual, she shocked everyone, and as usual, she did not seem to mind. "I urge all the ladies to wear pantalettes. They're comfortable, economical and save considerable cloth."[34]

Later in the month, Alice was a house guest of Mrs. Cornelius Vanderbilt, in New York City, and she came down with the mumps. A maid answered the phone when a reporter from *The New York Times* called to inquire about Mrs. Longworth's health. Alice spoke into the instrument, "I'm thirty-two years old, and I do *not* wish to have my mumps in the newspaper."[35]

Alice failed to recognize the similar traits of her father and the "despicable" Woodrow Wilson. Both men had brilliant minds—both tried valiantly to raise the moral and social status of America and the world. Reform stood at its apogee, but unconsciously, Alice had crossed from her father's liberal camp into the conservative thinking of her husband.

The Progressives wanted her father to stand as a candidate for the Presidency again in 1916, but this time Theodore refused the bait. Charles Evans Hughes, Associate Justice of the Supreme Court, carried the Republican nomination, and Wilson slipped back into the White House by a squeak.

"Almost everybody had gone to bed, but I stayed up and watched the returns come in from California. Two thousand votes the other way and Hughes would have won in the Electoral College," Alice noted. "I began wondering about the feasibility of that system then and there."[36]

Wilson's election slogan was, "He kept us out of war." But one month after he was inaugurated again, German policies became so offensive that Wilson sadly had to lead this country into the European conflict.

The humbling of Theodore Roosevelt began almost with the declaration of war. Having been successful in leading troops during the Spanish-American War, Roosevelt now offered to raise a division of fighting men for America. Wilson wouldn't hear of it. Although British and French commanders were in favor of Mr. Roosevelt's idea, Woodrow Wilson refused to consider any such thought. The Colonel pressed his notion until he succeeded in getting Congress to pass a law that would have allowed him to recruit and equip the doughboys. The bill died on Wilson's desk.[37]

Alice never forgave Wilson for his humiliation of her father. Although she sold bonds for the Treasury and made bandages for the Red Cross, Alice, along with Senator Borah, Senator Lodge, and others, decided not to go along with the President's concept of a League of Nations.[38]

She composed bawdy ballads about the President and repeated the libelous limericks her pals gleefully disseminated, "There once was a man named Woodrow. . . ."[39]

Not allowed to do anything for the war effort, Roosevelt confessed bitterly, "I don't want to be an old cannon loose on the deck in the storm, smashing everything I come near."[40]

Theodore Roosevelt had taken great pride in the knowledge that all four of his sons were in the service of their country during the war. Tragically, his youngest, Quentin, disappeared over German lines during the closing days of the conflict.[41] An aviator, Quentin had the misfortune of tangling with Baron Manfred von Richthofen's Flying Circus. Shot down, he was buried at Cambrai by the Germans.[42]

"If this war goes on," the Colonel said to a visitor, "none of the boys will come back." Mrs. Roosevelt overheard the words and went white.[43]

Shortly after this, an armistice was signed by the warring parties. On the eleventh hour of the eleventh day of the eleventh month of 1918, the firing ceased and the Great War ended.

On January 5, 1919, Alice's father decided to spend the day in the bedroom of his country home.[44] He worked on an article, and read a book as his wife stayed close by, playing solitaire. Now and again, they both gazed out of the large window at the wintry waters of Long Island Sound.

"I wonder if you will ever know how I love Sagamore Hill," he said to Edith.[45]

Earlier than usual he told his valet that he felt weary and wanted to retire. Mrs. Roosevelt kissed him good night. During the morning hours of January 6, 1919, Theodore Roosevelt died in his sleep.[46]

"Dive, Alice; now, dive!"[47] That's what T.R. had shouted to his eldest child when she trembled at the sight of the deep, cold water of the Sound. She'd felt persecuted that her father had forced her to do something of which she was afraid. Hike farther than you think you can, ride a horse until you are more fatigued than the four-footed animal, climb to the top of the cliff—never turn back. Adapt to all situations. It is not only possible, it is imperative. Those were T.R.'s rules for himself and his family.

"Dive, Alice; now dive!" Alice dived. There was no one to force her, only the training that her father had instilled. Alice became a new kind of Rough Rider, and her first ride took her to Oyster Bay where she helped plan her father's funeral. From then on, it would be life without T.R.

In the future, whenever Alice caught a whiff of geraniums or heliotrope, the scent would race her memory back to the early years at Sagamore Hill and she could smell again the handkerchiefs that her father had sprayed with his favorite colognes. When Americans think of the twenty-sixth President, they recall his power to "bust trusts," his strength to settle strikes, his diplomacy to end a war, the "Bull Moose," the Great White Fleet, the Big Stick, the rugged West—only his daughter Alice thinks of geraniums and heliotrope.

"He was buried without eulogy, music, or military honors, in a plain oak casket on a . . . plot near Sagamore Hill. . . . About four hundred personal friends came."[48]

Cabot Lodge paid his respects to T.R. in the Senate, and closed his emotional speech with, "So Valiant-for-Truth passed over and all the trumpets sounded for him on the other side."[49]

Eleanor Roosevelt recorded in her diary, "Another great figure off the stage."[50]

Irwin S. Cobb, a leading American humorist, wrote, "You had to hate the Colonel a lot to keep from loving him."[51]

Throughout the many unofficial tributes paid to her father, Alice seemed mesmerized. Her lips were tight, her eyes were cold. As the days turned toward spring, friends noticed that her grief took the form of fury directed at Woodrow Wilson. "I never forgive the persons who injure those I love," Alice said more than once.[52] She felt that Wilson's snubs of her father had hastened T.R.'s death. The President would regret what he had done. The lethargy of sorrow evolved into a host of plans—all of them designed to thwart Mr. Wilson's most cherished dream—the League of Nations.

Now it came time for Alice to humble the proud Woodrow Wilson. Although he took much credit for being an international statesman, Wilson carelessly or deliberately failed to invite any Republicans to join him on his first trip to Europe.

> The armistice had left a wake of trauma and bereavement, and the final score was formidable, [wrote Mrs. Wilson's biographer, Ishbel Ross] with 53,390 men killed in battle or dead from wounds. The wounded num-

> bered 234,000 and 4,500 men were missing.[53] The war was won but there were many who felt that America should revert to its well-established policy of isolationism—all of which ran counter to Woodrow Wilson's expansive vision of a united world. . . .
>
> The Wilsons had left Washington secretly in their private railroad car, *The Mayflower*, and embarked at Hoboken.[54] As they slipped their moorings, the racket began. Bands played and hastily assembled crowds gathered. The news could now be told. All New York knew what was going on as the fog horns blasted, gun salutes came from the forts, and the screech of whistles ripped through the air.[55]

Eleanor and Franklin Roosevelt had sailed on that ship with the President.

In Paris, the French greeted the Chief Executive with hand-printed placards that read, "Vive Wilson." The American party felt elated. After the public celebration, parades, visits to the tomb of Napoleon Bonaparte, excursions to Versailles, to the grave of Lafayette, to the Louvre, the Left Bank, Wilson and his advisers met with the heads of state of the Allied Nations.

He anxiously presented his Fourteen Points—a basis for the League of Nations. Clemenceau of France observed cautiously, "God gave us the Ten Commandments, and we broke them. Wilson gave us the Fourteen Points and we shall see."[56]

President and Mrs. Wilson and their entourage traveled by train, visiting the provinces of France and Italy. When they stopped in the station in Modena, a telegram was delivered to him with the news of Theodore Roosevelt's death. American correspondents watched the President through the window as he read it. A couple of them reported to Alice that after his initial surprise, his face could hardly conceal his satisfaction.[57]

When Wilson and his party steamed back to the United States, T.R.'s daughter awaited him. Upon their return from that first peacemaking trip to Europe, Alice and a friend drove down to Washington's Union Station to gauge the size of the crowd. It was small. Summer had taken hold of the capital. Most of the people who had gathered to greet the President were women wearing lightweight dresses. In the absence of a breeze, their voices floated high in the almost-empty railroad terminal.

Alice and her friend then drove to the White House. There, no more than two or three hundred curiosity seekers lined up outside the gate. Seeing Wilson approach Pennsylvania Avenue, Alice got out onto the running board of her car, crossed her fingers to make the proper "magicks," and muttered softly, "A murrain on him. A murrain on him." Her friend, fearing the Secret Service might spot her, urged her to get back into the car and clear away from the location.[58]

"Who are you afraid for?" Alice asked her fearful companion. "Me or Wilson?"

As the auto bearing the Wilsons neared the White House, the lamp under the porte cochere went on. Only then did Alice get back into her car, depress the clutch, slip the gear into its first position, and slowly drive away.

Henry Cabot Lodge, T.R.'s dear friend, opened the salvo against Wilson and the League of Nations with a speech from the well of the Senate. Caustic, sarcastic, this clever old professor, playing the warlock to Alice's witch, enjoined his fellow Senators to beware of international entanglements. Lodge, chairman of the Senate's Foreign Relations Committee, attacked Wilson's League from the floor of the Upper House. Invoking the warnings that George Washington had used against foreign entanglements, Lodge portrayed the League as a threat to the Monroe Doctrine. He saw American boys being pulled into foreign wars by intriguing powers. He called for consideration, time, and thought, before his countrymen were dragged "by any glittering delusions, through specious devices of supra-national government, within the toils of international socialism and anarchy."[59]

Above the floor, high in the visitors' gallery sat Alice Roosevelt Longworth. Each day she made her sacred pilgrimage to the Senate gallery. Each day, she listened intently to those men who debated the matter of the League of Nations. "The Battalion of Death" was the name given to her followers, and like her father she was awarded the rank of "Colonel."[60]

As a small child, Alice had fantasized that the grass terraces surrounding the Capitol were "Uncle Cabot's" private lawns. "Lodge himself," wrote Jonathan Daniels, "had some such idea about Republicans and the republic. He considered himself on guard for both."[61]

On March 19, 1920, the final vote was taken in the Senate. It tallied 49 in favor, and 39 against.[62] The League supporters assuredly lacked the necessary two thirds for passage of the measure.

Alice hastened down from the gallery. Lodge met her outside the cloakroom. In a rare display of open affection, Alice threw her arms about the exhausted chairman.

"Well, my dear," he said, "the issue is as dead as Marley's ghost."[63]

In the only serious political battle to which she admitted taking part, Alice emerged the victor. Wilson lost his League. He also lost his health and in time his Presidency. In the end, Theodore Roosevelt's eldest child triumphed.

10 □ THE DEUCES WILD

If he had lived, some historians believe Alice's father would have been elected the twenty-ninth President of the United States.[1] Fate decreed it otherwise. In 1920, a well-known Republican Senator was quoted as saying, "This year we have a lot of second raters. Harding is no world-beater, but he's the best of the second raters."[2]

To this, Alice told Thornton Wilder, Pulitzer Prize-winning playwright and novelist, "Saying that Harding is second rate is one of the biggest compliments anyone can pay him."[3]

Nick and Alice arrived in hot, steamy Chicago early in June and went to their favorite hostelry, the Blackstone, where they were given suite 404.

General Leonard Wood, T.R.'s old commanding officer and Alice's host in Puerto Rico, was the front-runner in the Republican Party, but as Harry Daugherty, successor to Mark Hanna as the Republican boss of Ohio, observed, "There's not enough money in the world to buy the nomination for a man with epaulettes on his shoulders in 1920."[4]

For this vital compaign, the Republicans had a formidable list of candidates. In addition to General Wood, Frank O. Lowden, governor of Illinois, had a strong following. Senator Hiram Johnson of California had equally powerful backing, as did Nicholas Murray Butler of New York, Senator William Borah of Idaho, another of Alice's favorites, Wisconsin's Senator Robert LaFollette—the inventory of the candidates went on and on. Alice assuredly gave no thought to her fellow Buckeye, Senator Warren G. Harding, but Harding's political mentor, Harry Daugherty, had other ideas. "I found him sunning himself like a turtle on a log, and I pushed him into the water," Daugherty wrote some years later.[5]

Of course, only Daugherty considered Harding a serious Presidential candidate, but when the balloting became deadlocked and the Party powers retired to a baking Blackstone hotel suite, where no food and no water were served but strong cigars and illegal whiskey were plentiful, the evening took on a different hue. Determined to find a man for the White House, a man who could get the vote and still be controlled, the oligarchs of the Republican Party settled at 2:11 A.M. on Warren Gamaliel Harding. When informed of the decision, Mrs. Harding replied, "I see but one word written over his head if they make him President, and that word is, 'Tragedy.'"[6]

In retrospect, most historians believe that the men in the smoke-filled room of the Blackstone Hotel in Chicago compromised and chose Harding for three reasons—he was easy to manipulate, his silver-haired portraits always came out perfectly, and he could be elected.

After the decision was passed on to him, Harding turned to no one in particular and said, "I feel like a man who goes in on a pair of eights and comes out with aces full."[7]

Alice, the poker authority, observed, "I always felt he had a fourth ace up his sleeve, and if he needed it, a fifth ace in his slipper."[8]

The Republican ticket was Harding and Coolidge, and since the Democrat Cox did not attract the electorate, the opposition coasted in on the men's lethargy and the women's votes. As Samuel Hopkins Adams wrote

"The country had made its choice, not that it loved Harding more, but Wilson less. Cox had manfully accepted the Wilson tradition; he was made the scapegoat." After the inauguration, Alice painted a memorable word portrait of the President.

"Harding," she said, "looks like a debauched Roman emperor."[9]

The journalist Mark Sullivan wrote, "Warren G. Harding was the only man in the Senate who could wear a toga and get away with it."[10]

While Alice appeared relieved that the ailing Wilson had moved out of the White House, she was far from taken in by Warren Gamaliel Harding. True, he was a Republican; true he had beaten Cox and Cousin Franklin Delano Roosevelt, the Democratic slate. Still, Harding's election in 1920 filled her with no rapture.

During the 1912 convention at the Coliseum in Chicago, the then-Senator Harding had sauntered over to the box that held Alice and Nick. If the Longworths would string along with their fellow Ohioan, Taft, Nick could have the governor's mansion in Columbus. Alice, enraged because she felt her father should receive the Republican nomination, snapped, "One should not accept favors from crooks."[11]

Harding left the box a bit stung, but not surprised. He'd heard about Alice's tart tongue. Everyone from Nick to Julius Fleischmann, Nick's wealthy backer from Cincinnati, tried to get Alice to apologize but that word did not exist in Alice's vocabulary. When her father accepted the Progressive Party's nomination for the Presidency, Harding, as editor of the Marion, Ohio, *Star*, called T.R. "every kind of traitor from Benedict Arnold to Aaron Burr."[12] Alice never forgot.

For Nick's political future she allowed the poker-playing Harding into her house on 21st Street, but she never set foot in the home in which he lived as Senator.

Born in an Ohio village, Harding moved to the town of Marion where he began work as a newspaper reporter. After marrying the daughter of the richest man in Marion, Harding bought the paper. His wife, Florence, had been married before and deserted by her first husband. She taught music until Warren came along. Five to eight years older than Harding, "Flo" possessed a harsh voice, a single kidney, and an incurable ambition for her handsome husband.[13]

By the time Harding worked his way through local politics and came to Washington as a Senator from Ohio, Alice ran the most influential salon in the capital. Invitations to her dinner parties were eagerly sought after by all branches of government and the diplomatic corps.

"You have to have a bit of malice to be a good hostess," Alice said. "I'm afraid I'm rather malevolent about people."[14]

Alice planned her dinners with controversy in mind. She worried over the place cards, and tried desperately to seat people who had completely divergent views side by side.[15]

"They hate each other," Nick would protest, and Alice would clap her hands and say, "Marvelous!"[16]

A militant would find himself passing the salt to a pacifist—the head of a corporation might learn that his neighbor spent his time trying to start a union—a bigoted Southerner would possibly have to give an example of his charm to a lady who devoted herself to the raising of money for black universities. If no argument ensued before cognac, Alice considered the evening a flop. "We'll try and do better next week," she'd say.

Another facet of Alice's personality showed flashes of kindness and generosity. Her brother Quentin had been engaged to marry Flora Whitney.[17] It is doubtful whether Alice knew the young Whitney girl. Being a member of an old New York family she did know the older Whitneys along with the Astors, the Vanderbilts, the Goelets, and other prominent members of Gotham's socially elite.

When the "boys" returned from Europe and Quentin was not among them, Flora Whitney became distraught.

"Flora is utterly heartbroken," the Colonel in his last days had written Ted. "She is young, and time will mercifully heal her sorrow, but she has had her golden dream and it proved only a dream."[18]

Upon her sister Ethel's report of the girl's condition, Alice promptly invited her to work in Washington. A telephone call secured her a job at Republican Headquarters. As for a place to live, she would stay at the Longworths.[19]

> Living with Alice was absolutely marvelous [Flora Whitney Miller recalls]. Of course, I'd have to report for work at nine o'clock in the morning, and every night there'd be a party so wonderful I couldn't think of missing it. Alice was kind and wonderful and invited me to all of them. The problem was, I never got enough sleep. Guests would leave at three or four in the morning, and Alice would sleep until noon or even later. She was so much fun to be with that I'd never get to bed until she did. But then *I'd* have to be up at eight.
>
> Then came the time when Alice went away for a few days and I said to myself, now I'm going to get a couple of good nights' sleep. Not at all. Nick wanted to sit up and talk, so I didn't get to bed until the usual hour at the Longworth's![20]

While those days may have been trying for the young girl, they accomplished precisely what Alice intended: they took Flora Whitney's mind off misfortune and set her back to feeling as a young girl should.

While Flora Whitney took readily to the social life of Washington, two significant changes in the history of this nation came about. The first was the sane, sensible, long-overdue woman's suffrage amendment (at Alice's prodding, Nick voted for it in the House), and then that prize curiosity of reformist ardor, the experiment noble in purpose, the Eighteenth Amendment.

Few thought of whiskey as contraband. If they had any liquor in their homes, Americans considered it their private stock. Thanks to the Prohibition Amendment, spirits could be obtained through a variety of means; a prescription from one's doctor could be filled at the corner drug store; a sometimes deadly concoction hastily distilled in the hills of West Virginia, Tennessee, Kentucky, and Arkansas called White Mule provided kicks for the thirsty. Then, of course, there were the local suppliers who got theirs from Canada, Mexico, or fast-running motor launches coming in from the sea on both coasts. With the arrival of hootch, appeared the gangster.

The transgressions caused by the Volstead Act titillated Alice's sense of mischief. She listened as her friends boasted of acquiring "the real stuff—bottled in bond." Many people drank in modern new speakeasies and even in the distinguished old homes of Washington.

The initials "B.Y.O." began to appear on the bottoms of engraved dinner invitations ("Bring Your Own"), but the Longworths beat the system by making wine, "bathtub gin," and home brew in their basement.[21] Although she sipped an occasional glass of claret or white wine, Alice frequently refused to accept invitations to the "dry" households because Nick couldn't manage to get through a long Washington evening without a few pick-me-ups. Two articles of dress became standard with Alice, broad-brimmed hats and enormous satchellike cloth purses. Into these voluminous pocketbooks, Alice placed a variety of items, ranging from copies of the Constitution to flasks containing bourbon or rye for Nick and his friends.

"I sometimes think I may have been one of the first bootleggers," Alice said.[22]

At the White House, the Hardings observed the law of the land for official functions, but the moment the guests departed, the President ordered an open bar. His wife, whom he called the Duchess, had gray hair, a jealous temper, and wore dog collars made of velvet or beads to hide the wrinkles on her neck. The Duchess had a little red book into which she wrote the names of those people who snubbed her. Alice's name appeared as regularly as model T's dropped off the assembly line in Detroit. When T.R.'s daughter spoke with Harding, she involuntarily recalled the 1912 convention, and her conversations with the President became saturated with condescension. Some say her tone bordered on contempt.

The man, not the office, Alice felt, deserved it. Publicly, Harding smoked cigars. Privately, he chewed tobacco. He insisted on toothpicks at his table, which was probably the first and last times they were to appear at the Executive Mansion. Sometimes he put his feet on his desk when officials called on him. "I'm just folks," he liked to remind his cronies.

Harding passed out favors faster than cigars. The only fame his father attained was from the sagacious observation he offered his son. "Warren," the senior

Harding said, "if you were a girl, you'd be in the family way all the time. You can't say No."[23]

Alice also held little regard for the President's wife. "Cheap" was the word she used to describe Mrs. Harding. Talk of Flo's daily facials, her boasting that she had propelled her husband into the nation's highest office, rankled Alice. True, Flo Harding had shaken a record 4,756 hands at a New Year's reception—her hand had been swollen for almost a week afterward. Her closest friend turned out to be an old chum of Alice's, Evalyn Walsh McLean, owner of the Hope diamond. Both Mrs. Harding and Mrs. McLean loved clothes, both coveted jewels, both were superstitious, both dashed to fortune tellers and crystal gazers. The only common ground the three women shared, at that time, was superstition.[24] But to a woman who had made "magicks" since childhood, Mrs. Harding and Mrs. McLean were late-comers.

Evalyn McLean's father had been a gold miner. His country place, Friendship, was where Alice and Nick spent the first night of their marriage. It was filled with gold knives and gold forks and gold spoons, and Evalyn McLean talked the First Lady into having the White House silver triple gold plated. It remains to be used only for state dinners.

Alice scoffed, "When we were there, we didn't *need* gold."[25]

On the death of Chief Justice Edward White in 1921, Warren Harding appointed William Howard Taft as the new Chief Justice. Taft began serving October 3, 1921. He felt comfortable in his full black robes, and he adapted well to the position. After a few months of handing down decisions and banging the hard oak gavel, he said to his fellow Justices, "I don't remember that I was ever President." Alice nodded when she heard his statement. "Neither does the country."[26]

Within a year of Harding's taking the Presidential oath, sounds of ugly innuendo began to circulate through Washington. Alice was among the first to hear them. She knew, for instance, of the poker games held at the little green house at 1625 K Street. Supposedly, many were rigged by the "Ohio Gang" so that the President would win. Even Mr. Harding noticed that the stacked blue chips stayed piled high in front of him, and the other players bragged of their losses and never objected.

Will Rogers, the humorist from Oklahoma, visited the White House.

"Want to hear the latest jokes, Mr. President?" he asked.

"Don't tell me, Will," Harding answered, "I appointed them."

And poker wasn't all. There were women. Loose women, wanton women, nude women fighting with broken bottles in their hands in front of the little house on K Street. And then came Nan Britton, the high-school newspaper reporter from Marion who had the President's baby.

Alice listened to talk of Harding and Nan Britton, talk of explicit sexual intercourse, of indiscretions on desks, in small closets in the White House.

"My God," she exclaimed, "we have a President of the United States who doesn't even know *beds* were invented—and his campaign slogan was 'Back to Normalcy!'"

Later, Nan Britton wrote more than a news story; after his death, she wrote an entire book called *The*

President's Daughter,[27] and the rumor persisted that Nan hadn't been the first to be blessed in that manner.

Apparently oblivious of everything about him, Harding continued to hum his favorite tune as sung by Jesse Smith, a member of the "Ohio Gang." Smith, who lived in the House on K Street, handled the vast sums of cash. The ditty he sang was:

> My father makes book on the corner,
> My mother makes synthetic gin,
> My sister makes love for a dollar,
> My God how the money rolls in![28]

The Duchess played the piano, and all the while she remained in the White House her favorite song was "The End of a Perfect Day." The end for the Duchess began on the return from a trip to Alaska in the summer of 1923. On August 2, the President collapsed aboard his train. He died in San Francisco.[29] At first the diagnosis was food poisoning—then a brain clot. When Mrs. Harding refused to allow an autopsy to be performed, the ugliest rumors began: he killed himself to avoid a scandal, she poisoned him for the same reason, his doctor administered the poison. Then the doctor, Charles Sawyer, who had been brought from Marion and made a general, died suddenly.[30] After that came the Teapot Dome scandal.

Teapot Dome was government-owned land that contained a large reserve of oil for the use of the United States Navy in case of war. Examiners hired by doubting Senators uncovered graft, bribery, and assorted forms of chicanery by various Harding officials and executives in the private sector; i.e., Harry Sinclair's company had siphoned off oil from Teapot Dome and sold it commercially. Then the Congress stepped in and began investigating. First to resign was the head of the Veteran's Bureau, Charles Forbes. Then, Secretary of the Interior Albert B. Fall. Charles Cramer, his legal counsel, committed suicide. Jesse Smith, who shared a house with Attorney General Harry Daugherty, took his own life.

Multimillionaire Tom Walsh, Evalyn McLean's father, had his son-in-law, Ned McLean, admit he gave Albert Fall $100,000 in a little black bag. Convicted and sent to prison were the Secretary of the Interior, the Custodian of Alien Property Thomas W. Miller, and Gaston B. Means of the Justice Department.

Alice Roosevelt Longworth viewed all this with skeptical eyes. The newspapers hinted that two of her brothers, Archie and Theodore, Jr., were involved. Archie had been an employee of Harry Sinclair, and Ted, Jr., once owned Sinclair stock. While Washington waited, the two Roosevelt brothers met with Alice, Nick, and their friend Senator Borah. The advice they received was to tell the truth. This they did, and the Congress and the press found both Roosevelts free of any complicity.

Harding's death brought an end to corruption in the White House—for a time. Although a marble tomb was erected in Marion, Ohio, to hold the bodies of the President and his wife, unofficial Washington felt Alice came up with a fitting epitaph when she said, "Harding was not a bad man. He was just a slob."[31]

II □ THE CRADLE ROCKS

In a scruffy hotel room off Boston's Public Gardens, sat the governor of the Commonwealth of Massachusetts, Calvin Coolidge, and his attractive wife, Grace. During the Boston police strike in 1919 the governor had gained nationwide attention by calling out the National Guard and wiring Samuel Gompers, head of the American Federation of Labor, "There is no right to strike against the public safety by anybody, anywhere, anytime."[1]

This, many Republicans considered to be just the right tone for the Presidential nomination in 1920. Disappointment came on the tenth ballot in Chicago, when Warren Harding was named the Party's choice. Coolidge was asked to remain close by; a Vice-President had to be picked. Eventually, the telephone rang, the governor picked up the receiver, listened for a moment, and then turned to his wife.

"Nominated," he said.

"You're not going to take it, are you?" she asked.

"I suppose I'll have to," he replied.[2]

So it was Harding and Coolidge against Cox and Roosevelt, the latter being that distant Hudson River Valley relative, Franklin Delano Roosevelt. The race for the Presidency proved no contest. Harding and "Normalcy" swept into the White House with the ease of a stick going over a waterfall. Author Jonathan Daniels noted that Harding's actual words were, "Not nostrums but normalcy." The national press selected only the last word and turned it into the banner of the Harding Administration.

The time: August 3, 1923, 2:47 A.M.

The place: John Coolidge's house in Vermont. The Vice-President and his wife are staying with his father. Because the gruff old farmer refuses to spend money on electricity and telephone, newspaper reporters drive twenty miles to inform the Vice-President of Mr. Harding's death in San Francisco. Awakened in their nightshirts, the Coolidges gather around a table on which rests the family Bible. The elder Coolidge, a notary public, is eligible by law to swear in his son as the next President of the United States. In the dim light of a kerosene lamp, the oath is taken, the first time an American President has accepted office in such humble and subdued circumstances.

Asked by the clamoring reporters for his thoughts, the laconic Coolidge, in his nasal New England twang says, "I think I can swing it."[3]

Alice Roosevelt Longworth's friend and ally Henry Cabot Lodge, Senator from Massachusetts, sneered down his Boston Brahmin nose at the thought of Calvin Coolidge as President of the United States. "I have known Calvin Coolidge only as long as it has been necessary to know him."[4]

Alice took a different view. If the Taft Presidency had been an insult and the Wilson years anathema, her feelings toward Harding had been ambivalent: she was euphoric that the White House was no longer occupied by a Democrat, but she was far from content with the Republican occupant.

Now, with Coolidge, the scandals, the women, the whiskey, the poker games were replaced by the proper family life of the short, redheaded New Englander who preferred few visitors over Nick and Alice Longworth. Pure New England on her mother's side, Alice appreciated his dry sense of humor, and found his wife to be an amiable conversationalist. She beamed when she heard the President had said, "I want things the way they used to be—before." What he meant, Washington soon learned, was that what he wanted was a White House patterned after T.R.'s White House. She blossomed when he made it clear that rather than a host of Republican swindlers, he would see more of the Roosevelts and the Longworths.

"Coolidge," Senator Lodge continued to patronize, "is the kind of man who lives in a two-family house."[5]

Alice matched him by noting that Mrs. Coolidge had once taught in a school for the deaf and mute. "That made it easier for her to live with Calvin,"[6] she said. But that was spoken before the Coolidges and the Longworths became friends.

The Coolidges waited patiently in the Willard Hotel, for three days, before Mrs. Harding moved out of the White House. Rumors flew that the waiters refused to serve them because the new President's tips were so small. Another favored canard was that Mrs. Coolidge intended to divorce the President the moment he left office. Alice knew this to be without substance the moment she met the couple. Coolidge adored his wife more than anyone on earth, except perhaps his sons, and Grace found Calvin an ideal husband.

Calvin, Junior, and John were teenagers, and while the high spirits of T.R. did not manifest themselves, the boys breathed a younger form of action into the old house. Even the President contributed a certain amount of levity. He would press all the buttons on his desk and then hide behind a door in his office. Secretaries, military and naval aides, assistants of all sorts, Secret Service men with drawn revolvers would rush in from all directions. Out from behind the door would step the President.

"Just wanted to see if everyone's working,"[7] he'd say.

Now a regular visitor to the White House, Alice became familiar with creatures that had not been there since her father's Presidency—dogs and cats abounded with collars that had WHITE HOUSE name tags so if they strayed, people would know where to return them. The two Coolidge boys, like Alice and her brothers and sister, received lion cubs as gifts, also bears, wallabies, and raccoons. As the Roosevelts had done before them, the Coolidges sent most of the animals to the National Zoo. Only the raccoon, named Rebecca, remained, and a special cage was constructed on the White House grounds.

Thrifty, as a New Englander should be, the President ordered two dozen chickens and placed them in a coop near the house, with orders that only Coolidge chickens were to be served at his table. His command was carried out to the letter, but Coolidge chickens had a curious minty taste. Investigation showed the chicken coop stood atop an old mint bed planted by Alice's father. The coop was moved immediately.[8]

Thanks to his impassive demeanor, the press named him Silent Cal. Alice, present at a White House luncheon for Republican women, sat on the President's right. On his left was a National committeewoman from Grand Island, Nebraska. Mr. Coolidge consumed his food in his usual silence, with an occasional mumble to Mrs. Longworth, but not once during the entire meal did he speak to the woman on his left. Painfully, the committeewoman tried gambit after gambit, but to no avail. The President did not answer. At the conclusion of the luncheon, she turned directly toward him and said, "Mr. President, I made a bet with one of my girlfriends back home that I could get you to say more than three words."

The President turned away from Mrs. Longworth and looked the woman straight in the eye. "You lose," he said, and arose from the table.

Alice is constantly credited with saying, "Coolidge looks like he was weaned on a pickle."[9] It is an excellent word caricature of Calvin Coolidge, but when she realized it was being quoted from the Senate to the salons, so as not to lose favor with the First Family, she refused to admit that the description was hers. She explained that she'd paid a morning visit to Dr. Worth Daniels, her physician. Supposedly, *he* had said it and she had only repeated it that afternoon at her hairdresser's. Those familiar with both the Longworths *and* the doctor say that the line has Alice's stamp on it. It is, they state, as identifiable as a fingerprint.

What did delight Alice was the tale of young Calvin, Junior, who spent the summer of 1923 working on his grandfather's farm in Vermont. One of the hired hands said to the youngster, "I wouldn't be doing the work you're doing if my father was President."

"Oh, yes, you would," Calvin, Junior, answered, "if *your* father was *my* father."[10]

The bubbling humor of Calvin, Junior, came to an end all too soon. While playing tennis in July of 1924, the young boy raised a blister on his foot. What seemed like an ordinary matter grew rapidly into a serious complication. Physicians and surgeons were called into the White House for consultation. The wonder drugs used today were unknown then. A staphylococcus infection raced through the boy's bloodstream. He was moved to the Army's Walter Reed Hospital where, to the dismay of the nation, he died on July 11, 1924.

Mrs. Warren Harding, whose year of mourning for her husband was not yet over, wrote a touching note to the Coolidge family. It included this sentence: "No matter how many loving hands may be stretched out to help us, some paths we tread alone."[11]

The summer of '24 proved a fateful time for Alice. She had a simple dream: Nick as President for two terms, then brother Ted as President for an equal time. Fulfillment of that hope would give her sixteen unbroken years back in the White House, back where she had come from, back where she belonged.

But her spells and incantations proved worthless. Coolidge had kept the country running smoothly. The chance of Nick getting the Republican nomination was hopeless. The convention began in Cleveland on June 12, 1924. Alice decided to skip it. She said the delegates could have sent in postcards, it was so cut and dried.[12] She had wished, and so had the President, that her close friend and confidant, Senator William Borah, be given the second spot on the ticket, but the convention chose Charles Dawes. Her interest in the Presidential contest waned when the Democrats nominated John W. Davis, a Wall Street lawyer, who couldn't have been more Republican than Alice herself even if he did run as a Democrat.

"Peace and Prosperity" was a Coolidge slogan, and who could vote against that? "Keep cool with Coolidge" was another political battle cry. Alice kept calm through Al Capone and his gangsters, through Leopold and Loeb and the murder they committed, and through the Ku Klux Klan burning their crosses not only in the South but in the North, too. But if Wilson had tried to make the world safe for democracy, Coolidge succeeded in making the nation safe for Wall Street. The stock market went on an upswing so high that nobody could see the end. Not at that time.

Perhaps the day was not right for Nick to ascend to the Presidency, but the other part of the dream seemed to be coming true. Brother Theodore received the Republican nomination to be governor of New York. The road to Albany was clear and straight. The Tammany Hall candidate, Catholic Al Smith, seemed easily beatable. Nothing stood in Theodore Roosevelt's way. Except two other Roosevelts, Eleanor and Franklin. Eleanor toured the state in a Ford shaped like a teapot, to remind voters of the Oyster Bay connection with the recent scandal. Franklin, improved miraculously from the polio he contracted at Campobello, campaigned as a Democrat with unexpected vigor, against his own cousin.

On the first Tuesday after the first Monday in November, Republican Coolidge trounced Democratic Davis, but Republican Roosevelt lost the governor's seat in New York to Democrat Smith by less than a hundred thousand votes. The difference between victory and defeat, apparently, were those political nobodies from Hyde Park. Alice would never forgive Eleanor and Franklin for her brother's loss, and Alice would live a long time. "Like the Republican elephant I am," she vowed, "I never forget."[13]

Even before the election of 1924, Alice had a secret. In Washington, D.C., where secrets last hours or even minutes, Alice managed to conceal this one from the world. Only two men knew anything about it, her husband and the President of the United States. Both men were politicians who could keep their mouths shut.

There are some secrets that nature does not allow to be kept hidden. While the President and Mrs. Coolidge were entertaining a group of ladies in the White House, Alice telephoned Grace Coolidge and asked if she might stop by. The First Lady's schedule being heavy with appointments, Mrs. Coolidge begged off. "But," as William Allen White, editor of the Emporia, Kansas, *Gazette,* and a friend of both women, wrote, "Alice being a Roosevelt refused to take no. A few minutes later she came bubbling into the White House, . . . " and told Grace about her forthcoming baby. She had just come from her obstetrician and there was no doubt. Was the news privileged? Must the secret be kept? Of course not, Alice laughed on her way out. One can't keep a baby a secret forever.[14]

At the luncheon, Mrs. Coolidge broke the news. The assembled ladies were delighted to be in on the gossip so early. The President, being the only man in the room, sat quietly and stared straight down into his plate. It didn't take long for one of the women to ask the obvious question.

"When will it be?" she called out.

"Now, if that isn't just like me," the First Lady answered. "In all the excitement I forgot to ask."

The women laughed and kept wondering aloud. Looking up, the President announced, "Some time in February, I understand."

"Calvin," his wife said, as a flush rose to her cheeks, "you knew all along?"

"Yup."

"And you didn't tell me?"

"Nope."

"How would you like to live with a man like that?" Mrs. Coolidge asked her guests. "He's known all along and never said a word to me!"

Within minutes, the telephone in Alice's home on M Street began to ring. The first call was from a wire service reporter.[15]

"Excuse me, Mrs. Longworth," he stammered, "I apologize for asking you this question, but are you pregnant?"

"Hell, yes!" Alice shot back. "There's nothing to be ashamed of."[16]

So there it was. Alice Roosevelt Longworth, age forty-one, married for eighteen years, was going to have a child!

A cradle had been waiting for ten years—a gift from a friend, Mrs. William Hitt (Katherine Elkins). Made of mahogany with a half hood, it was rich in historical background. At least one hundred years old—the donor advised the Longworths that antique experts believed it to be of English origin, and at one time it had rocked a baby in colonial days. Mrs. Longworth made certain that the empty cradle had been looked after carefully during the last decade. Soon it would be put to use.[17]

Paulina Longworth was born at 10:30 A.M. on February 14, 1925, in the Chicago Lying-In Hospital.[18] The hospital was chosen because it had the reputation of being one of the finest in the country for the delivery of infants. It was also in Chicago, where Alice's friend Mrs. Medill McCormick, of the Chicago *Tribune*, lived, and the mother-to-be wanted to spend her waiting time with her.

News of the child's birth flashed from the Associated Press in Chicago around the world.[19] Nowhere was there more celebrating than in the House of Representatives in Washington. Nick Longworth, recently elected

Speaker of the House, wielded his gavel and called for order. To no avail. His Congressional colleagues on both sides of the aisle rose to a man and applauded him for forty-five minutes.

Representative Upshaw of Georgia, under the impression that the newborn child was a boy, stood and addressed the chair.

"Mr. Speaker," he bellowed over the noise coming from the floor, "if legislative business were not so pressing, it might be fitting in the name of the Continental Congress and the great God Almighty to declare a holiday in the House to commemorate the perpetuation of the name of Theodore Roosevelt, Nicholas Longworth, and Nicholas Longworth, Jr.!"[20]

Representative Upshaw of Georgia could not be held entirely responsible for this error. Alice kept all news of her child from the press. Its sex, its weight, its name remained closely guarded. Eventually, the press learned that Alice had given birth to a girl, that the child weighed six and a half pounds, and, by the third or fourth day, Alice announced her daughter would be named Paulina, hard *i*, after Alice's favorite Saint in the Bible, Paul.[21]

Nick pulled back his shoulders, pushed out his chest, and announced, "She resembles the Roosevelts. She even has more hair than I have. Maybe when she gets older, she'll look like the Longworths," and then as an afterthought, "just so she keeps her hair."[22]

Two weeks later, mother and daughter emerged from seclusion. Alice wore a brown karakul coat, shook hands with the superintendent of the hospital and all the new mothers who lined up in the lobby to greet her. When it came to the members of the press, Alice answered questions with a smile. Paulina was carried by her nurse, and covered with a blue eiderdown quilt.[23] Mrs. Longworth gave firm orders that photographs were not allowed. Despite what her husband had told reporters, Alice explained, "A two-week-old baby can't be expected to have much more than a buttonlike nose and cheeks and eyes like any other two-week-old baby."[24]

They stayed at the Drake Hotel for a few days and then headed back home.

Mrs. Marshall Field sent Paulina her first *wedding* present—a check for a thousand dollars. She enclosed a note that said casually, "Since I won't be here when you're married, when that time comes, please select a gift with the compliments of an old family friend."[25]

When the party arrived in the capital, enthusiasm ran so high that troops had to be called out to control the well-wishers who lined the streets from Union Station to the Longworth home on M Street.[26] Reporters were quick to link the reception to that of royalty. The title of Princess was bestowed, in the prints at least, on Paulina. Alliteration made it fashionable for almost six months.

Within the Longworth home, the appellation "Princess" never existed. Paulina's father gave her a pet name that remained with her throughout her life. At this stage, it is not possible to know what made Nicholas Longworth decide to nickname his daughter Kitz. There was no German blood in his veins, but Cincinnati in his time was as German as Milwaukee, and the Teutonic word for tickle—an act which parents of that period considered to be loving rather than distressing toward their infants—is *kitzeln*. The Dutch employ a similar word, and while Alice may have been several generations from the Netherlands, she could easily have accepted the endearing contraction of Kitz for her daughter. In any case, to her intimates, that name became Paulina's.[27]

For many years, Nick and Alice had believed their quarters on M Street to be adequate, but for a baby and a nurse, the new Speaker of the House needed something larger. The Longworths found it in a grand mansion on Massachusetts Avenue abutting Dupont Circle. Called Embassy Row in those days, the location was the most fashionable in Washington. Even if it had not been, Alice's move into the neighborhood would have raised its social status greatly.

"A palatial house" the newspapers described it.[28] But how could the Speaker and his wife have anything less? They entertained the real royalty of the world and the would-be royalty of America.

The four-story, yellow sandstone building stood well back from the avenue. It was large and impressive looking. A bell-pull alongside the front door gave proof of the mansion's age. Inside, a steep, wide staircase pointed the way up from the foyer to the elegant drawing room.

The lady of the house decorated it with the finest antique furniture, mostly Empire style. Soft silks and satins covered the plump down sofas and chairs, and oriental rugs were strewn over the floors. On the tables and mantle, she placed the Longworths' precious wedding gifts and mementos.[29]

Alice and her sister Ethel vied for the many animal skins their father had left: tiger, bear, lion, coyote. They decided to play poker to see who would get them. Alice, inexplicably, lost. She pouted for a few days, but accepted the terms. Then Ethel telephoned her and said, "Let's divide them. I'll give you half."[30]

Perfect! Alice had known from the beginning where she would place them—on the wall beside[31] the stairs and on the shiny hardwood floors. Everyone who went there was affected by the sight of those animal skins and the memories they evoked.

To the right of the staircase, on the ground floor, a short corridor led into the kitchen, where uniformed maids, seemingly at all hours, busied themselves.

The sleeping quarters and study were on the floors above the formal entertainment section. Mrs. Longworth slept in a headless and footless bed. At each end of the bed, and on each side stood revolving bookcases. "On one side, I keep low-brow stuff like confession magazines and Nick Carter fiction," she admitted. "On the other side is the more lofty reading material: *American Mercury*, tomes on politics and law and history."[32]

The house had no elevator and the stairs did more for Alice than the iron braces of her childhood. She never walked; she dashed up and down constantly. "It's fine exercise," she said.

The basement of the Massachusetts Avenue home contained, among other items, the casks and tubs and various implements for the manufacture of wines and spirits Nick Longworth, host, found necessary during the Prohibition Era.

Servants' quarters were atop the Longworth domicicle, and though Alice forever told people how mean she was, those who worked for her found her a pleasant and kind employer.

A couple of them indiscreetly told reporters of Mrs. L.'s private stunts with her husband. Once, when President Coolidge walked arm in arm with Nick, at a charity affair sponsored by Alice, she said, "Nick was looking too dignified for words," so she stretched out a silver evening slipper and tried to trip him. Agile Nick avoided falling on his face.[33]

At home, she liked to chase her husband from room to room and spray him with her perfume atomizer. With no time to change clothes, he would arrive in the august chambers of the House emitting a strong aroma of Alice Blue fragrance. Then, to top the day, she would perch in the front row of the gallery, making faces at Nick, and the dignified Speaker feared he might break into laughter while the Congressmen carried on a serious debate on the floor of the House.[34]

Passersby on Massachusetts Avenue were amazed that Alice often pushed the perambulator around the block—just as proudly as the other mothers in the neighborhood. Then, as now, almost every carriage on the street held, not only an infant, but a teddy bear. Paulina had hers. When Alice took her baby *out* of the block to visit friends or do errands, she carried her in an ordinary market basket.[35]

After Alice learned to place complete trust in the child's nurse, she returned to her political schedule.

Almost every afternoon, she strode to the Capitol and sat in the Speaker's Box of the House. Mrs. Longworth peered down at the powerful men below through her lorgnette. Sometimes, they winked at her and waved.

"Those were happy and heady days," she said to a reporter who walked beside her, as her high heels clicked on the marble floors.[36]

The Speaker of the House of Representatives is traditionally the third most important elected official in the United States Government. Since 1947, lawmakers have legislated him directly behind the Vice-President in the succession to the Oval Office. Even in Nick's day, when the succession after the Vice-President went to the Secretary of State, the office of Speaker was both powerful and prestigious.

"Nick Longworth was considerably above the House level of intelligence," wrote Drew Pearson and Robert S. Allen. "He never grew serious about anything, and his anger was only peevishness. He ... dressed in luxurious elegance and viewed his political career as a source of amusement, and a means of keeping himself occupied."[37]

Alice remained the most envied of the Congressional wives, and Nick became the most popular Speaker the Republicans had put up since the founding of their party.*

If Nick was powerful and popular, no small amount of both qualities came from his wife. Although she continually denied having any political influence, Alice carried a clout that was similar to her father's Big Stick. It would have been unseemly, undignified, and unwise for her to have claimed any political power. She knew only too well that any assertion would diminish any power. The more Flo Harding told people she had political influence, the less she had.[38]

Alice, shrewd Washington observer and a woman filled with insight, had watched as Mrs. Taft ruined her popularity by insisting that she be included in every high-level discussion. She had watched dispassionately as the second Mrs. Wilson had tried to run the nation through the sick months of her husband's Presidency.

Being the daughter of a successful politician and the wife of another, Alice played the game according to the rules of the day: she was the Speaker's wife. Her wit,

*The first House office building is named the Nicholas Longworth Office Building.

her skill in the Washington of the 1920's enchanted her husband's friends and enemies alike. President and Mrs. Coolidge saw more and more of Speaker and Mrs. Longworth. Nick's worthy and honorable opponent across the aisle, Minority Leader "Cactus Jack" Garner of Uvalde, Texas, appreciated Alice more than any woman in Washington after his own wife.

Alice not only knew where the political bodies were buried in the capital, she knew which strings to pull and which buttons to push. More than that, she could, like no one in Washington, articulate the sense of her own day.

"It was a time," she said in describing the Republican years in the twenties, "when the golden calf gave triple cream."[39]

One of the creamier years in Washington was 1926. At the height of the season, the diplomatic event of the year took place. On October 21, Queen Marie of Rumania was the guest of honor at a state dinner in the White House.[40] The protocol officers had everything worked out to perfection. Following dinner, Mrs. Coolidge was to lead Her Majesty into one of the salons off the dining room. The two ladies were to share the same sofa. In this way, when Mrs. Coolidge was ready to leave, she would rise, the Queen would also rise, and the affair would terminate. In the middle of the evening, however, the President's wife got up to speak with one of Her Majesty's ladies in waiting. Seeing the seat beside her vacant, the Queen beckoned to Alice, and with that, protocol went out the window. No one could leave until the Queen rose, and Alice held the Queen with so much sparkling conversation, that the evening went into the night, and finally into the small hours of the morning.

Upon the departure of the Queen, Americans still had the Presidency on which they could focus their attention. After a year of reflection, the current man in the White House made a statement of significance.

On August 3, 1927, Calvin Coolidge cut a niche in American history by telling his constituents, "I do not choose to run." Insiders knew that he only meant he would not go looking for the nomination, but the politicians took him at his word. The Republican Convention of 1928 was considered to be wide open.

Regarding a leading contender, Herbert Hoover, Coolidge told his Secretary of Agriculture, William Jardine, his exact feelings. Jardine urged the President to sign a certain farm bill as a favor to Hoover. The Secretary continued to give the reasons Mr. Hoover had for the passage of the farm bill when the President cut in.

"That man," he said, referring to Mr. Hoover, "has offered me unsolicited advice for six years, all of it *bad*!"[41]

For Nick and Alice, the wave of their political influence neared its crest. All that remained was for Calvin Coolidge to select his successor, as Alice's father had named William Howard Taft. But the President sulked, waiting in vain for the convention to draft him. He even postponed his summer vacation in the cool woods of Superior, Wisconsin, until the convention acted. But Walter Lippmann, shrewd chronicler and judge of Washington affairs, wrote that Calvin Coolidge "had a political genius for effectively doing nothing."[42]

On June 12, 1928, the Republican Convention came to order in Kansas City. Alice, full of hope, but refusing to make any statement, arrived with her husband.[43]

Newspapers throughout the country speculated, some even predicted her reentry to 1600 Pennsylvania Avenue. Headlines blared:

> WILL PRINCESS ALICE RETURN TO
> THE WHITE HOUSE?[44]

The Longworths were ready to receive the nomination. Behind the scenes, at dinner parties, in state and national committee meetings, they had campaigned with discretion and tact. If the White House once again was to become Alice's home, the time for it to happen would have to be June 1928, and the place, Kansas City. Hearts pounded.[45] Anticipation ran high. Handshakes and smiles were exchanged. Hopes and fragments of acceptance speeches began to take form. And then. . . .

For reasons that are decided by luck, fate, or a higher authority, the Republican Convention chose Herbert Clark Hoover of West Branch, Iowa, as its Presidential nominee.[46]

With dignity, Alice arose and started to leave the convention hall. At the door opening onto the street, she began to open an umbrella.

"Oh, don't do that!" a friend cried. "It'll bring bad luck."

"If that is the case," Alice responded, "there must be an open umbrella over all of Kansas City!"[47]

12 □ THE DRY DIVERS

It seemed incredible to Alice Roosevelt Longworth that the Republicans, in convention in Kansas City, nominated a man who had never run for public office in his life. Herbert Hoover had been appointed Secretary of Commerce and "Assistant Secretary of everything else."

At the Democratic Convention, Alice's old friend, William Allen White, a dyed-in-the-silk Republican, covered the proceedings for his newspaper, the Emporia *Gazette*. There is a story concerning that visit, probably apocryphal. Reporting on the convention seemed bad enough, White told his pals, but when a committee composed of prominent Democratic leaders waited upon him and invited him to deliver the invocation on the eve of the convention, White drew the line. Alice relished repeating his refusal. "Thanks, boys," he said, "I'd better not. I don't even want God to know I'm here!"[1]

As wife of the Speaker of the House of Representatives, Alice remained loyal to the Republican Party, and campaigned beside Lou Henry Hoover, the candidate's wife. Mrs. Hoover, who had been a coed at Leland Stanford University, shared an interest in minerals with the man she had married. Together, they traveled around the world as Hoover, a mining engineer and promoter, amassed a fortune for himself and his family.[2]

While riding by train through the state of Ohio, Alice urged "my fellow Buckeyes" to vote for Hoover rather than the Democratic candidate, Al Smith.

Apparently, her fellow Buckeyes and much of the rest of America gave heed and cast their ballots as she suggested. In the election of 1928, Hoover won by 6.5 million votes, getting 444 electoral votes to Smith's 87.

Will Rogers said that Smith, a devout Roman Catholic, sent a cable to the Pope on the morning after the election. It contained a single word: "Unpack!"

Change in the White House is as inevitable as Leap Year, and frequently it occurs at the same time. The Coolidges brought no personal servants with them. They invited no one to lunch on Inaugural Day except members of the immediate family. By contrast, the Hoovers had 1,800 guests for a buffet luncheon in the State Dining Room of the White House.[3]

Other things changed, too. The new President worked in a room where Lincoln signed the Emancipation Proclamation. He even worked at Lincoln's desk.

A matter of delicacy arose when Hoover entered the White House. Irwin "Ike" Hoover had been there since Benjamin Harrison, and was then the Chief Usher. There could not, by any stretch of the imagination, be two Hoovers in the Executive Mansion, one a President, the other a Chief Usher. To cut this Gordian Knot, "Ike" Hoover was forced to have his name changed to Mr. Usher.[4]

Almost immediately upon the Presidential Hoover's taking office, a conflict flared between Alice and the half-sister of the new Vice-President. The War of Dolly Gann's Succession is even less familiar to Americans than the War of Jenkin's Ear. Not many people had heard of Dolly Gann and still fewer cared. But the new Vice-President was a bachelor and his half-sister agreed to serve as his hostess.[5] As such, she demanded to be placed above Alice on the official White House pecking order. Protocol officers wrestled with this weighty problem. It appeared to those men trained in diplomacy that the wife of the Speaker of the House of Representatives, also the daughter of an earlier President, should be seated higher than the half-sister of the new Vice-President.

Dolly Gann, who had visions of herself as another Dolley Madison, refused to accept this decision. Once the Washington press corps got hold of the story, it began to be splashed over the national front pages. The ultimate arbitrator in this comic-opera dispute had to be the President of the United States, and he decided in favor of Alice.

Headlines throughout the country blared of Alice's triumph, and Alice, never one to take victory lightly, smiled at Mrs. Gann in the visitors' gallery at the Senate, spoke to her charmingly in the House elevator, and sat immediately to President Hoover's right at most of the state functions.

Those who sided with Alice said Mrs. Gann should have been grateful to Mrs. Longworth, for without their feud no one would have ever heard of the name Dolly Gann.

On March 3, 1928, the stock of the Radio Corporation of America stood at 94½. By September 3, 1929, it had risen to 505. Other stocks gained with similar rapidity.[6]

"I have no fears about the future of our country," Herbert Hoover said in his Inaugural Address on March 4, 1929. "It is bright with hope."[7]

Then, a few months after Mr. Hoover had been sworn in, came Black Thursday. On October 24, 1929, prices dropped in a flood of liquidations.[8] Eight months after he took office, the market collapsed completely. So-called dry divers were leaping out of windows not only on Wall Street but all over the country.

"The Crash" became "the Depression." Not only were millions of dollars lost, millions of men and women found themselves out of work. Banks began to fail. When people lose their life's savings, the tenure of the President is predictable. Not to Alice.

"Blaming Hoover for the Depression," she told a visiting journalist from Ohio, "is like blaming the people of San Francisco for the earthquake of 1906."[9]

Although Alice's trust funds and other investments were relatively untouched by the Crash, Nick's stocks took a beating along with those of the rest of the country. Most people began to feel the pinch. They stayed at home—if they still had their homes—and listened to the Broadway and Hollywood comedian Eddie Cantor pretend each week that he was running for the Presidency. "We want Cantor, we want Cantor," his radio chorus would chant. Then the star would reveal melodically what he would do when he became President.

The real President stayed close to the White House and tried desperately but ineffectively to stem the economic slide.[10] He became morosely quiet, speaking to none of the servants. Rules for the White House staff called for them never to be seen in the halls or corridors. Tinkling bells softly heralded the approach of Mr. Hoover. Maids and butlers would race for closets and remain secreted there until the bells sounded the all-clear.[11]

Generally, the press saddled the Depression on the President. "How primitive!" Alice Longworth protested. "In some ancient religions, the King or High

Library of Congress Collection

The bride, flanked by the bridegroom and her father. Her father is the man with the hair.

Library of Congress Collection

A newspaper sketch of Alice's wedding. The bride, leaning on the President's arm, is preceeded by the ushers, among whom were Ted, Jr., and Major Charles McCawley, USMC. It was McCawley's sword that cut the wedding cake.

Culver Pictures, Inc.

Fashionable
but muddy.
Grandin Road,
Cincinnati,
summer of 1906.

United Press International

Still a bride abroad. London, 1906.

Library of Congress Collection

With the Girl Scouts, selling Liberty bonds early in 1918.

Library of Congress Collection

On solid ground and home turf. Mr. and Mrs. Nicholas Longworth in Washington, D.C.

Culver Pictures, Inc.

Always one step above the others. Alice, with Ted, Jr., and Will Rogers, February 1922.

United Press International

Princess Alice and Princess Paulina outside their Massachusetts Avenue mansion, 1927.

United Press International

At the Coolidges' garden party for veterans. Mrs. Nicholas Longworth and her brother, Colonel Theodore Roosevelt.

Wide World Photos

The victor of the War of Dolly Gann's Succession, taken prior to a dinner party hosted by Washington *Post* publisher Mr. Eugene Meyer and Mrs. Meyer.

Library of Congress Collection

Mother and daughter.

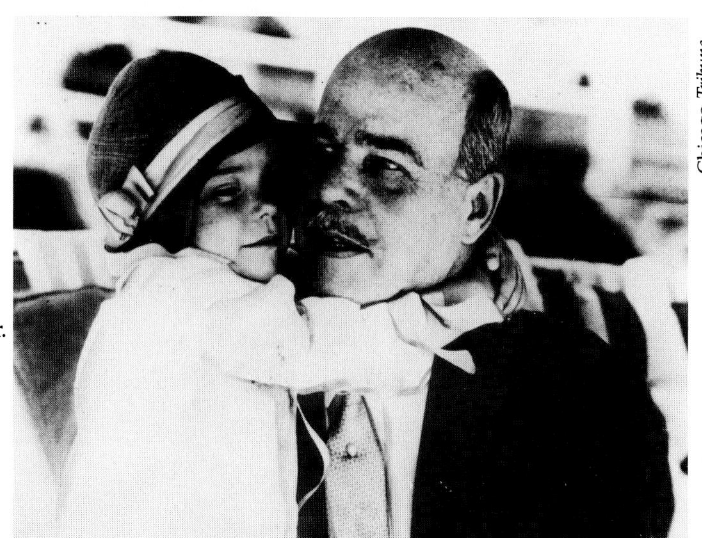
Chicago *Tribune*

Father and daughter.

Chicago *Tribune*

At the Congress Hotel in the Windy City. Nick, Mrs. Joseph T. Bowen, Alice, and Alice's best friend, daughter of Mark Hanna, Republican boss of Ohio, and wife of the publisher of the Chicago *Tribune*, Ruth Hanna McCormick.

Wide World Photos

Rushing to Nick's bedside in Aiken, South Carolina. On the left is Mrs. James F. Curtis, in whose home Nicholas Longworth died, April 9, 1931.

Wide World Photos

The granddaughter of the late Theodore Roosevelt, astride her dapple gray pony, makes her first appearance at a horse show. Her mother's hand is on "Dumpling's" withers. Her late father had been Speaker of the House of Representatives.

Wide World Photos

At last, Alice smiles enough to show her teeth for the cameras. The time, March 16, 1934. The place, the Senate airmail hearings. The witness, Charles A. Lindbergh.

Now at the Palmer House in Chicago. Never a candidate for public office, Alice supported her friend Ruth (Mrs. Medill McCormick) in the latter's successful campaign in the Republican Senatorial primaries in Illinois. Mrs. McCormick lost the election and settled for a seat in the House.

Priest was expected to see to it that the crops were good and the food plentiful. In return for this, he was given a position of power and comfort in the community. If he failed, however, he was killed and his place was handed on to another. In a measure," said Mrs. Longworth, "when one hears criticism that Hoover is responsible for bad times, it has just as much basis in reality as the beliefs of our far-off ancestors."[12]

No matter what Mrs. Longworth thought, the newspapers pounded away mercilessly at Mr. Hoover each day. A look at the gathered periodicals each morning would bring tears to the eyes of Lou Henry Hoover. It had not been the doing of her husband, but few listened to her.

By 1930, free-lance writers were a glut on the market. "Free lance" may sound impressive. In reality, it was another expression for "unemployed." To write on "spec" (speculation) or to snap photographs, paying for your own materials, meant that maybe—a big maybe—a discerning editor might buy your copy or purchase your pictures.

Alice and her young daughter answered the prayers of many columnists and their colleagues with the cameras.[13] A fast candid of Paulina enjoying the circus, standing with her parents on the deck of an ocean-going liner, or simply skipping rope in the park kept coffee and doughnuts on the lunchroom counters for the men and women whom Heywood Broun would eventually organize into the Newspaper Guild of America.

The Longworths did not encourage strangers around their daughter. More than one threatening kidnap note arrived in their mail. Neither Alice nor Nick was a person easily alarmed, but they felt it safer to keep Paulina in the background.

February was a month when the Longworths drew the most attention. Mother and child introduced the Age of Aquarius without realizing it. Valentine's Day was an important time on Massachusetts Avenue—Paulina's birthday and Alice's were celebrated together. Stacks of beautifully wrapped packages for the daughter always included red satin hearts filled with creamy chocolates. Alice received large boxes of her favorite flowers, long-stemmed yellow roses.[14]

When Paulina turned five, her mother presented her with a most unusual gift—a trip to Chicago—not to see old friends, but for an opportunity for the child to make a thorough tour of the Lying-In Hospital.

"I wanted her to see where her life started," Alice told the superintendent of nurses. "We must know where we came from to know where we are going."[15] The Longworths tried to keep the expedition out of the dailies, without success.

During these days of halcyon visitation through the corridors and rooms of the hospital, conditions throughout the country grew worse. Money became tight.

In 1930, in New York, a man named Darrow invented a game that utilized the names of the streets of Atlantic City. The Boardwalk, Park Place, Ventnor Avenue were part of *Monopoly*. Players could buy these sites for vast sums of paper money. It felt great to have money in one's hands, even if it was paper. The game was an instant success.

Alice, who always entertained well but informally, found her home growing in popularity. Nick's violin playing was an appreciated form of entertainment, but poker became more than popular.

"I cleared ten thousand dollars one winter," Alice said, "and that was after I paid for Nick's debts."[16] And that wasn't *Monopoly* money that Alice raked in.

Her sister-in-law, Mrs. Theodore Roosevelt, Jr., recalled a poker game at the Longworth home.[17] The butler was off that night so Alice answered the door herself, urging her guests to go up to the sitting room.

An Englishman, Lord Cavan, arrived late and dropped his sable-lined coat on a chair at the front door.

"It would be better," whispered Ted's wife, "not to leave it there."

"Why not?" asked his lordship.

"It's such a handsome coat. I'm afraid it might be stolen."

"Oh, but I say, you know it's most awfully good of you to warn me. Very, very kind, indeed."

With that, the Englishman took his coat to the poker table and sat on it throughout the rest of the evening.

Mrs. Ted always wondered if Lord Cavan thought Alice Longworth's home was a den of thieves. Mrs. L.—as those close to Alice referred to her—explained to Mrs. Ted, "Well, everyone from *this* country knows I run the best disorderly house in the capital."

Friends of the Longworths concurred. Alice's best idea for a party was the celebration she arranged for the twenty-fifth anniversary of her marriage to Nick. She instructed guests to wear an orginal outfit from 1906 or a costume that looked as though it had been worn that year.[18]

For those women who had not retained their 1906 finery, Alice laughingly decreed, "Shirtwaists, skirts, and sailor hats."

Alice overwhelmed them all—even Nick—by getting into an elegant gold satin gown she had preserved from her trousseau. She topped off her 1906 pompadour with a contemporary diamond tiara, and bolstered it back with a 1906 barette. Around her neck, she wore the diamond necklace Nick had given her as a wedding gift.[19] The "something blue" was a brooch, sapphire centered.

Those persons who had thought that Alice and Nick had grown far apart from each other as the years passed noticed the affection and warmth they showed each other the night of their anniversary.

The anniversary was one of many parties she gave. There were those affairs that Mrs. Longworth preferred to ignore. The wife of the Speaker of the House had certain obligations, but Alice, who had been breaking conventions for years, refused, for example, to hold an open house on New Year's Day. "People in Washington," she wrote, "seem as hypnotized by precedence as if they are hens with their beaks on a chalk line."[20]

Within the House itself, the "chalk line"[20] extended directly from Nick's seat to a small room within the Capitol itself. Here, just off the Rotunda, furnished with a dozen comfortable chairs and a similar number of quarts of good bonded whiskey, and a pitcher of branch water, met "the Board of Education." The unofficial biparty group, led by Nick and John Garner of Texas, would move to adjourn the House. "Gentlemen," either Nick or Garner would call out, "let's strike a blow for liberty!"[21] They would then retire to "the Board of Education" to consider means and methods of influencing recalcitrant Representatives to vote for or against legislation to aid the nation in the darkness of the Depression Years.

And darkness did spread over the land. There was tension in Washington and anxiety throughout America. Bonus marchers, reminding many of Coxey's Army, camped out on the green grass in front of the Washington Monument. Hungry, grim men erected tents or made "Hoovervilles" out of cardboard and tin.[22] They actually threatened Congress itself. For the first time in anyone's memory, the great bronze doors to the Capitol were closed. Riots broke out in front of the White House. Windows, doors, gates were locked. Extra Secret Service men and police were called out. Tear gas drove the rioters back to their dwellings in the "Hoovervilles." Units of the United States Army, consisting of infantry, cavalry, and tanks, under General Douglas MacArthur, who wore boots and spurs and "pink" riding breeches, were commanded to clear the area. MacArthur gave the order to a lowly major named Eisenhower, and the job was done.

Never could anyone in Washington recall anything like it.

A biography of Teddy Roosevelt came out in 1931. His daughter thought it brilliant, so did the Pulitzer Prize committee. Alice had a favorite section. Henry F. Pringle, the author, had written, "Theodore Roosevelt—talked about his Dutch, Scotch, English, Huguenot, and Welsh ancestors a great deal. It was convenient, when the day came to shake hands with assorted political supporters. 'Ah,' he could say, 'you have a Welsh name! I have Welsh blood myself! ... Well, so you are German; so am I!' In Washington there was a legend ... that a Jewish caller was once presented at the White House. 'Congratulations!' the President was rumored to have boomed automatically. 'I am partly Jewish, too!'"[23]

When Alice read Pringle's book, she told Alexander Woollcott, "I would have liked to have seen

George Washington Carver round the corner to shake hands with Father, and then sneak up and listen to the dialogue that followed."[24]

Early in April of 1931, Nicholas Longworth was stricken while on vacation in Aiken, South Carolina.[25] Physicians reported that Alice rushed to Nick's side and spent long hours with him, although he was in a comatose state.

Finally, with the end in sight, head bowed, she left by a back door. Newsmen outside held a deathwatch. The prearranged signal came—the lowering of the window shade in Nick's room notified them that the Speaker had passed away. Attending doctors explained that pneumonia had cut short the life of one of the nation's best-loved servants.

Alice told a friend, June Bingham, "Some things are too bad to talk about. If you must lick your wounds, do it in private."[26]

During the Taft Administration, Alice had once arrived before her host put in his appearance. She had taken Archie Butt's hand and drawn him to an area in the East Room. He wrote to his sister-in-law, Clara, about it.

"I was married just here," Alice had said, "I remember looking up and seeing Nick and thinking how hopelessly Middle West he did seem." And Archie added, "But for all that, she seems to be in love with him. Certainly no other man in the world would suit her as well—Middle West or Middle East."[27]

Alice does not admit reporters and other interviewers into the low points in her life. She admires the stiff upper lip of the British. But Nick's death closed a door on a large portion of what might have been. Gone were the hopes of her returning to the White House as something more than a visitor. Gone, too, were great sections of political influence. Years of being the wit of Washington, of her continuous charm and authority stretched before her, but at the time, she had no way of knowing that.

In all probability, a form of her own personal courage forced her to bear up under this loss just as her father had forced himself to overcome the illness of his childhood. Still, it could not have been easy for Alice. The man with whom she had lived for better than a quarter of a century, the man who had fathered her only child, suddenly ceased to exist. There are no photographs of tears running down Alice Longworth's cheeks. No diarist, no author has ever written of the depths of her emotion following Nick's death. For a few days, she wouldn't tell Paulina that her father had died. Somehow, telling her child, speaking the words, would make it more real. Nick had been a wonderful parent, and seeing him in that light had given Alice greater appreciation of her husband's positive qualities.

From South Carolina to Washington and then into Ohio the funeral train bearing Nick's body moved slowly and solemnly. In the family plot in Spring Grove Cemetery outside Cincinnati, they buried Nick. The President of the United States attended the rites. So did the Vice-President, and various delegations from the Congress. People from all over America attended, those high in station and those low.[28]

Thirty-one honorary pallbearers came from Cincinnati. Fifty honorary pallbearers came from the rest of the nation. Among them were Will Rogers, the humorist, and Congressman Sam Rayburn of Texas.*

*The second House office building would be named after this Speaker of the House.

When Nick's funeral was over, Alice returned to Rookwood. The silence of the present and the specter of the past made her realize that Cincinnati was Nick's town. The widow's walks she took now were lonely strolls through memories of picnics and musicales and sultry summer evenings under a parade of harvest moons and election-night victories that would come no more. Alice decided to divide her weeks between Cincinnati and Washington, and enrolled Paulina in an Ohio boarding school.[29] Part of the year she chose to live in the house on Massachusetts Avenue in Washington to be near the excitement of government, to mingle with those who rule and are ruled. From the time she had been a small girl she had liked Washington and the capital had liked Alice.

Following Nick's death, the voters of the First Ohio Congressional District urged Alice to run for her late husband's seat in the House of Representatives.[30] She was certain, they told her, to win such an election. But the last Roosevelt to run for public office had been her brother Ted, and he had stood for the governor's seat in Albany. And he had lost. Before him, the only Roosevelt to run had been her father. And he had lost the Presidency as a "Bull Mooser."

Alice was polite but firm. She declined, stating that her time had to be devoted to her daughter. Nick had once adjourned an entire day's session of the House in order to attend the child's birthday party.[31] Alice had to take his place in the home, not the House.

"Around this time," Archie Roosevelt, Jr., Mrs. Longworth's nephew, said, "Paulina had developed into a quiet and subdued child with an interesting face. She looked very much like her father, and as Nick wished, she had an abundant amount of dark brown hair."[32]

By 1932, Ohioans invited Alice to run for the Senate, while in Nebraska, there existed a strong move for her to accept the Number Two spot on the Republican ticket with President Hoover. Alice refused both offers.

Regarding the President, she told a New York reporter, "I am a Republican with a Progressive tradition-inclination. But if I were not a Republican, I would still vote for Hoover this time. I say this, of course, without the least personal feeling against my cousin."[33] Privately, she told intimates, "The Hoover Vacuum Cleaner is more exciting than the President. But, of course, it's electric."

After Franklin Delano Roosevelt received the Democratic Party's nomination as its candidate for the Presidency, Senator William Gibbs McAdoo of California, took him aside at the Chicago convention and told him, "Now, all you have to do is stay alive until the election."[34]

Confident of victory, certain that the electorate would vote out President Hoover, the Depression, and the economic malaise that had settled over the world, Roosevelt smiled as he sat in his wheelchair in the Presidential suite high atop the venerable Drake Hotel. Pumping McAdoo's hand, he promised he would follow the advice offered him.

On August 30, 1932, only a bit more than two months before Election Day, the Associated Press reported that Mrs. Longworth "... was intensely eager to bring about the defeat of the Democratic Roosevelt."[35]

Ten days prior to the election itself, the United Press, in a story out of Paris, France, cabled:

> Europe is more interested in the United States Presidential Election than ever before, and is confused about the Roosevelt family.[36]
>
> If Governor Franklin D. Roosevelt is elected, in the view of the French newspaper, *L'Intransigeant*, it will be due to the effort of Alice Longworth. In a two column copyrighted article yesterday, *L'Intransigeant* explained to its readers that the former Alice Roosevelt, daughter of the Late President, widow of Nicholas Longworth, and fifth cousin of Franklin D. Roosevelt, is now the wife of the present Democratic candidate.
>
> "She is twice a Roosevelt, " the article explained. "First, as a daughter of the great Theodore, and secondly, as the woman behind the scenes in Franklin Roosevelt's campaign, she may realize a lifelong ambition to return to the White House as First Lady." The article credits the famous Alice as dubbing her husband with the title, "Fearless Frank," and nursing him day and night for six months.

When reporters telephoned Alice for a reaction to the story, she shot out a single word in French that their editors would not allow them to print.[37]

Three days later, the New York *Herald-Tribune* carried a column by the same Associated Press crediting Mrs. Longworth and Mrs. Herbert Hoover with campaigning hard at dinners, parades, at governor's mansions, and from aboard Mr. Hoover's special train.[38] "Mrs. Longworth," Associated Press went on to report, "boarded the train in Cincinnati. She wore a black dress, black woolen sports scarf, black hat, black coat, and black shoes."[39]

Either she was still in mourning for Nick or her witch's intuition told her what the results of the election would be.

Neither her mysterious powers nor her ritualistic ways were of any help to Hoover. In 1932, a shaken and frightened American people delivered to Alice the worst personal and political blow she had ever suffered. On November 8 of that year, Franklin D. Roosevelt received more than 22 million votes compared to Herbert Hoover's 15 million. He carried forty-two of the forty-eight states and won overwhelmingly in the Electoral College, 472 to 59.[40]

"There we were—look at us—lovely creatures," Alice told Henry Brandon of *The New York Times*. "We were perfectly content. And what happens? A fifth cousin comes along and gets into the White House. Can you think of anything more distressing? We should be honest about it. There we were, swelling with pride and security, and what happens. Along comes Franklin, called by many in the family 'Feather Duster,' and hops into the Presidency. . . .[41]

13 □ THE FEATHER DUSTER

Suddenly, in 1932 when people said "Roosevelt" they meant Franklin, and, as Alexander Woollcott, the influential literary and dramatic critic of *The New York Times* and Town Crier of CBS, observed with affection, "The Oyster Bay Roosevelts have become the out-of-season Roosevelts."[1] They were old friends and she recognized and applauded his well-turned phrase. Her branch of the family had *certainly* become "the out-of-season" Roosevelts.

Exactly at noon, March 4, 1933, on the East Portico of the Capitol, Alice's gnarled chum from the House of Representatives, "Cactus Jack" Garner of Texas, took the oath and swore to protect and defend the Constitution and thereby became the Vice-President.[2] As Nick's widow, as Eleanor's first cousin, as Franklin's fifth cousin, and finally, as the daughter of an earlier President named Roosevelt, Alice received choice seats to the inauguration. She preferred to avoid the cold, the gusting wind, and the usual speeches. Remaining in her Massachusetts Avenue home, she listened to the proceedings via radio.

Shortly after Garner's few, clipped words of acceptance, Franklin Delano Roosevelt, wearing a heavy greatcoat, a winged collar, an ascot at his throat, and no hat on his head, became the thirty-second President of the United States.

With the exception of George Washington and—Alice grudgingly admitted—Abraham Lincoln, no man came to the Presidency with more trouble facing him than Franklin Roosevelt. As an avid reader, as one who lived in the capital and saw it all, Alice knew what serious problems were ahead of him. His first Inaugural Address—"the only thing we have to fear is fear itself"[3]—seemed merely words at the time, but those words would remain as long as she lived and after.

Alice reacted strongly. She could and did damn the new President, but let anyone outside the family say a single word against him, and she would glare icily and remind the offending speaker that Franklin was, after all, a Roosevelt, and members of her tribe were not to be spoken of in a derogatory manner.[4]

It would be all right for Alice to refer to the newly installed President as, "Ninety percent mush and ten percent Eleanor."[5,6] It pleased her to quote a story that the "brain trust" wanted "to get the pants off Eleanor and onto Franklin." She could sneer that "the marriage between her two cousins was not made in heaven but in Hyde Park" (by the groom's mother, Sara Delano). It would be acceptable to Alice for others to make many more degrading remarks about him, *but not in front of her*!

Even before F.D.R. took office, Alice Longworth had been known in Washington as "the Circe of Massachusetts Avenue."[7] She frequently seduced, so to speak, young radical Republican Congressmen, who after associating with Alice became good boys and obeyed their Party's leaders.

With the arrival of Eleanor and Franklin, Alice redoubled her efforts to get both chambers of the Congress to follow the conservative path. She automatically grabbed for the morning papers and checked the agenda of the Senate. If a good argument was on the schedule, she would present herself at the Senate Gallery on the stroke of noon. Even if the debate ran until two o'clock on the following morning, Mrs. Longworth remained. From time to time, she would race downstairs for a cup of coffee, or to encourage a Senator who saw matters through her eyes.

When Paulina was eight years old, she came up with a quip that her mother never tired of repeating. Alice had been in the Senate Gallery every afternoon for more than a week. One day, she dashed into her home, only to discover her daughter deep in the funny papers. "Paulina!" she commanded. "Stop looking at that trash. I buy you good books. Why don't you read them?" The child glanced up.

"Well," she began, as satisfaction crept across her face, "I notice you spend a lot of time in the Senate."[8]

James P. Warburg, the New York financial genius and author who wrote, among his other works, *Hell Bent for Election* and *The Money Muddle*, once commented, "No man can be conservative until he has something to lose."[9] Oyster Bay Roosevelts and Cincinnati Longworths had much in common. They all had something to lose, and they all watched and wriggled as it went down the drain called the Depression. With pride, even with a certain amount of arrogance, Alice clung to her conservative ideas, despite the acute shortage of cash she and Paulina were experiencing. In this attitude, she remained more Nick's widow than her father's daughter. Fiscal responsibility became the basis for Alice's personal and public economic stance.

Into this scene stepped one of America's great book editors. F. Scott Fitzgerald, Ernest Hemingway, Ring Lardner, Thomas Wolfe, and James Jones were among those authors edited by Maxwell Perkins.[10] The year of

Nick's death, the purse strings held so carefully by Alice began to cut into the firm flesh of her fingers. It wasn't the pinch she felt, it was more like strangulation. Perkins timed his proposal just right. A Harvard graduate (Alice always felt partial to Harvard men) his letter suggested that perhaps Mrs. Longworth might conceivably be interested in the royalties that would result from the publication of a book of her own memoirs.

"A book?" Alice replied to his letter. "I've never written anything longer than a postcard."

Max Perkins, who had lived through writers' blocks, their hangovers, good reviews, hideous reviews, wives, agents, business managers, strings of excuses, and procrastinations so finely conceived, would not be denied. Gently, oh, so carefully, he pointed her toward the desk.

She refused the help of a ghost writer. She even undertook the work of verifying dates and names, a big task in a book that dealt with so wide a background and such a procession of important people. Her memory, astonishingly good both for facts and times, forced her to demand a rigid standard of accuracy for herself.

"If I err," she told her younger sister, "it will not be on the side of the angels." [11]

Her third floor study hung with a variety of political cartoons and spilled over with hillocks of books. There was a great green couch, comfortable armchairs, and a tea service ready for duty. And for silent companionship, her dog Sandy. The fireplace, during that blazing summer, was filled with fresh leaves. On the long mantle shelf above it, set thick with bric-a-brac, stood another of her best loved possessions, a model of the Statue of Liberty, given to her for a wedding present by the widow of Bartholdi, its sculptor.

She wrote her memoirs in longhand. Then came the typewriter. Slowly, at first, then faster and faster her memories piled onto the pages. With equal speed, Perkins' blue pencil flew through the manuscript. During that dreadfully hot summer of 1932, when she wasn't aboard Lou Henry Hoover's campaign train, she sat alone in her home in the capital and typed out the final draft of her book.

After Franklin's first inauguration, Perkins sent her pages to the typesetter. By the summer of '33, review copies went out to the press. By late autumn, *Crowded Hours, Reminiscences of Alice Roosevelt Longworth,* moved onto the shelves of the nation's bookdealers, ready for what they fervently hoped would be a crisp seller for Christmas.

Crowded Hours received sparkling notices[12] from the country's leading literary critics. Curiosity shot it onto the best-seller list, praise for the author's writing kept it there. A minority report noticed her aversion to beginnings and endings. Even though Maxwell Perkins had urged her to reveal more, Alice failed to mention the death of her youngest brother Quentin, as well as the death of her father and husband. She also avoided any word of her daughter's birth and existence. Everyone thought tidbits and profundities would abound. They were mistaken. The author told only what she chose to tell.

Neither a pill nor a pal, a longtime Washington resident said of *Crowded Hours,* "It's colorful and well written—just like having a conversation with Alice. She discusses her opinions and prejudices, and takes you backstage at the White House, and upstage at many historical and social happenings. If Catherine de Médicis had kept a diary, I'll wager it would read a lot like *Crowded Hours*. Don't quote me!"[13]

When Maxwell Perkins begged Mrs. Longworth to do a second volume, she said with a twinkle, "I shall never write another book. My vocabulary is too limited."[14]

The literary life, however, lingered on for Alice in a syndicated newspaper column called "Capital Comment," similar in size and content to "My Day," the daily column written by Eleanor Roosevelt. For some time during the thirties, the two columns coexisted.

United Features handled Eleanor's literary output. A person named McNitt headed up the McNaught Syndicate. This mildly comical juxtaposition of names, McNaught's McNitt or McNitt's McNaught may very easily have lured Alice into writing her column. Actually, it wasn't the names that sold her; it was her sense of competition with Eleanor.

Dozens of editors had tried in vain to get the daughter of T.R. to put her name on the bottom line of a contract. McNitt started his intensive campaign on a sunny day in June 1935, in the most logical of all eating places, the Senate restaurant.[15] Aided by Frank Kent, the Baltimore *Sun's* Washington correspondent, McNitt hit the bell and got Alice Longworth's signature. Gossip went as high as the steam in Old Faithful, the geyser in Yellowstone National Park. Frank Kent, the rumormongers whispered, "was Alice Longworth's latest lover."[16] What Alice minded more were the hints that Frank Kent wrote her column.

Alice and Eleanor vied as to which of them could get the larger number of newspapers. Fortunes of journalistic war gave the total to Alice, one hundred to fifty.

Although she had outdistanced Eleanor 2–1, Alice's

friends and subscribing editors felt keenly that the saltiness and spice with which she ruled Washington for so many years did not pass onto the pages of her column.

"Why the hell do I roar hilariously when I'm with her and then only smile when her copy comes through?"[17] an editor from the McNaught Syndicate wondered. "Still," he admitted, "it's better to smile than read about Eleanor going from Pittsburgh to Cleveland to a CCC camp in Kentucky."[18] Perhaps the McNaught man felt that way, but millions of other Americans followed Eleanor's travels avidly. Eleanor's column continued. "My Day" became almost everybody's day. The interest in Alice's pieces dwindled and she tired of the work.

On December 8, 1933, Mrs. Longworth received the honor of drawing a number from a hat filled with coat checks at a tea given by the Author's League of America. The winner would receive a rare five-volume set of a first edition of Dickens' *Pickwick Papers*. Without hesitation, she plunged her hand into the hat held by Will Irwin, playwright, journalist, and promptly drew her own number. While the other guests enjoyed her embarrassment, Alice urged that another drawing be held. They overruled her. Mrs. Longworth, Louis Bromfield, the novelist, and Sidney Howard, the playwright, were guests of honor at the tea. The proceeds went to the Authors' League for needy writers, and Alice had a new set of books and friends.[19]

On February 12, 1934, Alice Roosevelt Longworth reached her 50th birthday. To celebrate the event, the President and Mrs. Franklin Delano Roosevelt invited her to a musicale at the Executive Mansion. When reporters asked her about the evening, she told them, "I've spent many of my birthdays in that house, almost always in the same rooms. It wasn't too different."[20]

Throughout the twelve years and thirty-nine days of F.D.R.'s tenure in office, Alice refused to call him Mr. President. Instead, she referred to him as Franklin, and each time she used his first name in his presence, he winced.[21]

Alice as "family" had been invited to the first dinner Franklin and Eleanor gave the evening they moved into the White House. No matter how harsh her words became about the New Deal policies, they continued to invite her to all the affairs, and she continued to accept the invitations.

Franklin's "First Hundred Days" she considered both remarkable and objectionable. When he temporarily closed all banks in America in order to stop what had already grown into a panic, the shortage of change—nickels, dimes, quarters—became acute. Who could buy a newspaper, make a telephone call at a pay station, ride a streetcar, bus or subway?[22] The absence of coins blocked the sale of food, medical supplies, gasoline. While most of America found itself in a state of paralysis, Alice remained unruffled. Paulina's piggy bank was loaded with coins, and the two Longworth ladies dipped into it without guilt. Delivery boys whizzed in and out of the house on Massachusetts Avenue. They were tipped well. Alice's chauffeur drove her plum-colored limousine to the service station. He not only had credit; more important, he had *change*.

When Franklin took the country off the gold standard, Alice arrived at a White House reception for the heads of government departments and stole the show.[23] From her ears to her shoulders and below dangled gold Hindu earrings shaped somewhat like horns of plenty. About her neck, she wore a heavy chain of red gold from which hung a Chiriqui Indian frog in green gold. Her watch-bracelet was white gold. She even wore amber-golden side combs in her hair. She was gowned in blue velvet and seemed to be having a fine time as she spent the evening chatting with Will Rogers. She spoke with reporters the next day, and conceded that what she had done was deliberate.

"I just wanted to show Franklin that all of the nation's gold wasn't in the vaults in Fort Knox," she stated.[24]

"If F.D.R. could have taken her to the Treasury and deposited her," columnist Cal Tinney wrote, "the deficit would have turned into a surplus."

Alice viewed with distaste the formation of Franklin's so-called Kitchen Cabinet. Men named Corcoran and Cohen appeared to be influencing him more than the Brain Trust. She looked suspiciously at the formation of the various new "alphabet agencies," the NRA, the CCC, the WPA, the TVA—the National Recovery Administration, the Civilian Conservation Corps, the Works Progress Administration, the Tennessee Valley Authority—the expansion of bureaucracy and the influx of bureaucrats into Washington filled Alice with misgivings. She dubbed it "The Alphabet Soup Society."

"When I think of Franklin and Eleanor in the White House," she hissed, "I could grind my teeth to powder and blow them out my nose."[25]

Society in New York went mad trying to forget the initials and the adversities of 1933. On November 13, *Time* magazine carried an article under the slug SPORT.[26]

The subject was scavenging. Mrs. Marshall Field III held the first scavenger hunt in London. Cole Porter, the composer, had organized a few in Paris.

For a Halloween charity affair that started at the Waldorf-Astoria Hotel, Elsa Maxwell, party giver to the world, served as hunt mistress. Mrs. Longworth sent her regrets, but her brother Kermit accepted, providing that he could be the barker and run the casino. Contestants, 199 of them, paired off in the east lobby, and received sealed envelopes that listed "bizarre objects" they were expected to collect within the next hour and a half.

At Kermit Roosevelt's signal, the frantic group dashed out into the New York night.

Time said that "Scavenging was a jittery version of the old fashioned Treasure Hunt." The items to be secured by the adventurers included a live goat, a hair from Kermit Roosevelt's mustache (he graciously handed out a few dozen hairs that he kept in an envelope in his vest pocket), a live turtle, any bird, the autographed step-ins of a popular Broadway actress, a lighted red lantern, the initialed handkerchief of New York's most charming and honest banker, one of Jimmy Durante's shoes, an unused foreign stamp, and Clifton Webb's red carnation—he was appearing in *As Thousands Cheer* at the Music Box.

When the scavengers returned, they deposited their trophies with Gene Tunney, heavyweight boxing champion, and Broadway producer Alfred de Liagre, Jr.[27] Marilyn Miller's step-ins were the chief acquisition of the couple who won first prize. Miss Miller had signed her silk-and-lace garment "With love and kisses from Marilyn."

Second prize went to the pair who willingly had settled on Fanny Brice's brassiere. Other actresses who "yielded their underclothes" were Hope Williams and Cornelia Otis Skinner.

Clifton Webb made arrangements for the theater's doorman to toss flowers at the passing cars of the scavengers.

Some collectors, in desperation, returned bearing monkeys, Great Danes, and even a bear cub.

Mrs. L.'s comments on the shenanigans? "I knew they'd never find an initialed handkerchief from an honest banker—and they didn't."

Washington is a city that swelters in the summers and steams with gossip all year round. There existed no greater gossip in the United States, at that time, than Alice's friend, Aleck Woollcott.

"Mrs. L. enjoys being bitchy even more than I do. I always thought *that* was impossible,[28] he told Noel Coward. Aleck also pointed out that Alice Roosevelt Longworth was responsible for the cigarette holders that F.D.R. clamped between his teeth at a jaunty angle. Finally, Woollcott coaxed Alice to his private island in Vermont, and introduced her to the sharpest and most satiric comedy writer America had produced in a generation or three. George S. Kaufman was shy as a maiden, as ascerbic as a disappointed despot.

"How did you happen to get into playwrighting?" Alice inquired.

"Stringent vagrancy laws," he replied.[29,30]

Woollcott, having learned a thing or so from Alice, placed Kaufman beside Mrs. Longworth at the dinner table. Instead of the argument he expected, Woollcott was distressed to see a warm and friendly Alice carrying the bulk of the conversation. Kaufman changed his eyeglasses and raised his eyebrows frequently.

All was not lost, for within months of their meeting, Kaufman, in collaboration with a Washington presswoman, Katharine Dayton, came up with a satire in which Alice clearly could be recognized as the leading character.

First Lady opened at the Music Box Theater on November 26, 1935, in New York and ran for 234 performances. Jane Cowl, a popular star of the Broadway stage, played the Alice Longworth role, only in the play she was called Mrs. Lucy Chase Wayne. Instead of her *father* having been in the White House, Lucy's *grand*father had occupied the Executive Mansion. And what an entrance Alice/Lucy gets! A door slams, the eyes of the two supporting players on the stage turn toward the sound and:

> LUCY CHASE WAYNE comes in. Having spent her girlhood in the White House, one hundred and twenty million* people know her age, but you would never think it to look at her. She has good looks, but they are subordinate to her vitality, charm, distinction. She carries an extra large handbag. Over the years, every newspaper and magazine in America has printed her picture—not once, but again and again. Everything she does, everything she says is News. Should her dog bite the most obscure man in the world, it gets a box on Page One. She is Lucy Chase Wayne.[31]

Drama critics gave the comedy rave notices. Alice didn't mind at all the attention she received. The spotlight shone on her again. She took bows and managed a blush or two because a frequently quoted line from the play referred to Mrs. Wayne as "the woman who owned Washington."

"Too bad the property values are down these days," she wrote George Kaufman.[32]

*Then the population of the United States.

Alice showed up as a delegate at the Republican Convention in Cleveland on June 9, wearing a light, flowered summer dress, topped off with a straw hat, the band around it proclaimed her newly found loyalty for a fellow Buckeye, Robert Alphonso Taft. This balding elder son of Nellie and Will Taft had found a seat in the Ohio Senate, to say nothing of Alice's endorsement.

1936 was hard on the New Deal. A crippling drought struck the Great Plains and Western farmers by the tens of thousands viewed their parched fields with horror, and then unceremoniously piled their families and bedding into their "flivvers" or "tin lizzies" and headed west for California. Her candidate, Bob Taft, unknown and untried, stood no chance against Herbert Hoover and the Establishment of the Republican Party. While Hoover savagely attacked his successor as both a communist and a fascist, Alice told acquaintances that she didn't think the GOP would dare nominate him.

Kansan Alfred M. Landon, born in Pennsylvania and educated as a lawyer, had made his fortune in the oil business. In 1932, when Franklin roared into office, Landon had been the only Republican west of the Mississippi River to be elected governor. No pal of the reactionaries, he had supported William Allen White in his campaign against the Ku Klux Klan. Landon believed in economy and had balanced his state's budget. Liberals screamed that he had done it by depriving Kansas schoolchildren and the insane.

"The only insanity is in the Old Guard of our Party," Alice told the people of Kansas in 1936. "Any man who has Bill White's backing, has mine."[33]

On the first ballot, the nomination went to Alf Landon. *The Literary Digest*, a weekly magazine with a spotless record for predicting Presidential victories, claimed that Landon would defeat F.D.R., carrying thirty-two states to Roosevelt's sixteen.[34]

When a publisher asked the editor of the Emporia *Gazette* if the *Digest's* views might be correct, he scoffed.

"You have a quaint sense of humor," William Allen White told him. "If Landon is elected, I'll write you a book about him, bind it in platinum, illustrate it with apples of gold and pictures of silver, and won't charge you a cent."[35]

"What a philanthropist Bill White is!" Alice grinned as she boarded the train for Cincinnati.

Her stay there was short because New York's *Herald Tribune* persuaded Alice to cover the Democratic Convention in Philadelphia for them. She only needed a nudge, she was happy to do it. She enjoyed the opportunity to "poke a pointed Republican pen at the Administration."[36] In one article that appeared on June 26, she wrote:

> The great mummers' parade sounded the real keynote of the convention on Thursday night. It was an elaborate spectacle and received the enthusiastic plaudits that were lacking during the week at the Auditorium.
>
> Speaking of mummery, the platform was read and adopted that same night with scarcely a ripple of applause.
>
> In my hotel room, I sometimes listened to the Convention on the radio. Commentators, apparently breathless with excitement, strained their vocabularies to paint word pictures of what they are pleased to call the historic proceedings. Fearing that I am missing a high point, I hasten to the hall where I find some stodgy individual chanting a litany of the New Deal while thousands of spectators and delegates are strolling about or catching up on much needed sleep. The radio audience gets a fantastically distorted presentation of what is actually going on.
>
> The lethargical reception of the platform is quite understandable. There is nothing in it to arouse fervor, even among the most susceptible of partisans. We must

> look to the campaign speakers for elucidation of its banalities. It is clear that they intend to continue lavish Federal spending and drastic Federal control of business and agriculture. . . .[37]

Later in the day, Alice was almost crushed in a crowd of exuberant Republican women who had assembled to honor the daughter of the late President and to demonstrate that Philadlephia Republicans had not been crowded off the scene by the Democratic National Convention.[38] Mrs. Longworth stood with Mrs. Barclay Warren before a platform decorated with palms and tall vases filled with red, white, and blue flowers which more than once tottered precariously as women pushed eagerly through the narrow aisles to shake her hand. The reception was held at a bank building at 1607 Walnut Street. On its window was posted a huge sign reading "Open House," and below it were the names of Mrs. Longworth, Ruth McCormick Simms, and Dorothy Thompson.

The locals heard that Mrs. Longworth had been persuaded by Mrs. Warburton to make a political speech, the first in her career. Those who attended in expectation of the event, however, were disappointed. Mrs. Longworth merely stepped to the edge of the platform and said, "I'm sorry I don't speak. I leave that to my sidekick, Mrs. Simms." Mrs. Warburton welcomed the crowd on behalf of what she called "an oasis in the tumult of Philadelphia." "Mrs. Longworth is here just in case you've been thinking there was nobody

"Do you know," Alice told Helen Ogden Reid, whose husband owned the New York *Herald Tribune*, "J.P. Morgan won't allow the name Franklin Roosevelt to be mentioned in his presence because it raises his blood pressure. I'm for Landon, but I do wish he'd stop *lowering* my blood pressure."[40]

As she told so many other people over the years, "Franklin very possibly wouldn't have emerged if my father hadn't emerged, and my father might not have emerged if Czolgosz hadn't killed McKinley. Who can tell? Were it not for Czolgosz, we'd all be back in our brownstone-front houses. That's where we'd be. And I would have married for money and been divorced for good cause."[41]

14 □ THE DIRTY THIRTIES

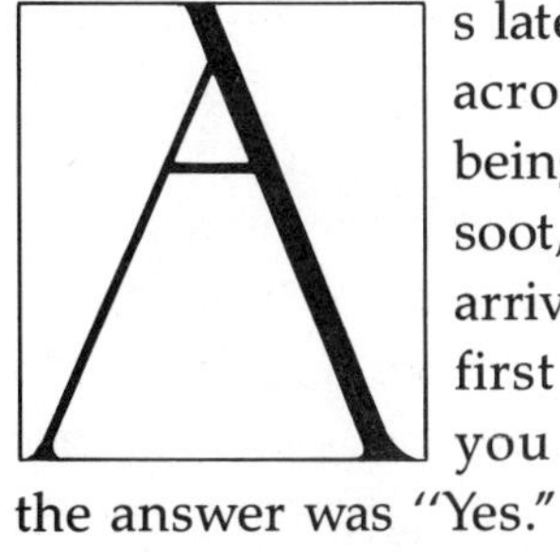

s late as the 30's, no one could move across America by train without being encrusted with layers of dust, soot, and cinders. The moment one arrived at his or her destination—the first question asked was, "Would you care for a bath?" Generally, the answer was "Yes."

Toward the end of August 1936, Alice and her daughter rode the Santa Fe's Chief from Chicago, across the flat fields of corn and wheat, over the mountains, and across the barren desert to the land of orange juice and green money—Hollywood.

Without doubt, Alice found more excitement in the movie capital than her daughter. Studio chiefs elbowed each other for the opportunity to lunch or have dinner with her. Stars had their egos punctured when they learned Mrs. Longworth "didn't recognize one actor from another."[1]

With her Roosevelt energy, Alice made a complete survey of Hollywood. She left no studio unturned. Backstage intrigued her; the technical side of movie making impressed Alice more than the actors.

She liked seventeen-year-old Mickey Rooney's personality. "He's fast on the uptake," [2] she said, "fun to talk with."

Having imagined Hollywood as "mostly a playground for grown-ups,"[3] she was astounded that the movie people worked so hard—even on Saturday!

Alice requested that she and Paulina be allowed to "bum around" the lots and be left alone, but it was about as easy for Alice to be left alone as for Greta Garbo. The actors and actresses wanted to have souvenir shots taken of themselves with the celebrated guest. Some even pushed scraps of paper in front of her and requested autographs.

Howard Dietz, vice president[4] in charge of public relations at MGM, scored a major coup when he arranged for Alice to lunch with the leading lady Norma Shearer and her husband, Irving Thalberg, Hollywood's leading "boy genius." "I rarely go to the pictures," Alice admitted as she nibbled her salad. Miss Shearer smiled enigmatically.[5]

Paulina took tennis lessons, while Alice listened with earphones to the voices coming in over the sound track from the set of *Libeled Lady*. A short time before, she had watched Myrna Loy and William Powell do innumerable retakes of a scene from that picture. "Practice wouldn't hurt a few politicians I know," Alice told Dietz.[6] She also confessed to him that she never had seen the film *The Thin Man,* which featured Loy and Powell. They ran it off for her in the projection room. "I thought it was fine," she said. "I particularly liked the dog."[7]

Alice studied how pictures were cut and edited. Paulina, sober-faced, with braids hanging below her waist, accompanied her mother on days that the weather refuted the Chamber of Commerce's "Sunny California" slogan, but Paulina showed little excitement until she caught sight of a horse race on film. "That's what I like," she said.[8]

"She's an excellent horsewoman—takes after her grandfather in the way she sits her saddle,"[9] said Will Roger's widow. Mrs. Rogers gave Paulina a horseback-riding party at her ranch—to which several of the screen's young "beaux" were invited—Jackie Cooper, Freddie Bartholomew and, of course, Mickey Rooney.

Even if Paulina failed to find Hollywood interesting—the inhabitants there thought the eleven-year-old looked "like a Swiss doll."[10] She wasn't the first girl who was told, "*You* oughta be in the movies," but *this* girl was told by Louis B. Mayer and Jack L. Warner.

While going through 20th Century-Fox, Alice dropped in on a rehearsal of the chorus girls and boys from the movie *Pigskin Parade*. She watched them dance to the "point of exhaustion"[11] and then drop down on the floor for a rest after they'd heard the dance director's whistle. A wide-eyed Judy Garland stopped by and shook hands with Paulina and Mrs. L.

Most intriguing at 20th Century was observing makeup experts turn a white man into an Indian for *The Plainsman*—Cecil B. DeMille, film producer and loyal Republican, explained the different cosmetics to mother and daughter.[12] Max Factor himself demonstrated the use of Max Factor Number 5. DeMille also introduced them to Jean Arthur and Gary Cooper, and they watched Wild Bill Hickok (Gary Cooper) dying with his head in Calamity Jane's lap (Jean Arthur). The scene brought tears to Paulina's eyes, and Alice put her arms around the child.

Years later, Howard Dietz included Alice Longworth when he told an acquaintance, "The names I knew were so heavy—you *had* to drop them."[13]

At the depot, in its enormous waiting room, Alice and Paulina were surrounded by questioning mobs. When asked about the Presidential election, Alice loyally supported Alf Landon, although she was frank to say that her hundred-dollar bet with Alexander Woollcott on the outcome of the election, stood in grave danger.[14]

Did she agree that the Republicans had launched a campaign to "save America from socialism"? Mrs. Longworth refused comment.

Did she believe that Landon was "the Kansas Coolidge"? Still no comment.

How about Landon as "the Kansas Sunflower"? Silence.

Had she seen the Democratic bumper stickers that proclaimed, "Sunflowers Die in November"? Alice sighed.

What about *The Literary Digest* poll showing Landon burying Roosevelt in a landslide?

"If they're not right," Mrs. Longworth answered, "I shall be forced to cancel my subscription!"[15]

By the time Alice and Paulina boarded the train to leave Southern California, Franklin and Landon met at a governors' conference in Des Moines, Iowa.

Queried as to what he thought of F.D.R., Alf answered, "He's a very fine gentleman."[16]

When Roosevelt departed, he told Landon, "Governor, however this comes out, we'll see more of each other. Either you come to see me or I'll come to see you."[17]

"Harmony dripped so steadily from every rafter," Kansas Senator Arthur Capper commented in disgust, "that I fully expected one candidate to withdraw."

The Literary Digest poll,[18] reenforced by the clear thinking of a Harvard professor of statistics, continued to predict an overwhelming victory for Landon.

On Tuesday, November 3, 1936, Franklin D. Roosevelt and John N. Garner won each of the forty-eight states except Maine and Vermont. Alfred M. Landon and

Frank L. Knox captured those sturdies. In one of the greatest landslides in modern American political history, Roosevelt and Garner gathered in well over 10 million votes. In the Electoral College, the tally stood at 523 to 8.

With regard to her subscription to *The Literary Digest*, Alice did not have to cancel it. What remained of *The Digest* found a purchaser in Henry Luce's newer, bouncier, *Time* magazine. "Sic Semper Victoribus!"

Shortly, after the second inauguration, on January 20, 1937, "Cactus Jack" Garner visited Alice in her Massachusetts Avenue home. "Presidents," he stated candidly, "are remembered as starters or enders of wars and other highfalutin policies, but Vice-Presidents, unless they hitch up a notch, are forgotten."[19] Alice, whose father had been a Vice-President briefly, tried to hush Garner. But his was a tongue sharp as a needle on a desert plant. And when it stuck, humor poured out. He told her about the time he and Mrs. Garner were invited to an official banquet, only Mrs. Garner came down with a heavy cold. "So I was sent packing by myself. When I got home, I went up to her bedroom and she gave me the third degree about what sort of dresses the ladies were wearing. 'Nothing *above* the table,' I told her. "I didn't look *under*.' "

Alice laughed and then turned the talk to her cousin:

"Poor Franklin, we used to say. As it turns out, the joke is on us."[20]

"Did you hear about his church up in Hyde Park?" she asked Mr. Garner.

"The young pastor proudly had printed under its name, 'The President's Church.' And under that," Alice laughed heartily, "some impish soul chalked, 'Formerly God's!' "[21]

In 1937, Alice and her brother Ted, Jr., edited *The Desk Drawer Anthology: Poems for the American People*. Selected from more than 40,000 poems sent in by listeners to the network radio show *Town Crier*, hosted by her still friend Alexander Woollcott.[22]

"The lovely but incautious Alice Longworth,"[23] as Woollcott called her, having paid her debt of one hundred dollars for backing Landon instead of Roosevelt, was now worthy of having her book trumpeted on the air by the *Town Crier* himself.

Within three years, the bantering between Mrs. Longworth and Alexander Woollcott stopped—by mutual agreement. They had grown far apart politically. She considered him and his chums "far left-pro-Russian," and as for Woollcott he wrote the publisher, Nelson Doubleday, what he thought of a novel called *Oliver Wiswell* by Kenneth Roberts.

"Historically, it is about as faithful a history of the revolution as would be an account of the last eight years in the White House written by Alice Longworth."[24]

By the time the Prince of Wales became the Duke of Windsor, and his wife, Mrs. Wallis Warfield Simpson, became the Duchess, Adolf Hitler's jackboots had marched unopposed into the Rhineland. The stench of war began to pollute the air of Europe, and Alice, who had lost a brother and imagined her father pounded into an early grave by the Democratic President Wilson, decided "to see if we can keep out this time."[25]

"Of course, a great deal was entirely mischief and dislike of Franklin," she said later. "Family feeling enters into it, you see. Anything to annoy Franklin."[26] To nettle her cousin Franklin further, she gathered a curious collection of new friends about her. Senator

Burton K. Wheeler, Senator Robert A. Taft, Senator Arthur H. Vandenberg, John L. Lewis, founder of the new labor organization the C.I.O., Charles Lindbergh, hero of the first transatlantic solo flight, Father Charles E. Coughlin, a Catholic priest who spoke on radio from his church in Royal Oak, Michigan, and those earnest people who believed in protecting "America First," the isolationists who agreed with them—all found a listener in Alice.

While she never joined any of these movements, she paid strict attention to their words. During the early summer of 1940, France fell. Hitler danced his jig, and the Wehrmacht marched under the Arc de Triomphe in Paris. Battered and beaten British troops crawled off the

The Luftwaffe blitzed London. England stood alone . . . almost. Cousin Franklin and Winston Churchill had plans. As though to circumvent these, Alice Longworth moved further and further to the right. It appalled Alice when "liberals with a left lean" such as Dorothy Thompson lectured on the platform, on the radio, and in the fourth estate, and the lectures brought them fortune and fame.

An agitated Miss Thompson—it seemed to Alice—tried ramming her philosophy down the American gullet. Utilizing a tartness for which she was renowned, Alice said of Miss Thompson, "She is the only woman who had her menopause in public and got paid for it."[27,28]

15 □ THE SECOND TIME AROUND

A tapestry of fresh faces greeted Alice when she arrived at the Republican Convention in June 1940. At fifty-six years of age, she was "unprepared for the youthfulness of the candidates and those would-be candidates."[1]

Thomas E. Dewey, the racket-busting, spectacularly successful district attorney of New York County, who had finished off the gunslingers of Murder, Incorporated, and found himself boosted into the governor's chair in Albany, was already a respected young man bitten by the insect that carries a disease known as White House Fever.

Another young Republican Governor, Harold E. Stassen of Minnesota, was dismissed by Mrs. Longworth because the party had scheduled him to deliver the keynote address, and she always suspected the keynoter as "someone who would try to stampede the convention in his own favor, but who generally fails."[2]

Governor John Bricker of Ohio showed up at the convention, hoping to be the Republican's compromise candidate. Bricker, an authentic farm boy, was the only Republican to serve three terms running as governor of his state. Intellectually, he was a blank who covered his inadequacies with a few clichés when he addressed the electorate.[3]

Asked what she thought of the man and his chances, Alice glanced at the silver-haired governor and said, "Bricker is just an honest Harding."[4] Those six words did not aid his cause, but after she said, "The trouble with Bricker is when he puts his foot in his mouth, he always forgets to take the horse off,"[5,6] Bricker was finished as a Presidential candidate.

Bob Taft stood number one in his class at the Harvard Law School, and could be as quick and deft in an argument as he chose. But Alice didn't even let *him* escape her barbs: "If he becomes President, Taft will follow Roosevelt like a glass of milk after a slug of benzedrine,"[7] she said candidly about her ex-protegé from Ohio.

The New Republic described Taft this way, "He is as magnetic as a lead nail."[8,9]

Wendell Willkie's candidacy incensed Alice Longworth. Here was a political amateur who'd been a Democrat all his life. A Wall Street lawyer who ran Commonwealth and Southern, the giant utility combine, he fell back on expediency and sought the Republican nod. This came about as a result of a suggestion by Mr. Harvey Firestone, of the tires of the same name.

"You'll never make it as a Democrat," Mr. Firestone pounded into him. "Wendell, you'd better come on to our side."[10] Willkie was forty-eight years old, handsome and a dynamic speaker. Alice considered him "an adventurer, but a dashing sort." True, he'd been born in Indiana, "but he hadn't been back since he was a pup."

The senior Senator from Indiana, James E. Watson, was even more scornful of Willkie than Alice. Watson, a conservative Republican, who had helped Lodge defeat Wilson and his League of Nations, when he heard of Willkie's intention to turn from the Democratic Party to the Republican, said:

"If a whore repented and wanted to join the church, I'd personally welcome her and lead her up the aisle to a pew, but by the Eternal, I'd not ask her to lead the choir the first night."[11]

At last Stassen delivered his keynote address. He sounded like a man laying the ground work for the '44 convention. He did not dare to offend any group.

"Where does Stassen stand?" a puzzled delegate asked Mrs. Longworth.

"He has one foot in Taft's camp, and one foot in Dewey's, and a third with Willkie,"[12] she answered.

The chanting in the galleries of the steamy Republican Convention, "We want Willkie! We want Willkie!" succeeded in securing his nomination.

"Willkie sprang from the grass roots of American country clubs,"[13] Mrs. L. cracked smartly.

Alice returned to Chicago for the opening of the Democratic Convention on July 15, 1940. She watched with amazement and horror as Franklin accepted an unprecedented "draft" for an unheard-of third term. Garner dropped out of the Vice-Presidency, and Eleanor backed the "radical" Henry A. Wallace of Iowa for the number-two spot on the Democratic ticket.

Stumping the country, even after his voice grew hoarse, Willkie manipulated the microphone to call out what Mrs. L. considered to be in questionable taste, "No man is good three times."[14]

Unlike the Landon campaign in 1936, this one turned nasty almost at once. Republicans warned that Roosevelt's aid to the English war effort would lead America into a conflict it did not need or want.[15] Alice's friends in the right wing assured her over and over that America had no reason to feel threatened by Germany, Italy, or Japan.

Democrats wisely asked the electorate to note that Willkie had actually contributed cold cash to the 1932 Democratic campaign fund.

Alice shuddered. When Willkie came out in favor of Franklin's foreign policy, she shook. She was ready to put a "murrain" on him when the American people did the job for her. On Tuesday, November 5, 1940, they elected F.D.R. for a third term, giving him 27 million votes to Willkie's 22 million. The count in the Electoral College went: Roosevelt, 449; Willkie, 82.

After his inauguration, Franklin scolded Alice for saying, "I like to be in the minority because it's more exciting." And then she continued, "Under the New Deal, Miss Columbia has become the girlfriend of the whirling dervish."[16]

By the time Alice and Nick had returned to the capital in 1914, Eleanor had hired a part-time social secretary, who was to help the young wife of the new Assistant Secretary of the Navy with her mail. Lucy Mercer was an attractive, well-bred girl who caught Franklin's notice immediately.[17]

Alice suspected a romance between Franklin and Miss Mercer. The next summer proved her right.

"I saw you driving in the country today," she told Franklin, "only your eye wasn't on the wheel in your hand. It was on that lovely young thing."[18] No disagreement came from her cousin. He only laughed. After that, Alice had the two of them to dinner now and then.

"Every man in Washington has a 'summer wife,'" Mrs. Longworth believed, "and Franklin deserves one because he's married to Eleanor."[19] That she should be encouraging the dalliance of one cousin at the expense of the other meant little to Alice.

Crushed when she learned of Franklin's unfaithfulness, Eleanor offered her husband a divorce in 1919.

Following councils with his mother, Sara Delano, Franklin gave his word not to see Lucy again. Mrs. Longworth, realizing that the Mercer family was devoted to the Roman Catholic Church, thought rightly that Lucy never would marry a divorced man. Instead, at the beginning of the Harding years, she chose a wealthy widower from New Jersey, twice her age, Winthrop "Wintie" Rutherfurd.

Eleanor was overjoyed, but Alice waited. When Franklin was inaugurated in 1933, he provided a limousine and chauffeur for Mr. and Mrs. Rutherfurd. Eleanor knew nothing of this. It would be years before any of it surfaced, and Alice carefully made sure she did not become the informant.

Following the inauguration of January 1941, rumors seeped into Eleanor's study, rumors unpleasant but not unfounded. The intimate dinners Alice had been arranging for Franklin and Lucy Rutherfurd were brought to her attention. With no small feeling of malice herself, Eleanor wrote to her cousin.

"Someone has told me that you say that you have to go to the White House and it is rather tough to go there. I don't want you to feel obligated to come."[20]

Alice caught the intent of the letter at once and replied, "How horrid people are, trying to make bad feelings. How can they say things like that? I adore coming to the White House."[21]

After that, the engraved invitations came with less frequency.

Mrs. L.'s verbal dissatisfaction with the Chief Executive built to such vitriolic proportion that one day in disgust, after having heard her latest criticism of him, Franklin Roosevelt said to one of his sons, "I never want to see that woman again."[22]

"Perhaps it gave them pleasure not to have me," Alice told an interviewer, "but they should have been better winners."[23]

There were a great many embarrassed Americans on the afternoon of December 7, 1941, Alice among them. For several years they had been telling each other the United States would never be attacked by the Axis Powers.

Senator Borah, from the great potato state of Idaho, held firm views on the possibilities of hostilities in the East, and never once doubted them. During a private meeting with Secretary of State Cordell Hull, Borah turned scornfully to the Secretary.

"We aren't going to have a war," he spoke with ease and assurance. "So far as the reports in your department are concerned, I wouldn't be bound by them."[24] He went on to say, "I have my own sources of information which I have provided for myself and on several occasions I've found them *more* reliable than the State Department."[25]

In February 1941, Senator Robert A. Taft said, "It is simply fantastic to suppose there is any danger of an attack on the United States by Japan."

On September 22, 1941, Senator Taft said with calm confidence, "There is much less danger to this country today than there was two years ago, certainly less than there was one year ago."[26]

Seventy-five days after the senior Senator from Ohio spoke, the Imperial Japanese Navy launched the most devastating attack American history had then known.

On December 7, 1941, the State Department received the following cable: JAPANESE PLANES ATTACKING PEARL HARBOR. THIS IS NO DRILL. HUSBAND KIMMEL, ADM. USN.

Admiral Kimmel, commandant of all American ships in the most powerful naval base in the world, had eighty-six vessels of war lined up neatly in what had been called "battleship row." His opposite number, Lieutenant General Walter G. Short, had two hundred and seventy-three Army war planes, fighters, bombers, and interceptors, lined up like sitting ducks on the runways of Hickam Field on the Hawaiian island of Oahu.

On December 7, 1941, *Life* magazine showed photographs of the Japanese envoys to Washington bowing and scraping. The caption beneath the photos read, "The defenses of Manila and Hawaii are stronger than ever. The Navy is ready for action."[27]

The Navy got action at 7:55 A.M. Honolulu time. One hundred and five Japanese fighters and bombers began hostilities over Hawaii.[28] The Navy and the Army received notice of war in the form of bombs dropping over Hickam Field and Pearl Harbor.

After the Japanese had completed their air attack, all planes on Hickam Field were out of commission. At Pearl Harbor, eight American battleships, ten other vessels, and a floating dry dock had been destroyed or seriously damaged. One hundred and fifty Navy planes had been bombed into rubble.

"Ships and aircraft are replaceable," Henry Morton Robinson wrote, "but dead men cannot be brought back to life. Of our armed forces at Pearl Harbor, 2,343 were killed outright, with 960 additional victims still reported as missing."[29]

Hundreds were wounded. One of them recollected, "It was just like a scene out of *Gone With the Wind* when they burned Atlanta. Here were these thousands of guys at a dressing station at Hickam Field, screaming, and bleeding, and dying. It was awful!"[30]

The next day, before a joint session of the Congress, Franklin Roosevelt called the sneak attack "a date which will live in infamy,"[31] and he asked Congress to recognize that a "state of war exists" with Japan, Germany, and Italy. He got that recognition at once.

When visitors arrived at Alice's drawing room after Pearl Harbor and saw a photograph of a Japanese emperor hanging on her wall, she would quickly speak up, "That's not Hirohito. It's the good one."[32]

Kermit volunteered to fight with the British and then switched over to join the Americans. As the war progressed, her other brothers, Ted, Jr., and Archie, entered the Army. All were officers. First to fall in his country's services was Kermit, who died in Alaska.

Typical of Alice, she kept her grief to herself. Quentin's death in World War I had been an underlying reason for Alice's antipathy toward this new war. Now, with Kermit's death, Mrs. Longworth had to hear in her mind the melancholy sound of "Taps" again.

Further grief lay in the offing. Her favorite brother had always been Ted. She'd loved each Roosevelt boy, but Ted and Alice had had a particularly close relationship dating back to his childhood.

After Kermit's death, members of the family reported that Alice's emotions were as near the surface as they might ever be. When she mentioned Ted and his V-letters from overseas, Ethel said she could see an unaccustomed apprehension in her sister's eyes.[33] As the days leading to the invasion of Europe counted down, that apprehension slowly turned to anguish.

On D-day, Brigadier General Theodore Roosevelt, Jr., landed with his troops on Utah Beach. His citation read:

ROOSEVELT, THEODORE, JR.

> *Rank and Organization:* Brigadier General, United States Army.
> *Place and Date:* Normandy Invasion, 6 June 1944.
> *Entered Service At:* Oyster Bay, N.Y.
> *Birth:* Oyster Bay, N.Y.
> *G.O. No.:* 77, 28 September.
> *Citation:* For gallantry and intrepidity at the risk of his life above and beyond the call of duty on 6 June 1944 in France. After two verbal requests to accompany the leading assault elements in the Normandy Invasion had been denied, Brigadier Roosevelt's written request for this mission was approved and he landed with the first wave of the forces assaulting the enemy-held beaches. He repeatedly led groups over the sea wall and established them inland. His valor, courage, and presence in the very front of the attack and his complete unconcern at being under fire inspired the troops to heights of enthusiasm and self-sacrifice. Although the enemy had the beach under constant direct fire, Brigadier General Roosevelt moved from one locality to another, rallying men around him, directed and personally led them against the enemy. Under his seasoned, precise, calm, and unfaltering leadership, assault troops reduced beach strong points and rapidly moved inland with minimum casualties. He thus contributed substantially to the successful establishment of the beachhead in France.[34]

Marquis Childs, veteran Washington journalist, said many years later, "T.R. was always spurring on his sons to be great athletes, great soldiers. Their ends were inevitable."[35]

Ted, Jr., died of a heart attack in the field on June 12, 1944. At fifty-seven the strain of leading one of the landing assaults had been much too strenuous. He received the Congressional Medal of Honor, the highest decoration an American serviceman may be awarded. His father had sought that Medal of Honor but always in vain. At last, his namesake had it, even at the cost of his own life.

Archibald suffered severe wounds that he carries with him to this day.[36] Throughout it all, Alice Roosevelt Longworth went about her usual routines and maintained her public silence.

Paulina, shy and cautious, grew slowly from childhood into adolescence. In Cody, Wyoming, in 1938, she met and enchanted a young boy who became Dr. Remington Patterson, acting dean of the faculty and chairman of the Department of English at Barnard College, Columbia University.

> I found her very attractive [he recalled]. We rode very tame horses on large Western saddles. Nobody worried much about us.[37]
>
> She was a very friendly person, fun to be with. We were pals, and there was a little occasional hand-holding and that sort of thing. It was part of a process of growing up and discovery for me. I was thirteen or fourteen and I thought she must have been a year older. We exchanged some letters during the next year. I never saw her again, but I liked her a lot and she stayed in my mind. It was the first time I had ever become good friends with a girl.[38]

The summer hand-holdings of teenagers are almost always forgotten, but not for the Yale-educated Patterson.

Paulina went on to a more permanent relationship. For two years she tried life at Vassar, but the collegiate world could not hold "Kitz" Longworth. Shortly before D-Day, Alice announced the engagement of her daughter to Mr. Alexander McCormick Sturm, another Yale man. Sturm, related to Alice's friends in Chicago, the McCormicks of reaper and *Tribune* fame, was the son of a playwright, novelist and sculptor, Justin. The husband-to-be had written and illustrated two books, and longed for a future in the arts.[39]

Difficult as it was, Alice arranged for her daughter's wedding a month after the death of her brother, Ted, Jr.

They had intended to have a very small ceremony in Magnolia, Massachusetts, where they spent the month of August. As with most weddings, the guest list grew, and the nuptials were held in a somewhat larger church in Manchester, Massachusetts, on August 26, 1944. The bride's mother wore an Alice Blue gown.[40]

Many Americans still credit Alice with personally causing the defeat of Thomas E. Dewey, when he ran against Franklin D. Roosevelt's controversial bid for a fourth term in November of 1944. Shortly after her daughter married, Alice appraised the political situation.

Dewey had black hair, a black mustache, and wore conservative suits on his body and a faint set smile on his lips.

"How do you expect people to vote for a man who looks like a bridegroom on a wedding cake,"[41] Alice mused aloud. Her summation spread like a chain letter.

The conservatives in the Democratic Party dumped Henry A. Wallace as their Vice-Presidential candidate, and substituted an almost-unknown Senator, Harry S. Truman of Missouri.

On November 7, 1944, even though Franklin's health was failing rapidly, he gained reelection, beating Dewey by 3.5 million votes.[42] His inauguration took place on the south portico of the White House on January 20, 1945.[43]

After traveling 14,000 miles to the Black Sea resort of Yalta, where he met for the last time with Winston Churchill and Joseph Stalin, Franklin Roosevelt returned to the Capitol, where he asked a joint session of the Congress if he might be permitted to deliver his speech sitting down. It would give him the chance, he said, to remove, "about ten pounds of steel from around my ankles."[44] It was the first public mention of Franklin's polio misfortune.

A few weeks later, in the spring of 1945, a massive cerebral hemorrhage took his life. Alice learned that Lucy Mercer Rutherfurd, whose husband had passed away during the previous year, was in the room when the President died.[45] Alice told no one about the incident until years had gone by. Suddenly, she felt a belated pang of sympathy for Eleanor.

"As far as I'm concerned, Eleanor really came into her own *after* Franklin died," Mrs. L. said. "Before, she was too noble—a person who had gone down in one coal mine too many."[46]

Alice had learned almost as much about coal mines as Eleanor—not first hand, but from an acknowledged authority.

John Llewellyn Lewis, born in 1880, near Lucas, Iowa, was the son of a pair of immigrants, both of whom had come from the mining towns of Wales. By the time he left seventh grade and went into the mines, young John realized that he and everyone else in the pits worked twelve hours a day, seven days a week. The pennies they received in wages hardly compared with the six-figure incomes of the men who owned the property and the coal.

The men who went beneath the earth's surface and dug appeared to have little opportunity in the land of opportunity. Because Theodore Roosevelt had settled the coal miners' dispute with the coal operators in 1902, Lewis joined the Republican Party. By 1905, he received appointment as the legal representative of the United Mine Workers of America. Soon he rose to the presidency of the UMW.

Corrupt and racket-ridden, the giant American Federation of Labor in the 1930s ceased to hold the loyalty of the average worker. Dues-paying members dropped out by the thousands each week. Lewis thundered onto the scene by forming the Congress of Industrial Organizations.

John L. Lewis became the instant hero of the unions, driving around the country, defending virtue—virtue in Lewis' lexicon always meant poor people or assembly-line workers—his booming voice exhorted his listeners to "Organize! Organize!"[47] During business hours, he defied Capitalism and the Wealthy. What an unlikely man to attract Alice Longworth. What an unlikely pair they made, but somehow this heavy-jowled crusader appealed to her.

The Communists have a catchphrase, "Nothing is too good for the workers." Certainly that applied to John

Llewellyn Lewis. When he wasn't making impassioned speeches for the downtrodden, he socialized with the Duponts of Delaware, Winthrop Aldrich of Equitable Trust and Chase Manhattan of New York, Ernest Weir of Pittsburgh Steel, Evalyn Walsh McLean of Washington and Fairfax County, Virginia, and Theodore Roosevelt's daughter, Mrs. L.[48] "Nothing too good for the 'head' worker."

Although he had been a Republican, in 1932 he urged his union to vote for Franklin Delano Roosevelt. "Where else could they go?"[49] he reasoned. Still, he never trusted F.D.R., and by 1940, he endeared himself to Alice Longworth by turning on her cousin in the White House.

Mrs. Longworth thought Mr. Lewis "an enchanting man."[50]

"He loved making trouble, and I loved watching him make it. It was natural that we should get together," Alice told Lewis' biographer, John Hutchinson.

"We had great fun. We used to dine together, sometimes at my home, sometimes at his house in Alexandria—just us. He was courtly and friendly. I was lucky in my middle age, to find a new delightful companion." Mrs. L. continued, in answer to the obvious question, "Marriage?" "I think it was in the wind. But I didn't take it seriously. I wouldn't have married anybody. Once is enough, but, for me, he was the best company there ever was."

Alice cozied up to her memories, "We didn't pretend at all. We laughed at ourselves. We were suddenly fellow thieves. We could have come straight from the Arabian Nights."[51]

16 □ THE SHADOWS

lice Longworth mellowed considerably during the second half of the forties. A most important person entered her life. To her only daughter, Paulina, was born an only daughter, Joanna.[1] The woman who forever poked fun at sentimentalists found herself fussing over the infant whenever she had the chance to get to Southport, Connecticut, where Paulina and Alexander Sturm lived.

Back in Washington, Alice realized the new occupant of the White House was a surprising change from Franklin. The man who had aspired to his county's road commission now led the United States.

"Harry Truman?" Alice recollected "I met him once—when the battleship *Missouri* dropped her anchor into the Potomac. We had a pleasant talk. He scared some people. He didn't scare me."[2]

He didn't scare the Republican Party, either. With Franklin out of the picture, they felt they were a cinch to win in 1948. However, some unknown prophet with a raucous voice called out to the President as his train paused at a campaign whistle stop, "Give 'em hell, Harry!"

Harry Truman gave 'em just that. He gave it to the Republicans, the Democrats, the Congress, and later, to a five-star general who failed to obey orders, and finally to a music critic who failed to fully appreciate his daughter Margaret's singing.

The morning the sun came up after the election of 1948, Alice snuffed out a cigarette in a tray filled with stubs and ashes. An unidentified man, tired, hungover, bewildered, turned to her and asked, "The Chicago *Tribune*'s headline last night called Dewey the winner. How could he have lost?"[3]

Alice removed her earrings and turned off the radio.

"You can't raise a fallen soufflé," she told him.[4]

Within twenty-four hours, that comment hopscotched into editorial offices of the newspapers and from there into print.

Truman's victory in 1948 was not the sole jolt. In that same year, Dr. Alfred C. Kinsey, a professor of zoology at Indiana University, published *Sexual Behavior in the Human Male*. Americans gasped!

Open discussions of sex were served with the main course at every dinner. Ed Sullivan, a likable but at times inarticulate newspaperman, started a variety show on television, a gadget with a six-inch black-and-white screen. Along with his guests, who included dancers, acrobats, animals and actors, came vocalists.

There was that big night in the early 50's when a boy named Elvis Presley appeared. Sullivan instructed the cameramen to "shoot" the gyrating singer from the waist up. No matter what Kinsey said, Ed Sullivan was trying to keep sex under control to please his family audience. The strange sound Presley emitted was as contagious as measles. As with measles, the young were the most susceptible. Electric guitars were *in*, saxophones were *out*. "Hound Dog" and black-leather jackets replaced "Dear Hearts and Gentle People" and three-piece suits. Rock began to roll.[5]

The kids watched *Howdy Doody*, chewed bubble gum, and squished something called Silly Putty in their hands.

All this new personal freedom and fun, and in the midst of it, Alice's son-in-law died of hepatitis. After seven years of marriage, Paulina was a widow in her twenties with a five-year-old child. Alice shunned the press. People who knew Paulina said she felt lost.

Mrs. Longworth rented a house for her daughter and Joanna in nearby Georgetown, and Paulina sought peace by converting to Catholicism.

By the time Dwight David Eisenhower came into the Washington arena, put on a civilian suit, a gray homburg hat, and his famous grin, Alice Roosevelt Longworth's appraisals were getting short and sour.

"Eisenhower," she said. "A nice boob."[6]

And lethal.

Concerning a woman acquaintance who bragged about her background, Alice didn't think twice.

"We must have a common ancestor—and I use the word 'common' advisedly."[7]

The much-admired Adlai Stevenson, who lost two Presidential elections to Dwight David Eisenhower, spoke at a gridiron banquet and said, "A funny thing happened to me on the way to the White House. . . . Don't let me discourage any of you from running for President. It's a wonderful way to meet a lot of people you wouldn't meet otherwise—at *any* price!"[8]

Even his opponents appreciated the Stevenson humor. "But if we'd wanted a truly witty President," said a Republican voter from Denver, Colorado, "we could have drafted Alice Roosevelt Longworth."[9]

In the early fifties, Mrs. Longworth's home attracted as many of the influential people as it had in previous years. Favored by summonses to the house off DuPont Circle were such conservative stalwarts as Senator and Mrs. Everett Dirksen, Senator and Mrs. Lyndon Johnson, Vice-President and Mrs. Richard Nixon, "a very nice couple," publisher Henry Luce and his beautiful and talented wife, Clare Boothe, Speaker of the House of Representatives Joseph Martin, and the man who alternated in the Speaker's seat, Sam Rayburn. These two bachelors played musical chairs much the way Nick and Jack Garner had during the twenties and early thirties.

Politics aside, she took particular pleasure in Rayburn's wry humor.

"There's an old saying around Washington," the Texan noted. "If you want to *get* along, *go* along."

He also observed, "When two men agree on *everything*, *one* of them is doing all the thinking."

Years before, Alice's husband Nick had come home one evening quoting a Rayburn maxim "Any fellow who will cheat *for* you, will cheat *against* you."

Mrs. L.'s favorite Rayburnism was "It's better to be silent and pretend dumb than to speak and remove all doubt."

At a dinner given by the Washington hostess Perle Mesta, Alice found herself seated next to Sam Rayburn. Throughout the meal they argued politics. Alice launched into a tirade opposing the Democratic proposal of a twenty dollar across-the-board tax reduction. After she dived into her ample purse, extracted a $20 bill, and waved it under Rayburn's nose, he seized it.

"Give me back my money," the astonished Alice demanded.[10]

"A Republican as good as you shouldn't be toting around a picture of old Andy Jackson," he told her.

Stuffing the currency into his pocket, Rayburn kept it until the end of the evening when he returned it to Mrs. L.[11]

People felt privileged to be allowed up to her second-floor drawing room. James Brough, a Briton based in Washington and an astute Mrs. L. observer wrote, "What she possessed and . . . exercised was snob power more than anyone in the United States . . . . The salon on Massachusetts Avenue served as an intellectual hothouse."[12] Mr. Brough pointed out that Mrs. Longworth's flattery prompted politicians to repay her graciousness by taking her aside and divulging juicy classified tidbits.

One of the politicos she seemed to have little desire to discuss matters with was the junior Senator from Wisconsin. Her antiliberal feelings had their limits. Even President Eisenhower took pleasure in hearing of her encounter with a man whom he disliked thoroughly.

During the height of the Red Scare, Senator Joseph McCarthy, chief baiter of the day, met Mrs. Longworth at a charity bazaar. She tried with success to be polite, but then, "I think I'll start to call you Alice," the junior Senator said in his smug, sure way.

Mrs. L. turned her head and lifted her chin just the slightest bit.

"My gardener may call me Alice, the trash man on my block may call me Alice," she said, "but you, Senator McCarthy, may call me Mrs. Longworth."[13]

A devotee of prizefighting, she and Turner, her chauffeur of many years, were en route to the bouts one evening when a South Carolina motorist cut in front of her antique Cadillac. On went the brakes, and both cars slammed to a halt.

"What do you think you're doin', you black bastard!" the other driver shouted.

Without a pause, Mrs. L. rolled down her window.

"Driving me to my destination, you white son-of-a-bitch!" Alice retorted.[14]

Mrs. Longworth's words could shock. She could clown on cue, or, if necessary, be dignified and proper. What she had trouble with was being sympathetic. Alice commiserated with few persons because she didn't want any sympathy for herself. A kind word is sometimes a tear away from breaking down the barriers that Alice had spent a lifetime erecting.

Marquis Childs, a journalist of great intuition who has known her well for many years and has enormous affection for Mrs. L., said, "I think if you have to sum it up, in many ways, her life has been tragic."[15]

Quite probably, the most tragic blow Alice received came from a bedroom of a very small house in Georgetown. There, her beloved Kitz died in January 1957 at the age of 31. Paulina had been under the care of a physician for migraine headaches and despondency. Emotional and physical pain engulfed her. She took medicine prescribed by her doctor.[16]

Then came the day when she lost count of how much she had taken.

The eleven-year-old child, Joanna, discovered her mother lying unconscious on a sofa.[17] Rushed to the emergency room of Georgetown Hospital, Alice Longworth's daughter was pronounced dead. An accidental overdose of medication.

Alice still held her head high, but her eyes occasionally were moist. Those lines of Flo Harding's to the Coolidges now pertained to Mrs. Longworth: "No matter how many loving hands may be stretched out to help us, some paths we tread alone."[18]

The Sturm family felt strongly that Joanna should be brought up by them, that Mrs. Longworth, at seventy-three, was too old a woman to raise a young child.[19]

Alice stood like a ramrod. The determination she had when she was twenty seemed to flow back into her body. There were no lawyers or judges or courts who could take Joanna away. If she had failed Paulina in the slightest, and she had not, she would make it up to her granddaughter.

They would be "free spirits" together. That was her life plan for her granddaughter and herself.

Telegrams and flowers poured into the house on Massachusetts Avenue. A letter arrived from a first cousin immediately. "My dear Alice, [it read]. . . . I am shocked that this great grief has come to you, and I am glad that you have the small Grandchild. If there is anything I can ever do for you, please let me know. With my deepest sympathy, Affectionately, Eleanor"[20]

It took five months before Alice could manage an answer.

"Dear Eleanor," it began, and her handwriting was scratchy and slightly unsteady, "for months after Paulina died, whenever I tried to write, I simply crumpled."[21]

She went on to relate how touched she was by her cousin's telegrams and spring flowers, and continued that she and Joanna would leave within days for a couple of months in Wyoming. It is a letter seeking a truce. It is also a letter in which she asks her cousin to come by when she is in Washington so that Joanna might meet her. It is signed, "Affectionately, Alice."[22]

The key word here is "crumpled." She revealed her inner feelings to few people. It was strange that she chose to expose her soul to her first cousin, Eleanor.

Another cousin, deeply devoted to Alice, is the brilliant author, Joseph Alsop. Regarding Mrs. L., he wrote:

> What is her secret which would be so useful for others to know? One part of the answer is clearly *guts*. She has been through some very bad patches, but she has never asked for sympathy (and has more than once bitten the hand that too effusively offered it).
>
> After a bad patch, it is a sight to see her entering a room full of people young enough to be her grandchildren, squaring her shoulders, stepping swiftly and lightly, all but seeming to say, "Don't you dare pity *me!*"[23]

17 □ THE LADY WHO SINGS FOR HER SUPPER

rs. Longworth valued her cook more than the gold and diamonds in her jewel cases. The dinners she gave were simple but elegant. The table was beautifully laid, everything perfect,[1] old silver settings, heavy sterling candlesticks holding flickering white candles, tiny filigreed silver baskets, filled with nuts, in front of each service plate.[2]

Rarely more than twenty-four guests sat at her table. Generally, twenty.[3] The servants seemed invisible, they did their jobs so well. A typical Longworth dinner menu consisted of crab bisque, tiny homemade Southern biscuits, filet mignon—rare and beautifully done—French string beans, salad, cheese, the finest of wines, and the cook's speciality, crème brulée, a rich Gallic custard.

"Positively sensual,"[4] recalled the Washington bureau chief of a major newspaper. "Eating that brulée has been known to cause a few moments of guilt in the more inhibited guests."

"You have to sing for your supper,"[5] that was an expression she used. If you didn't add your own flavor to her dinner party, if you weren't prepared to talk and be talked *at*, "You might not be invited back," said intelligent, petite, dark-haired Selwa "Lucky" Roosevelt, wife of Archibald Roosevelt, Jr.

"And I'll tell you something else about 'Auntie Sister'—that's what the younger relatives call her."[6] (Quentin, Ted, Kermit, Archie, and Ethel had referred to Alice as Sister. It was a logical step for their children to address her as Auntie Sister.) "She was the most marvelous guest I ever had in my house. She'd come and, of course, everyone was always enchanted that she was there, and everyone wanted to talk to her, and she was wonderful about talking to everyone. She had very good manners, old-fashioned good manners and tact. She'd call the next day to say what a nice time she'd had and she meant it. And then she'd add, 'Did you notice? I'm getting old, but I still sing for my supper.'"[7]

The newly elected President, John Kennedy, agreed that she did. Although Alice Longworth had voted for Richard Nixon in 1960, she recognized that a carbon copy of F.D.R.'s Brain Trust resurfaced with Kennedy.[8]

Under Franklin, there had been Raymond Moley, Rex Tugwell, A. A. Berle, Jr., Ben Cohen, and Tommy Corcoran. Into the Kennedy White House swept McGeorge Bundy, Theodore Sorensen, Robert S. McNamara, Pierre Salinger, Arthur Schlesinger, Larry O'Brien, and Dean Rusk, among many others. They were all eager and active products of their time.[9]

She admired the Kennedy clan's style and solidarity.[10] She told Jean vanden Heuvel:

> There's been nothing like the Kennedys since the Bonapartes, and like the Bonapartes, the Kennedys have these extraordinary women. I like the Kennedys, I have an affection for them. They are all for one and one for all among themselves, which is quite different from our family, who were completely individualistic. What an extraordinary upbringing they had. Everything was put behind the boys so that they could concentrate on power and success.
>
> They talk about the Adams and the Roosevelt families; poor, feeble creatures we were compared to the Bonapartes and the Kennedys. We never had a family

> that hung together. The Adams family, perhaps, but they were always being superior persons—most superior persons.[11]

The Kennedys considered Alice a favored guest, one who had to be invited to the White House for almost every state and private occasion.

During his too few years in office, the youthful Kennedy chose the Broadway musical *Camelot* as his theme, and Mrs. L. as "the best company in town." High ideals matched high jinks. At dinner parties, observers noticed that the seat of honor between Bobby Kennedy and McGeorge Bundy, the President's chief adviser, regularly went to Alice. "They are peppy parties, splendid,"[12] Mrs. Longworth told Roger Stevens, managing director of the Kennedy Cultural Center.

Chided that she antedated the Kennedy water sports by half a century, Alice protested that she did nothing remarkable.

"How outrageous can you get?" Bobby demanded of her.[13]

"There was nothing at all outrageous about what I did," Alice replied. "Had I jumped into a swimming pool *without* my clothes, *that* would have been outrageous."[14]

Doubtless, her memory had been stirred by the appearance of the cellist, Pablo Casals, at the Kennedy White House. The first time Casals had bowed his cello at 1600 Pennsylvania Avenue, her father had been President.

Mrs. Longworth admired the new First Lady for her taste in entertainment, art, furniture, fashion, culture, and she appreciated what Jacqueline Kennedy and her circle gave to America.

From *Webster's New International Dictionary, Second Edition, Unabridged*: "Martyr, One who voluntarily suffered death as the penalty of refusing to renounce his religion or a tenet, principle, or practice belonging to it;—a title of honor among the early Christians."

On November 22, 1963, in Dallas, Texas, John F. Kennedy was murdered.

> Why are the assassinated Presidents called martyrs? When a President is assassinated [Alice stated], he is not a martyr. . . . No, I have no use for the martyr epithet. I'm awfully sorry about Jack Kennedy, who was much too good for the kind of things that are being done about him, and who would not have liked a great deal of what he would have considered, I think, sentimentality. No one could have a drier, more delightful, humorous, ironic view of life. He was an engaging character of great ability who needed no window dressing.[15]
>
> Bobby Kennedy may have been my favorite public figure of the 1960s. We traded insults. I told him what my father had written in his diary about Irish politicians. He laughed. He would have been an excellent President. It's sad. Both brothers were first rate.[16]

Lyndon Baines Johnson was something else!

"A lovely rogue elephant,"[17] Alice called him. She considered him more western than southern. Like her father, LBJ had a ranch, where he raised cattle and hunted and played Texas-style politics.

Elevated to the Presidency after the tragedy in Dallas, Johnson and his bright wife, Lady Bird, as she chose to be called, carried out the plans that Jack Kennedy did not have the days to achieve. Desegregation of schools, greater effort toward voter registration, subsidies to college students, establishment of Departments of Health, Education, and Welfare and Housing, cultural centers, everything Jack Kennedy had dreamed about in his private Camelot, Lyndon Baines Johnson brought to pass during his years in the White House.

His wife had been careful to keep a tape-recorded diary of her days and nights in Washington and her travels around the globe. *A White House Diary* reads openly, frankly, and with good political judgment and poignant discernment.[18] Never has the wife of an American President detailed with such tenderness the glories and disappointments of that exalted office.

> Thursday, January 30, 1964 [Mrs. Johnson's journal reads]. One of the highlights of the day was that Mrs. Alice Roosevelt Longworth came . . . . It was one of those afternoons I had promised myself—one of those completely unofficial things, no duty at all, just pleasure. Mrs. Longworth has lived this life I've loved, in this town I've loved, and seen so much of it—has observed it with such caustic wit and at such closeup range, that I yearned to spend an hour with her. And it was a great one![19]

When Alice learned that Senator Goldwater of Arizona would oppose Lyndon Johnson of Texas for the 1964 Presidential race, she claimed her attitude "was one of malevolent indifference."[20] Her indifference didn't last. By the time the autumn leaves turned, so did Alice. Something revolutionary happened. For the first time in her eighty years, Alice Roosevelt Longworth voted for a Democrat. In the 1964 campaign, Lyndon Johnson triumphed over Barry Goldwater.* It turned out to be one of the greatest landslides an American President had won. And Alice had voted with the majority.

*Although she had voted for President Johnson, Mrs. L. held a fondness for Senator Goldwater because she never cared for those who took defeat seriously. Following his loss to LBJ, Goldwater returned to his home state and successfully campaigned for a seat in the U.S. Senate from Arizona.

"Do you think the DAR will take my voting privileges away from me?" she asked.[21]

The First Lady noted in her diary:

> Wednesday, April 21, 1965. This was a memorable day, primarily because Alice Roosevelt Longworth came to tea and brought her grandchild, Joanna Sturm. She is fiercely undaunted by old age, bristling with the quality of aliveness. It's said of her that she has an acid tongue, but I like her. We reminisced and she obviously enjoyed herself, recalling the days she spent in this house. She related that once her little half brothers were playing hide-and-seek in the attic (what is now the third floor) and that President Roosevelt, hearing the noise, went upstairs to investigate. It was nighttime, and he was in his pink pajamas, rotund and blustering. One of the youngsters looked up and said, "Here comes cupid."[22]

By the time President Johnson was well into the term to which he had been elected, he had a few words to say about living in the White House:

> It's not the kind of place you would pick to live in; it's a place you go to after work. . . . I feel like I'm in the middle of an air raid. Then at 8 A.M. when I am trying to read a report from a general, all the tourists are going by right under my bed. And when I'm trying to take a nap, Lady Bird is in the next room with Laurance Rockefeller and eighty ladies talking about the daffodils on Pennsylvania Avenue.[23]

When Alice heard this, she countered, "Yes, but he'll have to admit, it *is* a fine location."[24]

On Tuesday, July 19, 1966, Mrs. Johnson spoke into her tape recorder.

> I had invited Alice Roosevelt Longworth to come to meet with Luci and me this afternoon at four. I had planned it as a meeting of the bride of half a century ago with the bride of 1966. I hurried to the Diplomatic Reception Room about five minutes of four to greet her. She was wearing the big brimmed hat . . . this one in brown. I wonder where she gets them?! Lyndon came in and kissed her and had a word or two. He likes her and she him, I believe. I expect they both recognize in each other a strong, untamed spirit.[25]

Alice also liked to tease the President. Once, he said to her, "Mrs. L., it's hard to kiss you under that brim."[26]

"That's why I wear it," Alice responded.

Where does she get those hats? Eleni, fashion editor of the Washington *Star*, wrote, "Perhaps as well known to some as Nefertiti's headdress are the big-brimmed hats that have become her signature since she was a young girl living in the White House."[27]

A Connecticut Avenue milliner named Mrs. Sonia Sheftel is presently responsible for them. She has been for the last quarter of a century. In the spring, Mrs. L. orders the same Milan straw hat in black, brown, and navy. She gets the identical style made in the same colors for fall and winter. They are trimmed with grosgrain ribbon and bow.

"I wait eagerly for rain or snow," Alice Longworth says. "I love to hear the raindrops on my new hat."[28]

Mrs. Longworth gave the Johnsons advice on their daughters' weddings. "Who wants a cozy wedding in the country? That's horrible," she said.[29]

First to marry was Luci, who chose Patrick Nugent as her husband.

In the summer of 1966, Luci Bird and her twenty-six attendants marched down a church aisle longer than a football field. Everyone managed to get a TV set to watch the ceremony. The wedding reception took place at the White House. There was a hundred-voice male choir, a three-hundred-pound cake, seven hundred guests, and Peter Duchin led the orchestra. Barbecued cold beef sirloin was served. Texas had been transported to Washington.[30]

Mrs. L., glancing around the crowded White House, said, "Everyone's here except the Texas Rangers. Perhaps they're disguised as waiters."

Eleanor Howard, an engaging journalist with an enormous liking for Mrs. Longworth, took her husband Jack on an adventure to Massachusetts Avenue in the spring of 1967. Alice proudly showed the couple her magnificent four-story doll house—the house with no dolls. Sinking to the floor, Mrs. L. sat and pointed out the various delicate objects. When her guests had concluded their examination of the miniature antique furniture, Mrs. Howard noticed that her hostess, "rose like a ballet dancer, her lightness of foot and grace were amazing."[31]

On October 27, 1967, Alice and President Johnson unveiled a statue of her father on Theodore Roosevelt Island in the Potomac River. On a cloudless October day the eighty-three-year-old Mrs. Longworth—wearing sturdy lizard shoes—hiked vigorously from a parking lot on the Virginia shore to the wild little island in the middle of the Potomac. She was accompanied by Joanna and dozens of other relatives.[32]

President Johnson, in his few dedicatory remarks, chose to quote T.R. "Woe to the country where a generation arises which . . . shrinks from doing the rough work of the world."[33]

The sculptor was the late Paul Manship, who did the Prometheus Fountain in Rockefeller Plaza. Chief Justice Warren and Interior Secretary Udall spoke. As usual, Alice could not be lured near the waiting microphones. "An appropriate place to have a memorial to Father," she told the Chief Justice.

Together, Alice and the President pulled the rope that uncovered the seventeen-foot-high bronze statue of T.R. The United States Marine Corps Band struck up "America the Beautiful."

"I like it enormously," Mrs. Longworth said of the statue. "I have a rather mean disposition, I *specialize* in meanness, but I have nothing critical to say about it. I think it is excellent."[34]

The next White House marriage took place on December 9, 1967. Lynda and Captain Charles Robb, USMC, exchanged vows in the same room that Alice and Nick Longworth had been married in sixty-two years earlier. This time, however, there was no need for Major McCawley's sword. Captain Robb and his bride cut their wedding cake with the groom's own sword. Alice nodded in approval.

The most sobering effect of the wedding was cast by the pall of the Vietnamese War. Begun under Kennedy, the war escalated into riots at home and tragedies on the battlefield. College campus disorders grew into full-scale rebellions, as the entire country howled with curses and choked on smoke from coast to coast.

Hippies, Yippies, Black Panthers, antiwar liberals turned much of America into a divisive state, stunned by a conflict it had not sought, did not want, could not abide.

Although Lynda and Captain Robb marched under an arch of crossed swords, at least three members of the groom's party, who wore the "dress blues" of the Marine Corps, were scheduled for action on the Indochina peninsula within weeks.

In 1969, Alice visited Lady Bird Johnson again. Mrs. Johnson described Mrs. Longworth as getting out of the car and coming toward her "like a ship under full sail, exclaiming, 'Isn't it delicious? Isn't it delicious?'"[35] She was talking about Jackie Kennedy's remarriage and could barely wait to get within speaking range.

Alice kept it no secret that she did not approve of the match.

"Hasn't anyone ever warned Jacqueline Kennedy about Greeks bearing gifts?"[36]

The country listened with mixed feelings to LBJ's announcement that he would not seek another nomination for the Presidency. The Johnsons had become "family" to Mrs. Longworth, and she had said of the thirty-sixth President, ". . . a masterful man, the greatest I've ever seen at getting things done, and I've seen them all."

Alice Longworth had intended to go to the 1968 Democratic Convention in Chicago, but after a man with a handgun snuffed out Bobby Kennedy's life, she canceled her plans.

"Why him?" she asked her sister Ethel. "So young and attractive."[37]

Ethel told Mrs. Longworth it reminded her of Don Quixote's line, "Death devours lambs as well as sheep." Alice knew that.[38]

She would have felt even worse if she hadn't had such enthusiasm for an ex-Vice-President whom the Republicans were assuring each other "couldn't lose."

At eighty-four years of age, a refreshed and rejuvenated Alice Longworth stayed on the telephone most of the afternoon and a good part of the evening. "Vote for Dick," she urged her friends in her low, cultivated convincing voice. "Don't forget, vote for Dick Nixon."[39]

18 □ THE WOMAN OF ALL SEASONS

After he had taken the Presidential oath of office, after he had stood bareheaded in the reviewing stand watching the bands and marchers troop past the White House on January 20, 1969, after he had raised his arms countless times in the V for Victory sign, after he had forced his lips to part and show a semblance of a smile, Richard Milhous Nixon, thirty-seventh President of the United States, retreated to the Executive Mansion and even he was a bit surprised to find himself there.

In 1962, after Nixon had lost the California governor's race, he held an unscheduled, unprepared meeting with the press.

"Just think," he said, "you won't have Nixon to kick around anymore. Gentlemen, this is my last press conference."[1]

Now that he had proved himself wrong, and he sat at the head of the United States Government—one amazed patron of a downtown Washington bar was heard to say, "It's the greatest comeback since the Resurrection of Jesus."

The first dinner party in the Nixon White House was held toward the end of January 1969, in what once had been Alice Roosevelt's old bedroom.[2] Now it had been converted into the private dining room for the First Family. Only ten selected guests were honored: Secretary of State and Mrs. William Rogers; the President's National Security Adviser, Dr. Henry Kissinger;

Chief of the Federal Bureau of Investigation, J. Edgar Hoover; Counsel to the President and Mrs. John Erlichman; Mrs. Robert Low Bacon, a Republican hostess in Washington since 1923; the President and Mrs. Nixon; and, of course, Mrs. Nicholas Longworth who was close to her eighty-fifth birthday.

Astute Myra MacPherson, writing in the Washington *Post*, quoted Helen Smith, Mrs. Nixon's press assistant, as saying no advance word was given out about the party because it was "private and supposed to be off the record."[3]

"These are people he feels easy with," Smith went on, describing those attending the dinner.

An acquaintance of Alice said that, "If the Communists take over the White House tomorrow, Mrs. L. would be one of the first people invited to dinner, and Mrs. L. would be the first person to accept the invitation."[4]

"The boy wonder" from Whittier, California, Richard Nixon, didn't know that about the lady who lived on Massachusetts Avenue. He only knew that she had liked him and Pat for years, and she had always said that he was "level headed."[5]

A woman he once dared to call "the Pink Lady," Helen Gahagan Douglas, a woman whose political career he had ruined, said with amazing control, "Mrs. Longworth must have meant *flat* headed."

With the coming of Nixon to the White House, no small amount of zip returned to Mrs. L. She had been sharing sympathy and tea with the Nixons since 1948. Intrigue, spy stories, mysteries—she'd always loved them. And now, instead of being between the hard covers of a book, there were enticing, titillating clues in the daily newspapers. Microfilm hidden in a pumpkin on a farm! Who could have invented anything so bizarre?

A young Congressman's name kept appearing, she told Eleanor Howard. Alice couldn't resist.[6] What an idea! She darted to the Capitol Green Book and looked up the name. It was listed. Nixon, Richard M. He and his wife were living in an inexpensive apartment in Alexandria, Virginia. Alice called the number, and invited Congressman and Mrs. Richard Nixon to her Massachusetts Avenue home.[7] Their first meeting, and she never regretted making the call. "What if I read that Sherlock Holmes and Dr. Watson were working on a case and staying at the Hay-Adams, wouldn't I have rung them up?"

She found Pat Nixon to be a gracile redhead with an easy smile and a wide streak of generosity. That Dick had defeated Jerry Voorhis, a ten-term Congressman from California, meant only that a Republican had beaten a Democrat. That his victory had been bought at the price of smearing Voorhis meant little to Mrs. Longworth. Her father had been smeared, her brothers, her husband, her daughter, and not least of all, Alice Roosevelt Longworth had been pilloried in the public prints, and in fashionable and polite drawing rooms here and abroad for the better part of her life.

The frequency of her later visits to the White House were a result not only of Richard Nixon's insistence, but of Pat's as well.

"I've been for Nixon for the last twenty years," she told Wiley Buchanan, chief of protocol under President Eisenhower, "and I'm glad to see him back." She also admitted to having "2.7 dinners a year in the White House, no matter *who* is President."

Mrs. Longworth had scored heavily at the Women's National Press Club fiftieth anniversary dinner the previous year. The President and Mrs. Nixon attended the affair, along with a host of front-page celebrities. Werner von Braun, of the National Aeronautics and Space Administration, went to the wrong reception. Once he got straightened out, he arrived at the Women's Press Club and proceeded to the speaker's platform where he amused the audience by advising them, "There is only one moon so it is easy to hit."

Then the learned rocketeer asked, "Do you know of any other moon? We are having a difficulty to find what to do for an encore."[8]

Great laughter and much applause greeted Von Braun, but no speaker received the ovation that awaited Alice Roosevelt Longworth. Introduced by Marjorie R. Hunter, WNPC President, as "our woman for all seasons,"[9] Mrs. Longworth, gowned in Alice Blue, arose, smiled, and bowed to the crowd. The entire audience stood up and applauded for the longest time of the entire evening.

By 1969, reporters were bothering her with questions again.

"How do you feel on your eighty-fifth birthday?"

"Fine," came her answer. "Why, was someone expecting I'd be sick?"

Now a wisp of a woman who referred to herself as "a withered Twiggy,"[10] she gave a birthday party for herself in her own Massachusetts Avenue mansion. Dozens of her old friends stopped by, not the least of whom were President and Mrs. Richard Nixon. Alice began the evening by calling him "Mr. President," but before long, she eased the tension by referring to him as "Dick."

When the radical Weathermen stormed the South Vietnamese Embassy near her home in 1970, District of Columbia police used tear gas to break up the chanting demonstrators. Mrs. Longworth stuck her head out of a window. Why? Someone asked her. "To get a whiff of the gas," she answered. "It clears my sinuses."[11]

On March 15 of that year, columnist Maxine Cheshire reported that Bob Hope, the comedian, and his wife, were guests of Alice Longworth. Hope sat in Alice's drawing room, "laced-linen napkin on his knee, and one of her Chinese rose medallion teacups in his hand. The tea sloshed over in the saucer, as he heard Mrs. Longworth confide that she has smoked 'reefers' more than once in her life."[12]

The surprised comedian had nothing to say in answer to this confession.

Ms. Cheshire reported that as he left, he asked his wife Dolores what she thought about the tea. (Seldom is anything stronger served at one of Mrs. Longworth's afternoons-at-home.)

"Well," said Dolores Hope, "the tea was a little strong."

"Strong?" cracked Hope. "I don't think she *smokes* pot. I think she *drinks* it!"[13]

Hope had been too polite to ask if she meant marijuana, so he came away from that afternoon thinking that the revered "Mrs. L." had been experimenting with an illegal drug—"a not too remote pastime around her Dupont Circle neighborhood."[14]

> "How terribly amusing!" she said when the famed Washington *Post* columnist asked about the episode. "Everyone tried *reefers* in my day, but I thought they were those things children smoked behind barn doors—you know—corn silks. Are you sure people mean marijuana when they say *reefers* today?"[15]

Later, she told journalist Betty Beale, "I am always glad to learn something new. I am full of curiosity and overexuberance. And overexuberance is something I *hate* in the aged."[16]

A few days before her birthday, the First Family held a preanniversary affair for Alice at 1600 Pennsylvania Avenue. "So gruesome. Everyone looks at you and wonders if you'll last another year," Mrs. Longworth said. "Eighty-seven isn't a particularly interesting age. It's much more fun to be an age divided by five."

"I understand I am supposed to make a surprise announcement," President Nixon said in the East Room facing three hundred guests for an afterdinner, all-Irish gala honoring Prime Minister John M. Lynch of Ireland. "Trouble is, every time I try to make a surprise announcement, somebody leaks it, and this one is no exception."[17]

The jovial President wondered aloud, ". . . if making this announcement would be anticlimactic. But I talked it over with Pat—it's her birthday, you know—and the Prime Minister, and both Mr. Lynch and Mrs. Nixon told me, 'Do it, Dick. Even if they did leak it, it's not official until you say it is.'

"So Pat and I are very pleased to announce the engagement of our daughter Tricia to Edward Ridley Finch Cox."[18]

Most people, including Alice, had been aware of the forthcoming engagement for months. In the receiving line, the President introduced her "as someone who knows this old house extremely well." Mrs. Longworth kissed Mrs. Nixon and her newly betrothed daughter. The guest list included the groom-to-be; his parents; Vice-President and Mrs. Spiro Agnew; Robert Abplanalp, the Bronxville multimillionaire; Charles G. Rebozo, the President's pal from Florida; Dr. Henry Kissinger; singers Morton Downey and Dennis Day; and George Murphy, the film star who had once represented California in the Senate.

Patricia Nixon, elder daughter of the President, was married during a light rain on June 12, 1971, to a man who had been referred to by his fellow students at Harvard University as "Fast Eddie" Cox.[19]

In spite of rain plans to hold the ceremony in the East Room of the White House, the bride remained adamant that they go through with the sunshine plans to have it in the Rose Garden.[20]

"I am using all the powers I have to make the rain stop," the Rev. Billy Graham said.[21]

The President had set the tone earlier in the day when he looked up at the dark skies and remarked to his National Security Affairs Commissioner, Dr. Henry Kissinger, "It looks like it's going to be a beautiful day."

Nixon was wrong again.

The rain dampened everyone during the ceremony, but the minute the wedding concluded, "the guests scrambled for cover, many holding their white satin programs over their heads."[22]

When Alice Longworth was asked if the nuptials recalled her own wedding in 1906 she said, "Good God, not a bit. I was married twenty years before Hollywood. This wedding was quite a production."

As she accepted a glass of champagne, she turned to Press Secretary Ronald Ziegler and said, "I feel as though I've been sitting on a wet sponge."

The next day, President Nixon authorized the formation of the unit that later would be called "the Plumbers."

On that same day *The New York Times* undertook publication of the Pentagon Papers, a documented history of the war with the Vietnamese. They began to show that the people of the United States had been dealt with falsely by their own government.

June 28,1971, Daniel Ellsberg, senior research associate at Massachusetts Institute of Technology, Center for International Studies, admitted giving the *Times* the story because of his belief of the immorality of the war.[23]

September 3, 1971, the Plumbers, led by E. Howard Hunt, vandalized Ellsberg's psychiatrist's office.

June 17, 1972, Democratic headquarters at the Watergate Hotel were broken into by five men.

October 10, 1972, Bob Woodward and Carl Bernstein began their series in the Washington *Post* on the attempted disruption of the Democratic campaign by the Committee to Reelect the President, CREEP. Alice read the papers and stifled a few yawns. She was used to political pranks.

On November 7, 1972, Alice Roosevelt Longworth served caviar and scrambled eggs to the people who came to her home to watch the election returns. It pleased her that Nixon won.

When a friend telephoned a McGovern backer's complaint, "I am convinced God is a Republican," Mrs. L. responded, "*All* Big Business *is*."

"Coolidge would have liked that," she said.

The New York Times reported that President Nixon had noticed Mrs. Longworth missing from his second inauguration and the luncheon following it. "I worried about her," Nixon said in his most sincere voice.[24]

"Wretched flu," was Alice's excuse. "Simply wretched flu."[25]

By 1973, Mrs. Longworth stopped yawning at the news. She could hardly wait to arise at 1 P.M. to read the latest Bernstein-Woodward revelations, and to watch the fantastic proceedings on television. Senator Sam Ervin and his Select Committee held the nation glued to 200 million TV sets as the hearings went from May 17 until July 16, when the most unlikely person of all, White House aide Alexander Butterfield blurted out to the

Watergate Committee that Richard Nixon had operated a clandestine tape-recording machine, that tapes had been made and continued to exist. The audience in the room and those watching on the television tube became absolutely unraveled.

Alice, who had stopped smoking years before, almost reached for a cigarette.

"Watergate! Oh, how I love it. I thoroughly enjoy it. Oh, to see what comes next!" she said to a young acquaintance who spent part of the summer with her.[26]

She was in complete agreement with the Washington personality Fred Dutton, who remarked, "Watergate has done for politicians what the Boston Strangler did for door-to-door salesmen."[27]

Senator Robert Dole of Kansas, former National Chairman of the Republican Party before Haldeman, Erlichman, and Mitchell threw him out, was able to beat the Watergate rap.* Opponents went right after the Senator in hopes of splashing some Watergate mud on him. But Dole claimed he had never been taped while talking with President Nixon. Whenever he sat in the Oval Office, Senator Dole joked that he always nodded his head for "yes" or shook it for "no."

The Plumbers, who originally were brought together to plug leaks in White House and national security, dissolved before the Senate Select Committee. The gaps they left proved larger and far more dangerous than those they had been ordered to plug. Not only did the tapes reveal racism, prejudice, cowardliness, avarice, but—from the lips of the Commander-in-Chief himself, rumor had it—language more like a drill sergeant toward a particularly dumb batch of recruits than the country's leader. Alice didn't join the group

*Of course, slippery Spiro Agnew, pleading *nolo contendere* to a variety of charges, escaped prison. The term-and-a-half Vice-President resigned October 10, 1973.

that threw the first stones at Nixon. Instead, she pointed out, "They've always got the straitjackets ready for the inmates of the White House. Let's give him some time to see if he's a villain or a victim.[28]

David Bowes, a Cincinnati columnist, quoted Mrs. Longworth as saying, "Take Charles Bartlett's piece the other day. He wrote about how stylish Jack Kennedy was when he cursed. The press was captivated when Jack Kennedy said, 'son of a bitch,' but the press objects because President Nixon now and then says. . . ." And here Mrs. Longworth pronounced with clarity and elegance a four-letter word beginning with *s* which the American Heritage Dictionary lists and defines as "vulgar slang."[29]

When Pat Nixon and her daughter, Julie Eisenhower, came to visit at the mansion on Massachusetts Avenue, Mrs. Longworth treated them with dignity and charm. "I still long for those tapes," she advised her guests. "I'd like to hear what he called some of them on the tapes. I would doubt it's original profanity."[30] This from the woman who had heard "Cactus Jack" Garner cuss, who had listened to "Vinegar Ben" Bailey of the Rough Riders chew out a mule. *She* was an *authority* on profanity.

"This goddamn birthday is driving me crazy!"[31] she told both Helen Thomas and Jeanette Smyth, journalists. Despite her protestations, everyone knew that she looked forward to that special February day in 1974.

Her ninetieth birthday! She would see everyone from relatives and friends to politicians and Presidents. Gifts would flow in, flowers, telegrams, cables. No end seemed in sight.

She would have three birthday cakes. One in the shape of the numeral nine, one in the shape of zero, and one large round cake with the words "Happy Birthday to Me" written on it.[32]

Ten candles decorated the large round cake. Someone pointed out that the tenth "was to be good on."

"Not a chance!" Mrs. Longworth said.

President Nixon had three parties to attend the night of Alice's birthday, but he and Pat didn't even consider missing Mrs. L.'s.

The reporters caught up with him as he left a restaurant on his way to Mrs. Longworth's home. Without much prodding, the President volunteered his opinion as to why the celebrated lady has lived so long.

"If she spent all her time reading the *Post*, she'd have been dead by now— or the *Star*, for that matter." He uttered the words in that manner the reporters had become used to—the facade and facial expression that said "I am being light and amusing and stonewalling it."

"But Mrs. Longworth sees the world and brings people in from all over," he continued. "And as a result, she stays young by not being obsessed by miserable political things all of us, unfortunately, think about in Washington, instead of the great issues that will affect the world—which the *Post* unfortunately seldom writes about in a responsible way."[33]

And then he called over his shoulder, "Quote that exactly as I said it."[34]

The newspapers did as he requested, including the *Post* and the *Star*.

Mrs. Longworth wore a long black dress with tigers designed on it. Very appropriate, her guests thought. She tried to be a less active hostess than at most of her parties, but Alice had invited such distinguished persons that she had to keep popping up and down to greet them.

The President and Mrs. Nixon arrived with Julie and David Eisenhower. Mr. Nixon brought a music box decorated with the Presidential seal. It played Strauss waltzes and Alice found it delightful. The First Family sat on the worn sofa with Mrs. Longworth and her half sister, Ethel Roosevelt Derby. They chatted for over an hour.[35]

Marquis Childs, who along with his wife went to the party, said that the reporters stayed in a different room and actually tried to avoid speaking with the President. Mrs. Childs said to her husband, "Why don't we just go in and say hello as a kind of courtesy?" Following his wife's lead, Childs did just that.

Although some tension seemed to exist that night between the divided rooms, Childs said, "With Mrs. Longworth as hostess, there was always an easy atmosphere, and you could speak with the great and the near great if you wanted to."[36]

The guest list of impressive people included Senator and Mrs. Charles Percy of Illinois, Margaret Truman Daniel, former Ambassador and Mrs. Averell Harriman, the Sargent Shrivers, Mayor and Mrs. Walter Washington. Almost two hundred guests accepted Mrs. Longworth's invitation.

Mrs. Art Buchwald brought a Raggedy Ann doll with a card that explained, "Even naughty girls deserve dolls on their birthday."[37]

Asked to sum up the evening's events, Mrs. Longworth said, "I'm having a tidy old age, don't you think?"[38]

Toward the end of April 1974, the President, looking righteous and put upon, presented the American people with his own translation of the White House tapes. Almost immediately, reporters agreed that it was a doctored and lawyered version.

An acquaintance of Mrs. Longworth disclosed, "Mrs. L. still had a curious sort of admiration for Nixon because he was a trickster, and she rather was amused by tricksters."

"I've met some criminals over the years," Mrs. Longworth told chic Charlotte Curtis, editor of *The New York Times* Op Ed page and author of *The Rich and Other Atrocities*, "and I've liked them. Forty or fifty years ago I gave a party for a great friend of ours—Albert Fall. Meanwhile, his pockets were rustling with one hundred dollar bills. I'm afraid I keep up my associations whether people are criminal or not. I'm very careless about that."[39]

Formal inquiries on the impeachment of the President started early in May 1974.

"Dick is a weaker man than I thought him. Weak, weak, weak! Kennedy *never* would have shilly-shallied the way Nixon is doing. The tapes should have been destroyed and enough of this nonsense!" Mrs. Longworth told someone who preferred to have his name omitted.

The mud slide moved painfully downhill.

Witness after witness had appeared in the inquiry rooms of the Capitol. Slowly they poured out a variety of tales that would be woven into a noose for Richard Nixon. Dean, Erlichman, Haldeman, Hunt, Rebozo, Cox, Richardson, Bernstein, Woodward, all talked and talked as Rodino, Jordan, Holtzman, and other members of the House Judiciary Committee listened and learned and cast the votes that determined Richard Nixon's future.

Although she watched it all on her television set, everything from the House Judiciary Committee to the chambers of Judge John Sirica, Alice grew envious.

"Oh, how I wish I could be hidden away in some corridor and watch them pass by me," she confessed.[40]

When the Judiciary Committee voted for impeachment at the end of July, talk around Washington shifted to assumptions that Nixon would quit voluntarily.

"I don't think he'll resign. The great, rancid American people will forget."[41] Alice said . . . but not in her most definite voice. Her disillusion set in along with the rest of America.

On the evening of August 8, 1974, Alice Roosevelt Longworth listened to the President's resignation. She missed his emotional farewells the following morning.

"I was asleep. What did he say?"[42] she inquired of the reporters who telephoned her. They read her the passages that Nixon quoted from her father's diary, "When my heart's dearest died, the light went from my life forever."

"That was T.R. in his twenties. He thought the light had gone from his life forever—but he went on. He not only became President, but as an ex-President he served the country always in the arena, always tempestuous, always strong, sometimes wrong, sometimes right, but he was a man."

"I don't know why my father's recovery from my mother's loss gave President Nixon heart," Alice told the press. "My father was a very young man, at the very start of his life. President Nixon is in his sixties, and he has had a long career. So I don't know that my father's words are really applicable to the situation today."[43]

Later in the year, she said, "The whole damn thing has gone on far enough." And then she added, "I'll remember Watergate as good unclean fun."[44]

When asked about the new President, Gerald Ford, Mrs. Longworth struck.

"I've never met him, but I used to spend time in Ohio, and they turn out Jerry Fords by the bale!"[45]

19 □ THE ALL-AMERICAN SUBSTITUTE

It wasn't easy to go into the game after spending most of his life on the bench. Gerald Rudolph Ford, Jr., the long-term Congressman from Grand Rapids, Michigan, had ambition. He thought he might, in time, reach the rarified place of the Speaker of the House of Representatives. Throughout his political career he had pointed himself toward the post once held by Nick Longworth. Just as Nick never took Alice back to the White House as a resident, Jerry Ford never achieved the Speaker's seat. But the White House? Strong elements ruled that destiny.

In a series of lightning moves, Richard Nixon accepted the resignation of his Vice-President, and called upon likable Jerry Ford to take the recently vacated office. Ford once had promised his wife Betty that after his current term in the Congress expired, he would return to private life. The President's offer to accept the job of presiding over the Senate took precedence. In a brief ceremony on national television, "Gerald R. Ford, Jr., of Michigan," the President announced, was now his number-two man.

Then, on the evening of August 8, 1974, the numbers changed. The Pentagon Papers, Watergate, 2–1 votes of impeachment by the House Judiciary Committee, unanimous rulings against him by the Supreme Court brought Richard Nixon to the historic moment of being the first man in the nation's annals to resign as President of the United States.

As Nixon's plane was flying west toward Casa Pacifica, his retreat alongside the ocean, Gerald

Rudolph Ford, Jr., and his wife entered the jammed East Room of the White House. The hands on the clocks pointed to noon.

"Mister Vice-President, are you prepared to take the oath of office as President of these United States?" the Chief Justice of the Supreme Court asked.

"I am, sir," the President-to-be answered.

With Betty Ford holding the Bible, he put his hand on the passage that read, "Trust in the Lord with all thine heart . . ."

He took the oath, kissed his wife twice as the people in the East Room applauded and cheered.

A second of historic importance. Never had it happened before. Never had a man, unnominated and unelected, passed from relative obscurity to the highest office in the land. Who was he? How had this come about? Where would he lead his people? What would come next? Not only America but the entire world buzzed with questions.

To begin. He was not Gerald Ford. In Omaha, Nebraska, on July 14, 1913, he had been born Leslie Lynch King, Jr., the son of Dorothy Gardner King and Leslie King. After two years of an unsuccessful marriage, Mrs. King took her son and returned to her home in Grand Rapids. She obtained a divorce and married a Mr. Gerald R. Ford. The boy's name changed from King to Ford. Leslie became Gerald, Jr., and until he was sixteen years old, Jerry, Jr., remained ignorant of the facts.

Football, the game that Jerry played in high school and college with such skill, the game that he helped coach at Yale, turned the six-foot boy into a splendid all-around athlete.

Like Kennedy and Nixon, Ford, too, had served in the Navy during World War II. Discharged as a lieutenant commander in 1946, he went back to Grand Rapids and won election to the Congress as a Republican. His constituents returned him to the House twelve more times before Jerry Ford was asked to clean up the stain left by his predecessor.

Nothing came easily. Mistakes came quickly. His pardon of the ex-President, less than a month after Richard Nixon's resignation, may or may not have been such an error. Surely, it did not aid Ford's popularity.

His handling of himself both publicly and privately during the tragic days of his wife's mastectomy revealed a man of kindness and courage.

Among the messages Mrs. Ford received was one hastily written by ninety-year-old Alice Roosevelt Longworth. "Just a line to wish you well from one who a number of years ago had the experience you just had."[1]

Betty Ford's friends told her a remark made by Mrs. Longworth that brought a grin to the First Lady's face. Alice, after her own two breast cancer operations, had greeted Dr. Worth Daniels, her long-time physician, and cheerfully announced, "Now I'm Washington's topless octogenarian."[2]

The cheap shots, the old jokes about the President having played too much football, about not being able to walk and chew gum simultaneously, the stumbles, the falls, the comedians' imitations, did not keep Mr. Ford from carrying on affairs of state.

The Bicentennial Year pounced upon Americans before they expected it. The sale of American flags zoomed as never before. Red, white, and blue pencils, ball-point pens, books, pennants—all emblazoned with the magical dates 1776–1976—sold faster than they could be produced.

In February, the All-American Princess Alice had another birthday party.[3] This one was different. The white-haired enfant terrible of Washington, spry and cheery, invited only a few more than fifty relatives, friends and locals to her ninety-second birthday bash.

Heading up the guests were President and Mrs. Ford, who arrived at the Massachusetts Avenue "tenament," as Mrs. L. is fond of calling her home. A military aide followed, bearing a gold-wrapped box that contained a crystal bowl embellished with the Presidential seal.

Among the other guests who made the gathering most unusual was the presence of five small children, all Kermit Roosevelt's grandchildren.[4] For them, "Auntie Sister" had waiting hors d'oeuvres of warm peanut butter. They, in turn, happily wore the party hats and joyfully utilized the noise makers.

Kermit Roosevelt, age four, stationed himself at the top of the stairs.

"Are you really the President?" he asked Gerald Ford, who halted a few steps below.

"I certainly am," Mr. Ford admitted.

Without another word, young Kermit struck the President on the head with his orange balloon.

Mrs. Longworth said, "Audacious!" and young Kermit's mother, Kim, apologized immediately to the President.

Once the balloon wielder had been removed, the President and Mrs. Ford joined Mrs. Longworth for a leisurely chat and an examination of some of her other birthday gifts. Among them were a genuine rattlesnake rattle, a velvet frog, a T-shirt for ski buffs on which were printed the words "Deep Powder Is Better Than Sex."[5]

As the President and his wife made their way down the stairs, they were followed by all the children. At the door, his four-year-old assailant made peace with the President by kissing him on the cheek.

"There," Mr. Ford was heard to say, "we've made up, haven't we?"

"I guess so," replied Kermit.

Meanwhile, back upstairs, Mrs. Longworth was asked how she was doing at her age.

Grasping her right ankle until it crossed over her left shoulder, she allowed as how, "I'm feeling pretty fine."[6]

Early in the summer of 1976, Her Britannic Majesty Elizabeth II, Defender of the Faith and ruler of any number of crown colonies, dominions, and commonwealths throughout the world, visited Washington on her way to opening the Olympic Games in Montreal. Nowhere was there more pomp and protocol than at the White House in Washington, D.C.

Her Majesty first came ashore with her husband, Prince Philip, and an entourage of more than fifty ladies-in-waiting and gentlemen chamberlains. They had crossed the Atlantic in the royal yacht *Britannia*, landed at Philadelphia, presented to the citizens of the United States as a Bicentennial gift a six-ton bell that had been cast in London's Whitechapel Foundry, which had made the original Liberty Bell in 1752. Following that particular little visit, she and her royal group went down to Washington, D.C., for the most elaborate affair of her five-day stay in Britain's former colonies.

The state dinner was served in the White House rose garden, beneath a gleaming white canopy, bordered with Queen Elizabeth roses.

Dinner featured New England lobster en bellevue, saddle of veal, peach ice cream bombe, and three American wines.[7] Among the 224 guests were Alice Roosevelt Longworth, Lady Bird Johnson, Telly Savalas (star of *Kojak*, the Queen's favorite television serial),

Dorothy Hamill, the Olympic gold medal ice skater, and Alan Greenspan, the White House economic adviser. His dinner companion proved to be TV's Barbara Walters.

Television did not enjoy one of its greatest evenings. As Richard Schickel wrote in *Time* magazine:

> . . . An hour into *A State Dinner for Queen Elizabeth II*, one began to long for the mediating talents of a good film editor working up a show of highlights, which would have lasted about two minutes. To be sure, PBS was operating under restraints. It had been forbidden to show guests gulping and gnawing, leaving it with more than an hour-long hole right in the middle of the program, which it chose to fill with innocuous studies of the British monarchy's past and future. At times, the severe White House restriction on camera placement left viewers with the suspicion that the show could have been staged by Andy Warhol. . . .[8]

The affair was given by the President and Mrs. Ford in honor of the Queen. Candles burned, Air Force Strings played softly throughout the meal, pausing only for the toasts that were offered by the President, the Queen, the Vice-President, Prince Philip, and so on down the line.

After dinner, dancing was in the East Room, and the President, immaculate and handsome in white tie and tails, made all Americans proud as he danced with the luminous Queen. She wore her diamond tiara, a white organdy dress with the blue sash holding the Order of the Garter.

Midway through his dance with Her Majesty, the President was cut in on by the newly appointed Vice-President, Nelson A. Rockefeller. The Vice-President, a shade shorter than Mr. Ford, but possessing more blonde hair, said from a long experience, "This is the best party in six Presidencies."[9] With that, he danced away with the Queen.

During the course of the evening, guests were not at all certain if the Queen was going to curtsy to Mrs. Longworth or if Mrs. Longworth was going to curtsy to the Queen.

"Curtsy?" the ninety-two-year-old Alice whooped. "With these knees? I was afraid that I'd go in all directions." [10]

While she didn't attend the conventions of 1976, Mrs. Longworth peered at her television tube as Jerry Ford received the Republican nomination, and a man unknown to her, Jimmy Carter, easily picked up the nod from the Democratic delegates. The ensuing campaign, with its televised debates, left little doubt in her mind. Ford got her vote but Carter got the Presidency.

When she was asked for her opinion of the new President-elect, Mrs. L. commented, "Oh, the one who's always so happy and smiles so much?"[11]

Following Mr. Carter's inauguration and the treaty returning the canal to Panama, reporters began looking up quotes. President Theodore Roosevelt once boasted that he took the Panama Canal Zone.

Alice Roosevelt Longworth, his ninety-three-year-old daughter, said to an Associated Press reporter, "I don't care what they do with the canal. Who cares? It's there and I don't give a damn."[12]

Later, when asked what advice she might offer the President, Mrs. Longworth threw back her white head and laughed. It is a deep-throated merry laugh closer to a chuckle.

"What advice could I possibly give the Carters? That's silly. I wouldn't think of giving anyone advice, except to be themselves. If I should meet the President and Mrs. Carter, and they should ask me, that's exactly what I'd say to them. Be yourselves. Everyone has to learn for himself. Everyone has to do it his way."[13]

20 □ THE GRANDE DAME

ot too long ago, the most powerful woman in Washington's permanent social and political structure arose from a chair in the home of a local columnist, Tom Bradon.[1] She flopped down onto the floor, and placed her ancient legs in the almost impossible lotus position of India. This required her to sit cross-legged with each foot on top of the opposite knee. As open-mouthed observers stared, not believing what they were seeing, she twisted a live boa constrictor—the pet of a Bradon offspring—around her neck.[2]

Pandemonium reigned among the guests, but the ninety-year-old woman quieted them.

"I'm just one of the show-off Roosevelts," Alice explained. Then continuing, "I'm like an old fire horse. I just perform. I give a good show."[3]

❧

Girls under seven and over seventy can get away with anything. "Shhh," parents warn the little ones. To the grown girls who use wisecracks, charm, and cheekiness, people are inclined to say, "Bravo."

Mrs. Longworth, at ninety-five, is as rambunctious as a high-school freshman. She never has been particularly inhibited, but now this fragile, white-haired, self-admitted hedonist continues to deliver wall-to-wall witticisms and words generally confided from an analyst's couch.

After an interview with Washington *Post*'s blonde and bright Sally Quinn in 1974, the reporter wrote,

"Alice Longworth is a survivor in a town where the word is an anachronism."[4]

The article won Ms. Quinn plaudits, a better job on the Washington *Post*, and knocked the breath out of all who read it.

"Mrs. L. has the capacity to be outrageous," an admiring friend said, "and that's good for positive reasons. People ought to be shaken up. They ought to be caused to ask, 'Does it make any difference that women smoke? Does it make any difference that people dance all night? What is wrong and what is right?'"[5]

She's up to date in her attitudes, even ahead of some pacesetters.

"I don't think I've ever been scandalized,"[6] Alice Longworth revealed to Ms. Quinn. She also told about the time in 1904 when Marguerite Cassini, her double-dating companion, walked with her through the White House garden and whispered that a mutual friend was saying horrid things about her. Miss Cassini identified a young lady who professed to be in love with Alice.

"I don't think that's nasty. Why, I think that's lovely, I'm so glad she is," Mrs. L. recalled telling Miss Cassini. She then went on to tell her interviewer that, "Homosexuality and lesbians were very fashionable in those days."

Another example of her younger ideas appeared in the Quinn piece. If she were her granddaughter's age, would she marry?[7]

"No, I never would marry. I might live with people, but not for long. I might spend the night with them or the afternoon. . . ."

"I'm her silent accomplice," Joanna Sturm, her granddaughter, freely admitted.[8] The silent doesn't apply much these days—Joanna used to dart in and out to avoid the visitors, a sort of will-of-the-wisp inhabitant of the Massachusetts Avenue house. Recently, a woman, probably an ex-victim, said of Alice Longworth and Joanna Sturm, "Don Rickles could learn from both of them. They're the Dynamite Kids."

Honesty is what they dish out, and Washington, D.C., never has been the accepted place for unfiltered veracity.

☙

When *Newsweek* magazine wanted her to comment on the 1970s sexual scene she replied:

"I told them that I have nothing much to say on that subject except, if one wishes to talk about bodily functions, my philosophy is, 'Fill what's empty, empty what's full, and scratch where it itches.'"[9]

☙

Her opinion of Women's Liberation, delivered to Susan Sheehan of *McCall's* magazine, "It's—*so*—female!"[10]

☙

Years after the War of Dolly Gann's Succession, Mrs. Longworth confessed in a Washington *Post* article to the absurdity of seating arrangements. "Are people really taking this seating thing seriously?" Then she howls, "Isn't that wonderful, they're taking it seriously. I don't give a damn about it. I put people next to each other who are going to fight, who are disagreeable to one another . . . really, people must be suffering from idleness."[11]

Where, she is asked, does she think women of distinction should sit?

"Where?" she replies. "Why we should sit on our dear little tails."[12]

☙

Her method for staying young, "The secret of eternal youth is arrested development."[13]

☙

At eighty years of age, "It's just a birthday—you don't change between noon and midnight of one day unless you fall down and break something."[14]

☙

Even President Lyndon Johnson, whom she liked and voted for, felt the sting of her words. She referred to him as "Old Slyboots," and in the '60's, after the President had his gall bladder removed, and persisted in lifting his shirt to show off his scar to everyone, Mrs. L. said, "Thank God it wasn't his prostate."[15]

☙

Her most famous one-liner was uttered at a large Washington shindig. Alice Longworth called over an attractive, but for the moment, unattached lady guest—patted an empty chair and purred, "If you haven't got anything good to say about anyone, come and sit by me."[16]

Now, that line is embroidered on a large denim pillow in Mrs. Longworth's sitting room. It was a gift—some assume it came from the grateful guest at the party.

☙

June Bingham, author, biographer, and a familiar figure in Washington, wrote in the *American Heritage* magazine, that Congress had confronted Alice with an architect's plan for a spherical memorial to her father. Nothing ever came of the plan—it disappeared like a puff of smoke after Mrs. L.'s observation.

"It looks," she shook her head with disdain, "like a globular jungle-gym." [17]

☙

"Mrs. L. has never asked anybody for anything that she wasn't prepared to match," says the distinguished book publisher, Simon Michael Bessie. "You be smart—she's

Wide World Photos

With Gene Buck, master of ceremonies, and Chief Justice Charles Evans Hughes at Vice-President Garner's dinner for her fifth cousin, the "Feather Duster," F.D.R.

Wide World Photos

Hooray for Hollywood! Alice and Mary Pickford watch a polo game at an American Legion program in 1936.

At the 1940 Republican Convention in Philadelphia, Alice poses under the Ohio delegation's standard with Buckeye Governor John Bricker. Although Alice smiled, Wendell Willkie got the nomination.

Wide World Photos

Can it be? The right-wing Alice and the perennial Socialist candidate for the Presidency, Norman Thomas, agree. On January 22, 1941, he denounced Lend-Lease for Britain. She concurred strongly.

To the right, march! Alice, (dark hat, dark suit) sits beside Mrs. Martha Taft and Mrs. Burton K. Wheeler, wives of the isolationist senators. They are at an "America First" rally, less than seven months before Pearl Harbor was attacked by the Japanese.

Wide World Photos

Washington *Post* Photo

The Originator...

Wide World Photos

...and the Popularizer

United Press International

Paulina's coming out party at the fashionable Carmargo Club in the Queen City. June 13, 1942.

Wide World Photos

Alice and Pat and Dick and a 1900 poster of McKinley and Roosevelt. Dick is only Vice-President and Alice has no gray hair. The farther up the political ladder Dick went, the whiter Alice's hair became.

Wide World Photos

Three President's children. John Eisenhower, "Ike's" son, T.R.'s daughter, and William Howard Taft's boy Charles, at a Woman's National Press Club tea on April 30, 1959.

United Press International

Still another tea and more Presidential children. Alice, Helen Taft Manning, John Eisenhower, Mrs. John Harlan Amen (Grover Cleveland's daughter), John Coolidge, Mamie Eisenhower, James Roosevelt, Eleanor Wilson McAdoo, and Richard Cleveland. At the White House. Where else?

Wide World Photos

Fidel listens to Alice.
At a reception in the
Cuban Embassy in
Washington, 1959.

Wide World Photos

Glamour in the
White House:
President Kennedy,
Mrs. Longworth,
Mrs. Kennedy.
Dallas and Oswald
were less than a year
and a half away.

United Press International

L.B.J., his daughter Luci, his son-in-law Patrick Nugent, and A.R.L., 1966.

Wide World Photos

Alice and Bobby Kennedy
in his office in the Senate, 1966.

United Press International

Jackie and Alice
gossiping in McLean,
Virginia, 1969.

United Press International

Two White House brides.
Tricia Nixon Cox and
Alice Roosevelt Longworth.

Newsweek

Princess Alice and Queen Elizabeth at the White House during the Bicentennial bash, 1976. Flanking the Queen are President and Mrs. Gerald Ford. Next to the President is the chairman of the Bicentennial Commission, John Warner, now the freshman Senator from Virginia.

Washington *Post* Photo

Alice seated before Peter Hurd's portrait.

prepared to be smart. You give her gossip—she's got gossip to give you. You be difficult—she'll be equally difficult. In other words, she's a really fair trader."[18]

❧

"One of the things about Alice that always surprised me was that she never allowed a vacation to go unused," Mr. Bessie asserted. "I told her I was going abroad and she said, 'By any chance, are you going to Spain?'"

By no chance was Mr. Bessie going to Spain.

"The Spanish make the best switch-blade knives," Mrs. Longworth informed him. "I need a new one."

The publisher thought Mrs. Longworth was making sport of him.

The next time he saw her, was at Joe Alsop's.

". . . sitting, holding court—as she does so well."

As Mike Bessie approached Alice Longworth, he noticed her large handbag (which she refers to as "half filing cabinet, half psychosis"). The reticule rested on her lap.[19]

"Do you have a switch-blade knife in that handbag?" he asked, on an impulse.

"Of course," Alice beamed. "It's right here." She opened her purse and pointed. "You see, Mr. Bessie, someone *did* vacation in Spain."[20]

❧

While the tea brews, a visitor from Cincinnati, David Bowes, observes, "On a tabletop near her elbow is a stand holding an African tribal mask. Lifting the mask, she reveals the stand to be the miniature bronze Statue of Liberty.

"'I hang this mask right on the Goddess of Liberty,' she explains. 'It symbolizes Black Power in a free land. America's black citizens are not only winning liberty, they're discovering a wonderful heritage in art such as this. Don't you find that exciting?'"[21]

Can this be the same Mrs. Longworth who admired Father Coughlin in the thirties? "Why not?" someone says. "That's what's wonderful about her. The tinier she becomes in old age, the more she grows in human understanding and intellect. Perhaps that stimulating granddaughter Joanna has something to do with her new openness."

ꕥ

Another afternoon, she described her dress to an acquaintance as looking like "uncomfortable vegetables,"[22] and when a few minutes later, with extremely bad timing, her dressmaker called, Mrs. Longworth spoke to her in a sort of Bryn Mawr accent gone bad.

"I wore that dress with the stripes going round. I looked like a striped barrel," she informed the unlucky person on the other end of the wire. "Horrible. No, I don't want it let out. Unfortunately, it fits."[23] The phone went back on its hook as neatly as a period at the end of a sentence.

ꕥ

Near the stairwell in the sitting room rests a gong made of oriental metal. Held within a wooden frame, it is struck by one of Mrs. Longworth's maids when a visitor arrives. Summoned by the gong, Mrs. L. immediately points out the change of order.

"Notice how different everything is?" she asks. "I used to ring for my *servants*. *Now*, my servants ring for *me*."[24]

ꕥ

When you leave Mrs. L.'s Massachusetts Avenue home, you realize how much like a jungle the front yard has become. Only in 1976 could Joe Alsop persuade Alice Longworth, much against her own judgment, to have the gardener remove the poison ivy that had flourished for years right outside her curtained windows near the front path that leads to her door.

She has left untouched the clusters of pachysandra and thick bushes. The trees have grown tall and strong in the last fifty-three years, in contrast to the older occupant of the house.

"I hate the term 'Senior Citizen,'" she will tell you. "It's condescending."[25]

ꕥ

Alice ignores all critics. One day in 1977, Mrs. Longworth's neighbors became nervous when they looked up at her roof, and saw Ms. Sturm sitting on the chimney reading a book. The lady of the house shrugged. "It's nothing to worry about. I used to do it. Perhaps it's heredity."[26]

ꕥ

Don't ever try to reach Alice Longworth before afternoon. "I'm allergic to morning," she tells you. "The servants come in to wake me at 11:30 A.M., and I say, 'Get out. It's too early.' "[27]

She generally breakfasts at 1:30 or 2 P.M. Why not? Alice is a night person. She loves the small hours. On winter nights, she "lolls" in her study, curls up in front of a crackling fire, and reads as many books as her eyes permit.

"You can't live to be my age without having a few diseases," Mrs. L. wisely informs a caller. "I have glaucoma—cuts into my reading. Then there's emphysema—obviously too many cigarettes, and the more serious things." She leaves the last without more comment.

"At least, I still have all of my marbles,"[28] she says with pride and relief.

ꕥ

"I'm not as recognizable as I used to be," Mrs. Longworth says. "*Everyone's* wearing hats these days. I look at my hat on so many heads. My good old hat. I think it's that attractive Bella Abzug who made them popular, and I'm glad."[29]

ꕥ

In 1924, Anne Hard, writing for the Bell Syndicate, painted a word picture of Alice.

> I once watched a professor in a laboratory. He took some iron filings and shook them lightly over a sheet of paper. Then he placed a magnet beneath and the tiny bits of iron at once arranged themselves into a pattern. The professor called it a "field of force." But neither that learned person nor any other learned person yet has been born who could define or understand what happened. He could give it a name. That was all.
>
> And it always seems to me when I think of Alice Longworth that we may exhaust our adjectives, but we will never be able to define her. That unknown something which the scientist calls "power" and "energy," that unknown something which a Frenchman attempted to describe as the "life force" exists in her to a degree not touched by any other woman I have ever known. She is energy, she is power. She does not simply possess them.[30]

What held true in 1924 holds true to this day, even though time has eroded some of it.

ꕥ

One of Mrs. Longworth's stories deals with the time someone brought Charles A. Lindbergh to her home. It was shortly after his nonstop flight to Paris. The evening still retained the heat of the day and the Longworth windows remained open. As Colonel Lindbergh entered, in flew a bat that soared to an upper floor.

"Don't write that," Mrs. Longworth said to a reporter. "One has bats in the belfry, not in the boudoir."[31]

❦

She still calls herself "a combination of Scarlett O'Hara and Whistler's Mother."[32]

❦

If it depended solely on Mrs. Longworth, the United States Post Office could go out of business tomorrow. She never reads her mail. She merely tosses it onto the window seat and allows it to pile up for six months or a year. Then, it is removed and a new stack of unopened letters starts to come in.[33]

That tradition began with the two-cent stamp and has continued right through the current fifteen-cent issue.

Not even if the word "URGENT" is printed on the envelope does Mrs. L. peek inside. She plunges her hands into the two deep pockets of her dress, and notes, "*Nothing* is urgent these days."

❦

About her thoroughbred background, Mrs. Longworth scoffs, "The Roosevelts? A group of upstart Dutch who made a couple of bucks."[34]

❦

Charlotte Curtis, now editor of the Op Ed Page of *The New York Times*, once asked Mrs. L. to go through the fifty states and tell her who was what in society in each state. "My favorite," Charlotte Curtis reported, "was when she stopped at Alaska, and she said, 'Y'know, you just don't see anybody crawling out of those igloos.' And that was the end of the list."[35]

❦

Most Americans think of 1966, if they think of it at all, as the year James Meredith was shot while on a march through Mississippi; Sam Sheppard's conviction for murdering his wife was overturned in Cleveland; a sniper at the University of Texas shot forty-four people from the campus tower; and of course, the bloody, futile Vietnamese war dragged on. Do you remember Breezie and Blackie, two dogs the Russians sent into orbit around the earth? But to the real society "upper dogs," 1966 signifies the year of Truman Capote's Black and White Masquerade Party at the Plaza Hotel in Manhattan.[36]

If you weren't invited, you either left town to hide out, or pretended you had refused the invitation. The affair was given—so the talented author announced—as a token of affection for his friend Katharine Graham, publisher of the Washington *Post*.

"I asked Mrs. Longworth, Margaret Truman, and Linda Bird," Mr. Capote told Charlotte Curtis. "I guess that's enough of the White House."[37] Five hundred and thirty-seven other prominent people were on the guest list—a list which Ms. Curtis managed to obtain through some devious way that she refuses to divulge—except to assure her readers, she did *not* steal it.

The host made it an absolute rule that everyone wear masks, even the orchestra (Mr. Duchin, again) and the Soul Brothers Rock Group.

Mrs. L., at eighty-two, traveled from Washington for two reasons, she told the *Times* editor: "Truman Capote's one of the most agreeable human beings I know, and the ball sounds like the most exquisite of spectator sports."[38]

While many ladies spent hundreds of dollars on masks, and thousands of dollars on fancy gowns, Mrs. Longworth, who says, "I haven't bought a new dress since I was eighty," went to Woolworth's and selected a thirty-five-cent full mask. She cut off the top and the bottom, and before she entered the ballroom, she put on the tiny white part of what was left and secured it to her temples with adhesive tape. In place of her hat, Mrs. L. wore two small egrets in her hair—one black, one white. Her black velvet evening dress swept the floor—long sleeves, as usual.[39]

The Plaza ballroom, decorated by Mrs. George Backer, shone with bright red tablecloths, white lighted tapirs, and an internationally elegant set. Besides Mr. Capote and Ms. Curtis, someone else seems to have found a list of those attending the affair, because while Mrs. L. sat at a table, smiling, sipping white wine, and chatting, an enterprising thief was slowly and selectively robbing Alice Longworth's home.

First evidence of a nocturnal visitor came from a Longworth maid, who noticed that a pane of glass had been neatly cut in the front door, on the morning of November 29, 1966. On Mrs. L.'s arrival home, she was informed of the robbery. "Are you certain?" she asked the maid. "How can anyone *tell* in my room? It always looks ransacked."[40]

After going to her quarters, Mrs. Longworth admitted that her room appeared "less orderly than usual." Police were summoned. Her initial amazement added a slight flush to her face. Then Alice made a record of her losses for the local constabulary and her insurance company. It included two diamond-studded bracelets given to her by Kaiser Wilhelm II, a medal with crossed rifles on it, a souvenir of the United States First Volunteer Cavalry, a pen, several twenty-dollar gold coins, many French and British coins, all were the contents of two small jewelry cases that Mrs. Longworth said "had ridiculous trinkets in them."[41] If the burglar thought that he might get Mrs. Longworth's famous pearl necklace, her wedding gift from the

Cuban people, his information was very poor. Alice Longworth wears that necklace every place she goes, and it went with her to the Plaza Hotel.

The alleged thief was apprehended after he had removed the diamonds, and sent the metal to a Chicago smelting firm. The smelter, noticing the name "Roosevelt" on one item, and the initials ARL on another, telephoned the Chicago Police who, in turn, contacted the Federal Bureau of Investigation.

ꕥ

"Would you please state your name and spell it for the court reporter?" the young assistant United States attorney for the District of Columbia asked Alice as she prepared to testify against the man who robbed her house.

"I'm Mrs. Roosevelt Longworth," Alice replied. "That's R-o-o-s-e-v-e-l-t-L-o-n-g-w-o-r-t-h."[42]

There she was, the eighty-eight-year-old daughter of President Theodore Roosevelt, making her first appearance ever in a public courtroom. The time was early August 1972, and Mrs. Longworth, giving testimony before a judge and jury of her peers (if any existed), seemed excited by the entire proceeding.

The defendant, described in the public prints as a fifty-five-year-old man with a gentle face and a pot belly, listened to Mrs. Longworth enunciate. When she completed testifying, his shoulders sagged, and he chose to plead guilty to a lesser charge.

When it was over, Mrs. Longworth said her court appearance was "a brand new experience." As she left, she spoke to her granddaughter, and said regretfully, "I didn't bellow enough."[43]

ꕥ

The incredible grande dame can still remember the poetry she learned as a child. "The whole family could do that," Mrs. Longworth explains.[44] "A couple of my brothers could memorize whole books. I like to recite. I can rattle off Pope, Kipling, Chesterton, Longfellow, lots of others. One of my favorites—I read it in my stepmother's scrapbook—is:

> The little green lizard on
>   Solomon's wall
> Heard what the King said
>   All alone.
> Secrets that only the Djinn's
>   could recall,
> Graved in the magic ineffable stone.
> Yet when the little lizard
>   was led to speak
> Of the King when the King
>   was dead
> He had only kept track of the
>   flies on the wall.
> For he was but a lizard
>   after all.[45]

"I've always identified with that little lizard on the wall," Mrs. Longworth says. "It describes me with humiliating accuracy. I've been every place, I've talked with all kinds of people. I've listened to Kings and Queens and like the lizard, I don't remember as much as I should."[46]

☘

On nostalgia: "God, no! What is a more interesting time than today?"[47]

☘

When she was asked where she thought she would fit into the history books a hundred years from now, she pondered a few seconds and answered.

"Perhaps . . . perhaps I'll be a footnote."[48]

21 □ THE LAST WALTZ

Reconsider Cinderella. Only the circumstances are drastically altered. Edith the stepmother is gone. The stepbrothers Quentin, Kermit, and Ted, Jr., have departed. Only Archie remains.

Cinderella's child, Paulina, and the stepsister, Ethel, have exited, too.

Her father, the King, Theodore Roosevelt, lies in the earth beside Edith, overlooking the North Shore of Oyster Bay, high above Long Island Sound.

No longer do his flashing teeth glisten beneath the lights of the palace on Pennsylvania Avenue. No longer does his high-pitched voice ring out with booming cries of "*dee*-lighted!"

Beside his grave is a stone on which is written in letters of steel, "Keep your head in the clouds and your feet on the ground."

Cinderella doesn't go there anymore. The climb is too steep.

Prince Charming rests quietly in the Spring Grove cemetery near Cincinnati, Ohio.

The glass slipper is forgotten.

The United States Marine Corps never sends its band to serenade her with their tunes of glory, the "Hymn," "Hot Time in the Old Town Tonight," "The Washington Post March."

Major McCawley, the leatherneck who claimed the first dance with her at her debut in the White House in 1902, went to "Heaven's scenes" as a brigadier general.[1]

They are all gone now.

All of the Presidents of the United States she has known from Benjamin Harrison, the twenty-third, to Lyndon Johnson, the thirty-sixth, have perished. Richard Nixon writes books. Gerald Ford patiently waits for a renomination.

And the Senators and Speakers she knew and called by their first names, they, too, sleep like the Presidents, scattered through the American soil. Taft and Harding in Ohio, Wilson in Washington, Coolidge in Massachusetts, Hoover in Iowa, her cousins, Eleanor and Franklin, in Hyde Park, New York, Harry Truman in Missouri, "Ike" near the waving fields of wheat, in Abiline, Kansas, J.F.K. on a hillside in Arlington overlooking the capital. Near him is Bobby, his brother, whom she enjoyed so much. Lyndon lies close to the floodwaters of the Pedernales in Texas.

To their rewards have been delegated her "unloved lovers," the Western Senator and the Eastern journalist.

The palace on Pennsylvania Avenue has been altered once or twice since she romped through it. She opposes each change—fiercely.

The present occupant, a gentleman farmer from Georgia named Carter, hasn't invited her to visit. Nor has he come to see her.

The house she owns on Massachusetts Avenue stands with quiet dignity. Next door to it is a new hotel. At her front curb, a bus stops to pick up passengers on its regularly scheduled run—passengers who have no idea of who lives in the house behind them.

The Embassy Row of the Princess's day is not nearly as fashionable as it used to be, but her very presence there keeps it up.

The fragile lady of the house still serves tea in the afternoon—Jackson's of Piccadilly[2]—poured through a silver strainer. These days, she prefers someone else to fill the delicate porcelain cups and her tall glass in the sterling holder. Thin white bread spread with sweet butter, chocolate cakes, sugar cookies are passed around by the maid in the gray-silk uniform, with a white collar and cuffs and a white starched apron.

For Cinderella, there is dancing no longer. Yet, the old house is filled with hundreds of tunes to which thousands of long-departed guests still dance.

Presently, she is guarded by a granddaughter who has long, light hair, and whose keen green eyes watch and protect the Princess. The granddaughter's young legs are long and straight, no need here for those iron braces so many of the Roosevelt children had to endure.

Very slowly over the years, Cinderella has divested herself of her title. Perhaps she has abdicated in favor of that granddaughter.

The animal skins ranged along the wall of the staircase and on the floors of her home are dusty with time. An ancient tiger, next to the staircase, is missing a paw.[3] A jovial nephew, in a playful mood, once attempted to shake hands with the fellow, and to the nephew's horror, the paw came off. The Oriental rugs are worn. The backs of sofas have been clawed by generations of disobedient Siamese cats.

"The rooms are cluttered, everything is wearing out ... like the owner of the house," says a frequent visitor.

But Cinderella's spirit and her voice and the blue in her eyes remain true.

She eats little and she naps often. The telephone bell still jangles throughout the afternoon and into the evening. Quite often, she answers it herself. After listening to the latest gossip, she throws back her head and laughs the laughter of a woman whose anxieties have long ceased to exist.

"I'm not afraid of death," she says. "I'll consider it just another special occasion."[4]

□ NOTES

Chapter 1
THE DEBUT
(Pp. 1-6)

1. Washington *Post*. Washington *Star*. *The New York Times*, January 4, 1902.
2. New York *Sun*, January 4, 1902.
3. Ibid.
4. Henry F. Pringle, *Theodore Roosevelt*, (New York: Blue Ribbon Books, 1931), p.42.
5. Ibid.
6. Colonel Robert H. Rankin, *Uniforms of the Marines* (New York: G. P. Putnam's Sons, 1970).
7. *The New York Times*, January 4, 1902.
8. New York *Sun*, January 4, 1902.
9. New York *Tribune*, January 4, 1902.
10. Gunnery Sergeant Robert Hoffman, USMC, interview.
11. Alice Longworth, *Crowded Hours* (New York: Charles Scribner's Sons, 1933), p.46.
12. New York *Sun*, January 4, 1902.
13. *The New York Times*, January 4, 1902.
14. Joseph Lash, *Eleanor and Franklin* (New York: W. W. Norton Company, Inc., 1971), p. 140.
15. Longworth, op. cit., p. 47.
16. Owen Wister, *The Virginian* (New York: The Macmillan Company, 1902), dedicated to Theodore Roosevelt.
17. Owen Wister, *Roosevelt, The Story of a Friendship* (New York: The Macmillan Company, 1930), p. 87.
18. Longworth, op. cit., p.47.

Chapter 2
THE IDES OF FEBRUARY
(Pp. 7-13)

1. "Theodore Roosevelt Birthplace," National Park Service, U. S. Department of the Interior, U. S. Government Printing Office, Washington, D.C., Stock #024-005-00224-3, 1977.
2. Pringle, op. cit., p. 4.
3. William H. Harbaugh, *Power and Responsibility, The Life and Times of Theodore Roosevelt* (New York: Farrar, Straus, and Cudahy, 1961), p. 13.
4. Pringle, op. cit., p. 41.
5. John Kouwenhoven, *Columbia Historical Portrait of New York*. (Garden City, N. Y.: Doubleday, 1953), p. 380.
6. "Theodore Roosevelt Birthplace", op. cit.

7. Harbaugh, op. cit., pp. 7–8.
8. Ibid., pp. 15-16
9. Ibid., p. 20.
10. Ibid., p. 20.
11. Pringle, op. cit., p. 48.
12. Harbaugh, op. cit., p. 50.
13. Ibid., p. 51.
14. Ibid., p. 51.
15. Ibid., p. 47.
16. Ibid., p. 47.

Chapter 3 THE BELLE ON THE BICYCLE *(Pp. 15-27)*

1. Nicholas Roosevelt, *Theodore Roosevelt, The Man as I Knew Him* (New York: Dodd, Mead and Company, 1967), p. 25.
2. Harbaugh, op. cit., p. 68.
3. Ibid, p. 69.
4. James Brough, *Princess Alice* (Boston: Little, Brown & Company, 1975), p. 34.
5. Harbaugh, op. cit., p. 68.
6. Pringle, op. cit., p. 108.
7. Longworth, op. cit., p. 8.
8. Ibid., p. 8.
9. Harbaugh, op. cit., p. 69.
10. Theodore Roosevelt, *An Autobiography* (New York: The Macmillan Company, 1913), p. 7.
11. Longworth, op. cit., p. 13.
12. Hermann Hagedorn, *The Roosevelt Family of Sagamore Hill* (New York: The Macmillan Company, 1954).
13. Hapgood, David, "The Tax To End All Taxes," *American Heritage*, April, 1978.
14. Longworth, op. cit., p. 17.
15. Ibid.
16. Theodore Roosevelt, op. cit., pp. 168–203.
17. Hagedorn, op. cit., p. 70.
18. Ethel Roosevelt Derby interview.
19. Hagedorn, op. cit., p. 19.
20. Ibid., p. 21.
21. Ibid., p. 21.
22. Longworth, op. cit., p. 6.
23. Hagedorn, op. cit., p. 60.
24. Ibid, p. 26.
25. Longworth, op. cit., p. 155.
26. Nicholas Roosevelt, op. cit., p. 25.
27. Ernest Jones, M.D., *The Life and Work of Sigmund Freud* (New York: Basic Books, Inc., 1957), Vol. 3, p. 378.
28. Longworth, op. cit., p. 285.
29. Ibid., pp. 20–21.
30. Pringle, op. cit., pp. 181–195.
31. Ibid., p. 207.
32. Longworth, op. cit., p. 26.
33. Pringle, op. cit., p. 119.
34. Ibid., p. 222.
35. Frederick Lewis Allen, *The Big Change* (New York: Harper & Bros., 1957), p. 86.
36. Pringle, op. cit., p. 231.
37. Harbaugh, op. cit., p. 145.
38. Associated Press *Biographical Service*, July 1, 1957.

Chapter 4 THE WITCH IN THE WHITE HOUSE *(Pp. 29-46)*

1. *Current Biography*, 1943.

2. Charles Hurd, *The White House Story* (New York: Hawthorn Books, Inc., 1966), p. 132.
3. Melchiorre Grillo interview.
4. Harbaugh, op. cit., p. 146.
5. Derby interview.
6. Irwin Hoover, *42 Years in the White House* (Boston: Houghton Mifflin Company, 1934), p. 29.
7. Ibid., pp. 28–29.
8. Derby interview.
9. Longworth, op. cit., p. 59.
10. Derby interview.
11. Iphigene Ochs Sulzberger interview.
12. Ibid.
13. Ibid.
14. James Reston, *Sketches in the Sand* (New York: Alfred A. Knopf, 1967), p. 308.
15. Henry Brandon, "A Talk with an 83-Year-Old Enfant Terrible," *The New York Times Magazine*, August 6, 1967.
16. Nelson M. Blake, *American Heritage*, Volume VI, No. 2.
17. Nina S. Hyde, "Color It Blue," Washington *Post*, February 12, 1973.
18. New York *Sun*, January 19, 1906.
19. *Current Biography*, 1943.
20. Lash, op. cit., pp. 92–93.
21. New York *Sun*, December 11, 1905.
22. Ibid., May 7, 1903.
23. Special to the New York *World*, June 13, 1903.
24. Allen, op. cit., p. 122.
25. Harbaugh, op. cit., p. 232.
26. Ibid.
27. Ibid., p. 292.
28. *The New York Times*, March 2, 1905.
29. New York *Sun*, May 28, 1905.
30. Ibid.
31. New York *Sun*, July 5, 1905.
32. Hagedorn, op. cit., p. 265.
33. Ibid., p. 266.
34. Longworth, op. cit., p. 76.
35. Ibid., p. 77.
36. Ibid., pp. 78–79.
37. Michael Teague, "Alice in Plunderland," *Vogue* magazine, February 1, 1972.
38. New York *Sun*, August 18, 1905.
39. New York *Tribune*, August 19, 1905.
40. *The New York Times*, August 23, 1905.
41. Cassini, op. cit.
42. Teague. *Vogue*, February 1, 1972.
43. Ibid.
44. Hagedorn, op. cit., p. 267.
45. *The New York Times*, November 7, 1905.
46. New York *Sun*, December 16, 1905.
47. Chicago *Tribune*, December 20, 1905.

Chapter 5
THE MAID OF HONOR
(Pp. 47-52)

1. Longworth, op. cit., pp. 61–62.
2. Brandon, op. cit.
3. New York *Tribune*.
4. Derby interview.

5. Alfred Steinberg, *Mrs. R., The Life of Eleanor Roosevelt* (New York: G. P. Putnam's Sons, 1958), p. 89.
6. Lash, op. cit.
7. Steinberg, op. cit., p. 35.
8. Ibid, p. 35.
9. Lash, op. cit., p. 103.
10. Ibid, p. 138.
11. Associated Press *Biographical Summary*.
12. Lash, op. cit., p. 138.
13. Ibid., p. 140.
14. Ibid., p. 146.

Chapter 6
THE BRIDE
(Pp. 53-62)

1. Clara Longworth de Chambrun, *The Making of Nicholas Longworth* (New York: Roy Long & Richard R. Smith, Inc., 1933), p. 39.
2. New York *Sun*, December 14, 1905.
3. De Chambrun, op. cit.
4. New York *American*, January 22, 1906.
5. New York *Sun*, January 22, 1906.
6. Ibid.
7. *The New York Times*, February 10, 1906.
8. Ibid.
9. Ibid.
10. *The New York Times*, January 2, 1906.
11. There are many variations to these lines. Thaddeus Stevens was reputed to have made the comments. Simon Cameron also is credited with words similar in nature.
12. New York *Sun*, February 10, 1906.
13. Archie Butt, *The Letters of Archie Butt* (Garden City, N. Y.: Doubleday Page & Company, 1924), Vol. 1.
14. *Congressional Record*, February 17, 1906.
15. Washington *Star*, February 18, 1906.
16. New York *Sun*, February 18, 1906.
17. Derby interview.
18. World Wide Photos.
19. New York *Sun*, February 19, 1906.
20. Washington *Post*, February 21, 1906.
21. Longworth, op. cit., p. 116.

Chapter 7
THE MARRIED WOMAN
(Pp. 63-75)

1. Washington *Star*, March 4, 1906.
2. Derby interview.
3. Jean vanden Heuvel. "The Sharpest Wit in Washington," *Saturday Evening Post*, December, 1965.
4. Derby interview.
5. Cassini, op. cit.
6. Archie Butt, *Taft & Roosevelt, Intimate Letters of Archie Butt* (Garden City, N. Y.: Doubleday, Doran & Company, Inc., 1930), Vol. 1, p. 175.
7. London *Times*, June 16, 1906.

8. New York *Sun*, August 13, 1906.
9. Ibid.
10. Cincinnati *Enquirer*, August 17, 1906.
11. Ibid., August 18, 1906.
12. Ben Hayes, Columbus *Citizen*.
13. Derby interview.
14. Boston *American*, September 6, 1907.
15. Ibid.
16. Butt, *Letters*, Vol. 1.
17. Longworth, op. cit., p. 170.
18. Cincinnati *Enquirer*, October 9, 1907.
19. Harbaugh, op. cit.
20. Ibid.
21. Derby interview.
22. vanden Heuvel, op. cit.
23. Columbus *Journal*, June 21, 1908.
24. William Allen White, *The Autobiography of William Allen White* (New York: The Macmillan Company, 1946), p. 401.
25. Ibid.
26. Denver *Post*, 1908.
27. Longworth, op. cit., p. 156.
28. Mary Randolph, *Presidents and First Ladies* (New York: Appleton Century Company, 1936), p. 212.
29. Ibid.
30. Longworth, op. cit., p. 159.
31. Butt, *Letters*, Vol. 1, p. 379.
32. Ibid., p. 378.
33. Ibid.
34. William Walton, "Presidents She Has Known," The Washington *Post*, February 12, 1969.
35. Longworth, op. cit., p. 165.

Chapter 8
THE PARTY'S OVER
(Pp. 77-90)

1. Walton, op. cit.
2. Butt, *Letters*, p. 381.
3. Ibid., p. 257.
4. Ibid., p. 41.
5. Hoover, op. cit., p. 251.
6 Randolph, op. cit., p. 211.
7 Harbaugh, op. cit.
8. Butt, *Taft & Roosevelt*, Vol. II, p. 715.
9. Pringle, op. cit., p. 529.
10. New York *Sun*, April 3, 1911.
11. Boston *Globe*, May 8, 1911.
12. Butt, *Letters*. Vol. 1, p. 169.
13. Ibid.
14. Randolph, op. cit., p. 220.
15. Ibid.
16. Derby interview.
17. Ibid.
18. Butt, *Letters*. Vol. 2.
19. Ibid.
20. Pittsburgh *Press*, June 9, 1908.
21. Ibid.
22. Cincinnati *Enquirer*, July 5, 1908.
23. New York *Sun*, July 16, 1908.
24. Ruth Gordon, *Myself Among Others* (New York: Atheneum, 1971), p. 336.
25. Butt, *Letters*, Vol. 1, p. 143.
26. Ibid.
27. Boston *Record*, January 17, 1912.
28. Boston *American*, January, 1912.
29. Helen Hayes interview.
30. Butt, *Letters*, Vol. 1, Introduction, p. xxvii.

31. Cleveland *Plain Dealer,* April, 1912.
32. Longworth, op. cit., p. 186.
33. Pringle, op. cit.
34. Chicago *Press,* June, 1912.
35. Harbaugh, op. cit., p. 435.
36. Pringle, op. cit., p. 564.
37. White, op. cit., Introduction.
38. Derby interview.
39. Letter to William Allen White.
40. Harbaugh, op. cit., p. 445.
41. Longworth, op. cit., p. 211.
42. Associated Press, October 14, 1912.

Chapter 9
THE SWEET REVENGE
(Pp. 91-108)

1. Milwaukee *Journal,* October 15, 1912.
2. Pringle, op. cit., p. 569.
3. Ibid.
4. Derby interview.
5. Richard Harding Davis, New York *World,* October 30, 1912.
6. Milwaukee *Journal,* October 15, 1912.
7. Derby interview.
8. Harbaugh, op. cit.
9. Ishbel Ross, *Power with Grace, The Life Story of Mrs. Woodrow Wilson* (New York: G. P. Putnam's Sons, 1975).
10. New York *Sun,* August 25, 1916.
11. Cincinnati *Enquirer,* November 7, 1912.
12. *The New York Times,* November 7, 1912.
13. Cincinnati *Enquirer,* November 9, 1912.
14. Longworth, op. cit., p. 225.
15. Associated Press, April 15, 1913.
16. Ibid.
17. Simon Michael Bessie interview.
18. William Miller and Frances Spatz Leighton, *Fishbait* (Englewood Cliffs, N. J.: Prentice Hall, Inc., 1977), p. 103.
19. Derby interview.
20. Sally Quinn, "Alice Longworth At 90," Washington *Post,* February 12, 1974.
21. Inauguration speech, Washington *Post,* March 4, 1913.
22. Jonathan Daniels, *Washington Quadrille* (Garden City, N. Y.: Doubleday, 1968), p. 52.
23. Malcolm Moos and Stephen Hess, *Hats in the Ring* (New York: Random House, 1960), p. 27.
24. Derby interview.
25. Ibid.
26. Beatrice Kaufman and Joseph Hennessey, *The Letters of Alexander Woollcott* (New York: The Viking Press, 1944).
27. Harbaugh, op. cit., p. 465.
28. Ibid, p. 463.
29. Longworth, op. cit., p. 234.
30. Washington *Star,* December 29, 1914.
31. *American Heritage* magazine, August, 1964.
32. Jonathan Daniels, *The Time Between the Wars* (Garden City, N. Y. Doubleday, 1966).

33. Ibid.
34. Chicago *Tribune*, January 2, 1915.
35. New York *Sun*, January 11, 1915.
36. Cincinnati *Enquirer*, November 9, 1916.
37. Pringle, op. cit., p. 590.
38. Senator Borah was an "Irreconcilable," while Senator Lodge was a "Revisionist."
39. Derby interview.
40. White, *Autobiography*, p. 339.
41. New York *Tribune*, July 21, 1918.
42. Hagedorn, p. 414.
43. Ibid., p. 116.
44. Harbaugh, op. cit., p. 519.
45. Hagedorn, op. cit., p. 424.
46. Ibid.
47. Longworth, op. cit., p. 5.
48. Harbaugh, op. cit., p. 520.
49. *Congressional Record*, January 8, 1919.
50. Lash, op. cit., p. 231.
51. Irwin S. Cobb, *Exit Laughing* (Indianapolis: The Bobbs-Merrill Company, 1941), p. 282.
52. June Bingham, "Before the Colors Fade: Alice Roosevelt Longworth," *American Heritage*, February, 1969.
53. Ross, op. cit., p. 125.
54. Ibid, p. 126.
55. Ibid., p. 126.
56. Mike Wallace, *Biography*, Channel 11, New York City.
57. Pringle, op. cit., p. 602.
58. Daniels, *Washington Quadrille*, p. 174.
59. *Congressional Record*, February 4, 1920.
60. Mark Sullivan, *Our Times* (New York: Charles Scribner's Sons, 1926–1935), Volume VI.
61. Daniels, *The Time Between the Wars*, p. 27.
62. *Congressional Record*, March 19, 1920.
63. Ross, p. 213.

Chapter 10
THE DEUCES WILD
(Pp. 109-119)

1. Samuel Hopkins Adams, *Incredible Era* (Boston: Houghton Mifflin Company, 1939), p. 119.
2. Ibid., p. 163.
3. Thornton Wilder interview.
4. Adams, op. cit., p. 132.
5. Daniels, *The Time Between the Wars*, op. cit., p. 63.
6. Adams, op. cit., p. 163.
7. Adams, op. cit.
8. Derby interview.
9. *Newsweek*, May 5, 1965.
10. Sullivan, op. cit., Vol. VI.
11. Longworth, op. cit., p. 203.
12. Adams, op. cit., p. 112.
13. Ibid., pp. 18–19.
14. Associated Press *Biographical Service*.
15. Washington *Post*, March 10, 1921.
16. Associated Press *Biographical Service*.
17. Flora Miller interview.
18. Hagedorn, op. cit., p. 415.
19. Miller interview.
20. Ibid.
21. Longworth, op. cit., p. 314.
22. Longworth, op. cit., p. 61.

23. Adams, op. cit., pp. 7–8.
24. Daniels, *Times Between the Wars*, op. cit., p. 89.
25. Boston *American*, May 16, 1921.
26. Chicago Daily *News*, October 4, 1921.
27. Nan Britton, *The President's Daughter* (New York: Elizabeth Ann Guild, Inc., 1927).
28. Robinson, op. cit., p. 64.
29. Adams, op. cit., pp. 377–378.
30. Ibid., p. 379.
31. Longworth, op. cit., p. 325.

Chapter 11 THE CRADLE ROCKS *(Pp. 121-138)*

1. Adams, op. cit., p. 165.
2. Ibid., p. 167.
3. Daniels, *Time Between the Wars*, op. cit., p. 119.
4. William Allen White, *Puritan in Babylon* (New York: Macmillan, 1958), p. 177.
5. Daniels, op. cit., p. 65.
6. Derby interview.
7. Lillian Rogers Parks and Frances Spatz Leighton, *My Thirty Years Backstairs at the White House* (New York: Fleet Publishing Corp., 1961), p. 178.
8. Hoover, op. cit., p. 129.
9. Ishbel Ross, *Grace Coolidge and Her Era* (New York: Dodd, Mead & Co., 1962), p. 90.
10. Parks, op. cit., p. 176.
11. Randolph, op. cit., p. 87.
12. Cleveland *Plain Dealer*, June 13, 1924.
13. Chicago Daily *News*, November 9, 1925.
14. William Allen White, op. cit. preface, IXX.
15. Associated Press, November 1, 1924.
16. Ibid.
17. Chicago *Tribune*, November 25, 1924.
18. Ibid., February 15, 1925.
19. Associated Press, February 14, 1925.
20. *Congressional Record*, February 14, 1925.
21. Chicago *Tribune*, February 19, 1925.
22. Chicago *American*, February 21, 1925.
23. Chicago *Tribune*, February 21, 1925.
24. Ibid.
25. Ibid.
26. Washington *Star*, February 28, 1925.
27. Robert Morgenthau interview.
28. Washington *Post*, May 8, 1925.
29. Derby interview.
30. Ibid.
31. Alice and Ethel tell different stories regarding the division of the skins incident. In addition to poker, Parcheesi, and chess, Alice finally claimed to have paid for her share of the skins by check.
32. Allene Sumner, New York *Telegram*, March 11, 1927.

33. Ibid.
34. Ibid.
35. Chicago *Tribune*, May 4, 1926.
36. Drew Pearson and Robert S. Allen, *Washington Merry Go Round*. (New York: Horace Liveright, Inc., 1931), p. 130.
37. Ibid.
38. *Personality*, 1926.
39. Longworth, op. cit., p. 328.
40. Randolph, op. cit., pp. 56–60.
41. White, *Puritan in Babylon*, op. cit.
42. Walter Lippman, *The New York Times*.
43. Kansas City *Star*, June 13, 1928.
44. Uthai V. Wilcox, Brooklyn *Eagle*, February 26, 1928.
45. St. Louis *Post-Dispatch*, June 13, 1928.
46. Kansas City *Star*, June 14, 1928.
47. "Bad Luck for Longworth," *The New York Times*, June 15, 1928.

Chapter 12
THE DRY DIVERS
(Pp. 139-153)

1. White, *Autobiography*.
2. Columbus *Citizen*, June 17, 1928.
3. Randolph, op. cit., pp. 118–120.
4. Ibid.
5. Elsa Maxwell, *R. S. V. P.* (Boston: Little Brown & Company, 1954).
6. *The New York Times*, March 3, 1929.
7. *Congressional Record*, March 4, 1929.
8. *The New York Times*, October 24, 1929.
9. Columbus *Journal*, December 11, 1929.
10. Hoover, op. cit., p. 184.
11. Parks, op. cit., p. 219.
12. New York *Sun*, October 14, 1932.
13. *The New Yorker*, June 9, 1934.
14. Derby interview.
15. Douglas Gilbert, New York *World Telegram*, February 28, 1931.
16. Brandon, op. cit.
17. Mrs. Theodore Roosevelt, Jr., *Day Before Yesterday* (Garden City, N. Y.: Doubleday, 1959).
18. Chicago *Tribune*, February 18, 1931.
19. Ibid.
20. Longworth, op. cit.
21. Turner Catledge, *My Life and The Times* (New York: Harper & Row, 1963), p.68.
22. Allen, op. cit., p. 148.
23. Pringle, op. cit., p. 7.
24. Alexander Woollcott to George S. Kaufman (as told to author).
25. *The New York Times*, April 10, 1931.
26. Bingham, op. cit.
27. Butt, *Letters, Taft and Roosevelt*, Vol. II, p. 792.
28. *The New York Times*, April 10, 1931.
29. Brough, op. cit., p. 286.

30. Cincinnati *Enquirer*, June 17, 1931.
31. New York *Herald-Tribune*, April 16, 1930.
32. Archibald Roosevelt, Jr., interview.
33. *The New York Times*, October 14, 1932.
34. Chicago *American*, July 5, 1932.
35. Associated Press, August 30, 1932.
36. United Press *Paris Bureau*, October 26, 1932.
37. Derby interview.
38. Associated Press, October 29, 1932.
39. Associated Press, October 29, 1932.
40. *The New York Times*, November 8, 1932.
41. Brandon, op. cit.

Chapter 13
THE FEATHER DUSTER
(Pp. 155-170)

1. Kaufman and Hennessey, op. cit.
2. *The New York Times*, March 5, 1933.
3. Ibid.
4. New York *Sun*, June 8, 1933.
5. Dick Lee, "Capitol Stuff," New York *Daily News*, February 14, 1933.
6. Here again there are variations in the quotation. Often, it is quoted as "one-third mush and two-thirds Eleanor."
7. *World's Work*, August, 1950.
8. Washington *Post*, September, 1933.
9. Clifton Fadiman and Charles Van Doren, eds., *American Treasury, 1455-1955* (New York: Harper & Brothers, 1955) "Our Government and Politics," p. 336.
10. *Esquire* magazine, July 18, 1978
11. Derby interview.
12. Lewis Gannett, New York *Herald-Tribune*, October 28, 1933. Edward M. Kingsbury, *The New York Times*, November 5, 1933.
13. Margaret Leech Pulitzer interview.
14. *Esquire* magazine, July 18, 1978.
15. *Newsweek*, January 4, 1936.
16. Lee, op. cit., February 14, 1933.
17. Harry Anderson, McNaught Syndicate, November 28, 1938.
18. Ibid.
19. New York *Sun*, December 8, 1933.
20. Washington *Star*, February 13, 1934.
21. Brandon, op. cit.
22. New York *Sun*, May, 1933.
23. New York *Herald-Tribune*, February 1, 1934.
24. Cal Tinney, *Saturday Evening Post*, June 3, 1936.
25. *Newsweek*, January 4, 1936.
26. *Time* magazine, November 13, 1933.
27. de Liagre interview.
28. Alexander Woollcott to Noel Coward (as told to author in 1970).
29. George S. Kaufman (as told to author in 1958).

30. Kaufman, in one of his rare moments, may have borrowed a line from his fellow critic and playwright, Ashton Stevens of Chicago. Stevens, however, appears to have taken a version of "Vagrancy laws" from Edwin Booth, actor and founder of The Players Club in New York, who employed the words in terms of *his* profession.
31. Katherine Dayton and George S. Kaufman, *First Lady*. (New York: Dramatists' Play Service, 1935).
32. As told by George S. Kaufman.
33. Emporia *Gazette*, 1936.
34. Literary *Digest*, July, 1936.
35. Daniels, *Time Between the Wars*, op. cit. p. 275.
36. New York *Herald-Tribune*, June 26, 1936.
37. Ibid.
38. Philadelphia *Bulletin*, June 27, 1936.
39. Ibid.
40. Helen Reid interview.
41. vanden Heuvel, op. cit.

Chapter 14
THE DIRTY THIRTIES
(Pp. 171-177)

1. Howard Dietz interview.
2. Boston *Globe*, August 30, 1936.
3. Ibid.
4. Dietz interview.
5. Miss Shearer had been asked by her husband to remove her elaborate Juliet costume.
6. Dietz interview.
7. Ibid.
8. Boston *Globe*, op. cit.
9. Ibid.
10. Jack L. Warner interview.
11. Boston *Globe*.
12. Ibid.
13. Howard Dietz, *I Could Have Danced All Night* (New York: Quadrangle, 1974), p. 197.
14. Los Angeles *Journal*, August 17, 1936.
15. Ibid.
16. Daniels, *The Time Between the Wars*, p. 274.
17. Ibid., p. 274.
18. Ibid., p. 275.
19. Will Rogers op. cit. *Autobiography* (Boston: Houghton Mifflin Company, 1949).
20. Lash, op. cit., p. 103.
21. Steinberg, op. cit.
22. Edwin Hoyt, *Alexander Woollcott: The Man Who Came to Dinner* (New York: Abelard-Schuman, 1968) p. 303.
23. Ibid., p. 283.
24. Samuel Hopkins Adams, *A. Woollcott* (New York: Reynal and Hitchcock, 1945), p. 259.
25. Henry Brandon, *The New York Times*, August 6, 1967.
26. Ibid.
27. Brough, op. cit., p. 297.

28. Alice Roosevelt Longworth, Dorothy Thompson wrote, "has wit, spiced with malice and warmed by humor." M. K. Sanders, *Dorothy Thompson* (Boston: Houghton Mifflin Company, 1973).

Chapter 15 THE SECOND TIME AROUND *(Pp. 179-192)*

1. Philadelphia *Bulletin*, June 12, 1940.
2. Philadelphia *Inquirer*, June 14, 1940.
3. John Gunther, *Inside U.S.A.* (New York: Harper & Brothers, 1947), Chapter 26.
4. Ibid.
5. Ibid.
6. Newspapers disagree. She also is supposed to have used "the foot in his mouth" about Taft.
7. Gunther, op. cit., p. 434.
8. Ibid., p. 434.
9. Still, Robert A. Taft remained the only candidate whom Mrs. Longworth could back.
10. Daniels, *The Time Between the Wars*, p. 307.
11. Ibid., p. 309.
12. Gunther, op. cit., Chapter 19.
13. New York *Herald-Tribune*, June 16, 1940.
14. New York *Daily Mirror*, July 6, 1940.
15. Gunther, op. cit., p. 434.
16. *Biographical Service 1934*.
17. Lash, op. cit., p. 225.
18. Ibid., pp. 225–226.
19. Ibid., p. 226.
20. Henry Brandon, *The New York Times Magazine*, August 6, 1967, p. 12.
21. Ibid.
22. Ibid.
23. Ibid.
24. Gunther, op. cit.
25. Ibid.
26. Gunther, op. cit., pp. 433–434.
27. *Life* magazine, December 7, 1941.
28. Henry Morton Robinson, *Fantastic Interim* (New York: Harcourt, Brace & Company, 1943), p. 324.
29. Ibid. p. 325.
30. I. Leonard York interview.
31. *The Congressional Record*, December 8, 1941.
32. Linda Charlton, *The New York Times*, February 11, 1974.
33. Derby interview.
34. *The Medal of Honor* (Washington, D.C.: U.S. Government Printing Office, 1948), p. 289.
35. Marquis Childs interview.
36. Archibald Roosevelt, Jr., interview.
37. Remington Patterson interview.
38. Ibid.
39. *The New York Times*, August 7, 1944.
40. The Boston *Globe*, August 27, 1944.
41. John O'Connell, New York *Daily News*, October 8, 1944.

42. *The New York Times*, November 8, 1944.
43. Ibid.
44. New York *Post*, March, 1945.
45. Derby interview.
46. Jean vanden Heuvel, *Saturday Evening Post*, December, 1965.
47. Daniels, op. cit., p. 269.
48. Ibid., p. 266.
49. Henry Morton Robinson, op. cit., pp. 266–267.
50. John Hutchinson, "What Alice Said About John at Tea," The Boston *Globe*, August 17, 1975.
51. Ibid.

Chapter 16 THE SHADOWS *(Pp. 193-200)*

1. Joanna Sturm interview.
2. William Walton, "Presidents She Has Known," Washington *Post*, October 12, 1969.
3. John O'Connell, New York *Daily News*, November, 1948.
4. Ibid.
5. Paul Sann, *Fads, Follies and Delusions of the American People* (New York: Crown Publishers, Inc., 1967).
6. *Time*, 1974.
7. Bingham, op. cit.
8. Adlai Stevenson, *Papers* (Boston: Little Brown & Company, 1972–1977).
9. Denver *Post*, October 11, 1954.
10. Perle Mesta, *Perle* (New York: McGraw-Hill Book Company, 1960), p. 230.
11. Ibid.
12. Brough, op. cit., p. 310.
13. Barbara Howar, *Laughing All the Way* (New York: Stein and Day, 1973), p. 225.
14. Ibid.
15. Childs interview.
16. Associated Press *Biographical Service*, July 1, 1957.
17. Derby interview.
18. Mary Randolph, *Presidents and First Ladies*. (New York: D. Appleton-Century Company, Inc., 1936), p. 87.
19. *Current Biography*, 1975.
20. Franklin Delano Roosevelt Library, Hyde Park, New York.
21. Ibid.
22. Ibid.
23. Joseph Alsop, "Washington's Other Monument," *Vogue* magazine, February 1, 1966.

Chapter 17 THE LADY WHO SINGS FOR HER SUPPER *(Pp. 201-212)*

1. Selwa Roosevelt interview.
2. Ibid.
3. Ibid.
4. Childs interview.
5. Selwa Roosevelt interview.
6. Ibid.
7. Ibid.
8. Brandon, op. cit.
9. vanden Heuvel, op. cit.
10. Ibid.

11. Ibid.
12. Roger Stevens interview.
13. *Time* magazine, 1962.
14. Ibid.
15. Vanden Heuvel, op. cit.
16. *Time* magazine, 1974.
17. *Newsweek,* February 11,1974.
18. Lady Bird Johnson, *A White House Diary* (New York: Holt, Rinehart, & Winston, 1970).
19. Ibid.
20. Mary Gallagher, Cincinnati *Enquirer,* January 10, 1965.
21. Derby interview.
22. Johnson, op. cit.
23. *The New York Times* News Service, Washington, D.C., May 6, 1965.
24. Ibid.
25. Johnson, op. cit.
26. Eleni, Washington *Star,* August 4, 1968.
27. Ibid.
28. Jean Powell, Washington *Star,* September 24, 1969.
29. Nan Robertson, *The New York Times,* February, 1966.
30. Marcia Seligson, *The Eternal Bliss Machine* (New York: William Morrow & Company, 1973), p. 175.
31. Eleanor Howard interview.
32. Nan Robertson, *The New York Times,* October 28, 1967.
33. Ibid.
34. Nan Robertson, *The New York Times,* December 3, 1967.
35. Johnson, op. cit.
36. Derby interview.
37. Ibid.
38. Ibid.
39. Ibid.

Chapter 18 THE WOMAN OF ALL SEASONS *(Pp. 213-226)*

1. Los Angeles *Examiner,* April 4, 1962.
2. Myra MacPherson, Washington *Post,* January 31, 1969.
3. Ibid.
4. Susan Sheehan, *McCalls,* January, 1974.
5. Helen Thomas, *UPI,* February 12, 1974.
6. Howard interview.
7. Ibid.
8. *The New York Times,* July 8, 1970.
9. Special to *The New York Times,* July 8, 1970.
10. *Time* magazine, February 21, 1969.
11. *Newsweek,* February 11, 1974.
12. Maxine Cheshire, Washington *Post,* March 15, 1970.
13. Ibid.
14. Ibid.
15. Ibid.
16. Betty Beale, Washington *Post,* June 14, 1970.
17. Charlotte Curtis, *The New York Times,* March 17, 1971.
18. Ibid.
19. Washington *Post,* June 13, 1971.
20. Ibid.
21. Ibid.
22. Ibid.
23. *The New York Times,* June 29, 1971.
24. *The New York Times,* February 9, 1973.
25. Ibid.

26. Anonymous.
27. William Lee Miller, *Of Thee Nevertheless I Sing* (New York: Harcourt, Brace & Jovanovich, 1975), p. 180.
28. Anonymous.
29. David Bowes "In Search of Cincinnati," Cincinnati *Enquirer*, November 30, 1973.
30. Ibid.
31. Helen Thomas, Washington *Post*, February 11, 1974.
32. Ibid.
33. Jeanette Smyth, Washington *Post*, February 14, 1974.
34. Ibid.
35. Ibid.
36. Childs interview.
37. Ibid.
38. Linda Charlton, *The New York Times*, February 11, 1974.
39. Charlotte Curtis, *The Rich and Other Atrocities* (New York: Harper & Row, 1976), p. 143.
40. Linda Charlton, "Washington's Princess Alice At 90," *The New York Times*, February 11, 1974.
41. *Newsweek*, February 11, 1974.
42. Dorothy McCardle, "A Daughterly Vantage," Washington *Post*, August 10, 1974.
43. Ibid.
44. Susan Sheehan, *McCalls*, January 1974.
45. *Time* magazine, 1974.

Chapter 19
THE ALL-AMERICAN SUBSTITUTE
(Pp. 227-234)

1. *The New York Times*, October 3, 1974, "Mrs. Ford Cheered by Mail."
2. Letter from Jonathan Daniels to author.
3. Nina S. Hyde, Washington *Post*, February 13, 1976.
4. Ibid.
5. Ibid.
6. Ibid.
7. *Newsweek*, July, 1976.
8. *Time*, July, 1976.
9. Ibid.
10. Chicago *Daily News*, 1976.
11. Eleanor Adams, "With Washington's Grande Dame," Cincinnati *Enquirer*, January 2, 1977.
12. Associated Press, October 12, 1977.
13. Margaret McManus, Washington *Post*, April 4, 1977.

Chapter 20
THE GRANDE DAME
(Pp. 235-247)

1. *Time* magazine, February 18, 1974.
2. Ibid.
3. Ibid.
4. Sally Quinn, Washington *Post*, February 12, 1974.
5. Bessie interview.
6. Sally Quinn, op. cit.
7. Ibid.
8. Ibid.
9. *Newsweek*, May 18, 1970.
10. Susan Sheehan, *McCalls*, January, 1974.
11. Washington *Post*, 1976.
12. Ibid.

13. *Newsweek*, February 11, 1974.
14. Ibid.
15. Susan Sheehan, *McCalls*, January, 1974.
16. Ibid.
17. June Bingham, *American Heritage*, February, 1969.
18. Bessie interview.
19. Ibid.
20. Ibid.
21. Bowes, op. cit.
22. Susan Sheehan, *McCalls*, January, 1974.
23. Ibid.
24. Ibid.
25. David Bowes, op. cit.
26. Washington *Post*, September 30, 1975.
27. Myra MacPherson, "Alice Longworth At 85," Washington *Post*, February 12, 1969.
28. Sally Quinn, Washington *Post*, February 12, 1974.
29. *The New York Times*, November 27, 1972.
30. Ann Hard, Chicago *Tribune*, 1924.
31. *Time* magazine, December 18, 1973.
32. Ibid.
33. Howard interview.
34. Charlotte Curtis interview.
35. Ibid.
36. Curtis, op. cit., pp. 87–97.
37. Ibid.
38. Ibid.
39. Ibid.
40. Washington *Star*, August, 1966.
41. Ibid.
42. Jim Mann, Washington *Post*, August 7, 1972.
43. Ibid.
44. Betty Beale, "Alice Longworth Enthusiastic 86," Washington *Post*, June 14, 1970.
45. Longworth, op. cit., p. 335.
46. Chicago *Daily News*.
47. Susan Sheehan, *McCalls*, January, 1974.
48. Jean vanden Heuvel, *Saturday Evening Post*, December, 1965.

Chapter 21
THE LAST WALTZ
(Pp. 249-252)

1. United States Marine Corps, Historical Branch, Washington, D. C.
2. Bowes, op. cit.
3. Myra MacPherson, Washington *Post*, February 12, 1969.
4. Derby interview.

□ *BIBLIOGRAPHY*

Adams, Eleanor, "Tea with Washington's Grande Dame," Cincinnati *Enquirer*, January 2, 1977.

Adams, Samuel Hopkins, *A. Woollcott*. New York: Reynal and Hitchcock, 1945.

———, *Incredible Era, The Life and Times of Warren Gamaliel Harding*, Boston: Houghton Mifflin Company, 1939.

Allen, Fredrick Lewis, *The Big Change*. New York: Harper & Brothers Publishers, 1952.

Alsop, Joseph, "Washington's Other Monument," *Vogue*, February 1, 1966.

Arne, Sigrid, "'Princess' Alice in Minority Role," *AP Feature Service*, March 21, 1941.

Barrymore, Ethel, *Memories, An Autobiography*. New York: Harper Brothers, 1955.

Beale, Betty, "Alice Longworth Enthusiastic 86," Washington *Post*, June 14, 1970.

Beebe, Lucius, *The Big Spenders*. New York: Doubleday, 1966.

Berg, A. Scott, *Editor of Genius*. New York: Thomas Congdon Books/ Dutton, 1978.

———, "The Elusive Man Who Was America's Greatest Literary Editor," *Esquire*, July 18, 1978.

Bingham, June, "Before the Colors Fade: Alice Roosevelt Longworth," *American Heritage*, February, 1969.

Blake, Nelson Manfred, "Ambassadors to the Court of Theodore Roosevelt," *American Heritage*, February, 1956.

Bowes, David, "In Search of Cincinnati," Cincinnati *Enquirer*, November 30, 1973.

Braden, Tom, "Some Rules for the Newcomers," Washington *Post*, December 25, 1976.

Brandon, Henry, "A Talk with an 83-Year-Old Enfant Terrible," *The New York Times Magazine*, August 6, 1967.

Britton, Nan, *The President's Daughter*, New York: Elizabeth Ann Guild, Inc., 1927.

Brough, James, *Princess Alice*. Boston: Little Brown & Company, 1975.

Brown, John Mason, editor, and the editors of the Ladies' Home Journal, *The Ladies' Home Journal Treasury*. New York: Simon and Schuster, Inc., 1956.

Bugbee, Emma, "Mrs. Alice Longworth Wins Dollar at a Political Interview," New York *Herald-Tribune*, June 8, 1936.
Butt, Archie, *Taft & Roosevelt, Intimate Letters of Archie Butt*. Vols. I and II, Garden City, N.Y.: Doubleday, Doran & Company, Inc., 1930.
———, *The Letters of Archie Butt*, edited by Lawrence F. Abbott. Garden City, N.Y.: Doubleday Page & Company, 1924.
Butterfield, Roger, *The American Past*. New York: Simon & Schuster, 1947.
Byrnes, James F., *Speaking Frankly*. New York: Harper & Bros., 1947.

Cassini, Countess Marguerite, *Never a Dull Moment, The Memoirs of Countess Cassini*. New York: Harper & Bros., 1956.
Catledge, Turner, *My Life and The Times*. New York: Harper & Row, 1963.
Chamberlin, Anne, "Malice in Wonderland," Washington *Post*, April 6, 1975.
Chambrun, Clara Longworth de, *The Making of Nicholas Longworth*. New York: Roy Long & Richard R. Smith, Inc., 1933.
Charlton, Linda, "Harriman, 82, Honored," *The New York Times*, May 16, 1974.
———, "Washington's 'Princess Alice' at 90; A Tidy Old Age," *The New York Times*, February 11, 1974.
Cheshire, Maxine, "Alice Roosevelt Longworth and Bob Hope at Tea," Washington *Post*, March 15, 1970.
Cobb, Irvin S., *Exit Laughing*. Indianapolis: The Bobbs-Merrill Company, 1941.
Curtis, Charlotte, *The Rich and Other Atrocities*. New York: Harper & Row, 1976.

Daniels, Jonathan, *The Time Between the Wars*. Garden City, N.Y.: Doubleday, 1966.
———, *Washington Quadrille*. Garden City, N.Y.: Doubleday, 1968.
Daniels, Josephus, *The Life of Woodrow Wilson*. Chicago: The John C. Winston Company, 1924.
Dayton, Katharine, and George S. Kaufman, *First Lady*. New York: Dramatists Play Service, 1935.
De Young, Ruth, "Party Rivalry as Dissolved by Women Leaders," Chicago *Tribune*, June 21, 1936.
Dietz, Howard, *Dancing in the Dark*. New York: Quadrangle, 1974.
Douglas, Harvey, "Dry Dinner Was 'Wet Blanket,'" Brooklyn *Eagle*, October 27, 1933.

Edwards, Willard, "Senator Johnson Rips Attack as 'Vile and Indecent,'" Chicago *Tribune*, July 17, 1946.

Eisenhower, Julie Nixon, "Teddy Roosevelt's Daughter at 90." *Saturday Evening Post*, March, 1974.
Eisenhower, Milton, *The President Is Calling*. Garden City N.Y.: Doubleday, 1974.
Eleni, "Alice Longworth's Signature at the Top," Washington *Star*, August 4, 1968.

Frazier, Sir James George, *The Golden Bough*. New York: Macmillan Company, 1951.
Freidel, Frank, *The Presidents of the United States*. White House Historical Association, with the cooperation of the National Geographic Society, 1975.

Gallagher, Mary, "President Writes of Theodore Roosevelt," Cincinnati *Enquirer* Bureau, January 10, 1965.
Gannett, Lewis, "Books and Things," New York *Herald-Tribune*, October 28, 1933.
Gatewood, Willard B., *Theodore Roosevelt and the Art of Controversy*. Baton Rouge: Louisiana State University Press, 1970.
George, Alexander L., and Juliette L. George, *Woodrow Wilson and Colonel House*. New York: John Day Co., 1956.
Gezycka (Patterson), Eleanor, *Glass Houses*. New York: Minton, Balch & Company, 1926.
Gilbert, Clinton Wallace, *Behind the Mirrors, The Psychology of Disintegration at Washington*. New York: G. P. Putnam's Sons, 1922.
Gilbert, Douglas, "Capital Climbers Fear Her 'Big Stick,'" New York *World-Telegram*, February 28, 1931.
Gilman, Mildred, "We Photograph Alice," *The New Yorker*, June 9, 1934.
Gordon, Ruth, *Myself Among Others*. New York: Atheneum, 1971.
Gunther, John, *Inside U.S.A.* New York: Harper & Brothers, 1947.
———, *Roosevelt in Retrospect*. New York: Harper & Brothers, 1950.

Hagedorn, Hermann, *The Roosevelt Family of Sagamore Hill*. New York: Macmillan, 1954.
———, *Roosevelt in the Bad Lands*. Boston: Houghton Mifflin, 1930.
Hale, Henry, "Washington Memoirs," New York *Telegram*, January 21, 1930.
Hapgood, David, "The Tax to End All Taxes," *American Heritage*, April, 1978.
Harbaugh, William Henry, *Power and Responsibility: The Life and Times of Theodore Roosevelt*. New York: Farrar, Straus and Cudahy, 1961.
Hard, Anne, "People You Read About, Alice Roosevelt Longworth," Chicago *Tribune*, January 28, 1925.

Harrington, John Walker, "World Wonders," New York *Herald-Tribune*, February 22, 1925.

Hayes, Ben, "That Was Columbus," Columbus *Citizen*, September 9, 1956.

———, "The Flankers," Columbus *Citizen*, January 26, 1976.

Hemphill, Essex C., "Personalities," Washington *Post*, October 13, 1977.

Herrick, Genevieve Forbes, "Mrs. Longworth Reveals Threat to Seize Paulina," Chicago *Tribune*, March 24, 1932.

Hoover, Irwin Hood, *Forty-Two Years in the White House*. Boston: Houghton Mifflin Company, 1934.

Howar, Barbara, *Laughing All the Way*. New York: Stein & Day, 1973.

Howland, Harold Jacobs, *Theodore Roosevelt and His Times; a Chronicle of the Progressive Movement*. New Haven, Conn: Yale University Press, 1921.

Hoyt, Edwin P., *Alexander Woollcott: The Man Who Came to Dinner*. New York: Abelard-Schuman, 1968.

Hurd, Charles, *The White House Story*. New York: Hawthorn Books, Inc., 1966.

Hutchinson, John, "What Alice Said About John at Tea," Boston *Globe*, August 17, 1975.

Hyde, Nina S., "Alice's Birthday," Washington *Post*, February 13, 1976.

———, "Color It Blue," Washington *Post*, February 12, 1973.

James, Marquis, *Mr. Garner of Texas*. Indianapolis: The Bobbs-Merrill Company, 1939.

——— (*Quid*), "Princess Alice," *The New Yorker*, February 28, 1925.

Johnson, Lady Bird, *A White House Diary*. New York: Holt, Rinehart & Winston, 1970.

Jones, Ernest, M.D., *The Life and Works of Sigmund Freud*. Vol. 3. New York: Basic Books, Inc., 1957.

Kaufman, Beatrice, and Joseph Hennessey, editors, *The Letters of Alexander Woollcott*. New York: The Viking Press, 1944.

Kay, Virginia, "The Toughest Tea Leaves: Alice Roosevelt Longworth," Washington *Post*, January 26, 1969.

Kelly, Frank K., *The Fight for the White House*. New York: Thomas Y. Crowell Company, 1961.

Kottmeir, Jane, "Princess Alice Recalls the President's Table," Washington *Star*, March 11, 1958.

Kouwenhoven, John A., *The Columbia Historical Portrait of New York*. Garden City, N. Y.: Doubleday, 1953.

Krock, Arthur, "In the Nation," *The New York Times*, April 2, 1937.

Lash, Joseph P., *Eleanor and Franklin*. New York: W. W. Norton & Company, Inc., 1971.

———, *Eleanor: The Years Alone*. New York: W. W. Norton & Company, 1972.

Lee, Dick, "Capital Stuff," New York *Daily News*, August 8, 1935.

Lewis, Fulton, "Washington Sideshow," Boston *American*, November 21, 1933.

Longworth, Alice Roosevelt, *Crowded Hours, Reminiscences of Alice Roosevelt Longworth*. New York: Charles Scribner's Sons, 1933.

Longworth, Alice, "Landon Platform Wire Peak," New York *Herald Tribune*, June 12, 1936.

———, "New Deal's Confidence," New York *Herald-Tribune*, June 21, 1936.

———, "Robinson Wore Delegate's Patience Thin," New York *Herald-Tribune*, June 25, 1936.

———, "Roosevelt's Speech Is the Proof," New York *Herald-Tribune*, June 11, 1936.

Longworth, Alice Roosevelt, and Theodore Roosevelt, Jr., *The Desk Drawer Anthology, Poems for the American People*. Garden City, N. Y.: Garden City Publishing Company, Inc., 1937.

Lyons, Eugene, *Herbert Hoover, a Biography*. Garden City, N. Y.: Doubleday, 1964.

McCardle, Dorothy, "A Daughterly Vantage," Washington *Post*, August 10, 1974.

McManus, Margaret, "Alice Roosevelt Longworth at 93," New York *Post*, April 4, 1977.

———, "Princess Alice Still Reigns in D.C.," Chicago *Daily News*, March 27, 1977.

MacPherson, Myra, "Alice Longworth at 85," Washington *Post*, February 12, 1969.

———, "It Was All Very Cozy," Washington *Post*, January 31, 1969.

Mallon, Winifred, "She Sponsors No Causes," *Personality*, October, 1928.

Mann, Jim, "Alice Longworth Has Day in Court," Washington *Post*, August 7, 1972.

Maxwell, Elsa, *R.S.V.P., Elsa Maxwell's Own Story*. Boston: Little Brown & Company, 1954.

Means, Gaston Bullock, *The Strange Death of President Harding*, as told to May Dixon Thacker. New York: Guild Publishing Corporation, 1930.

The Medal of Honor of the United States Army. Washington, D.C.: U. S. Government Printing Office, 1948.

Mesta, Perle, with Robert Cahn, *Perle, My Story*. New York: McGraw Hill Book Company, Inc., 1960.

Miller, William Lee, *Of Thee Nevertheless I Sing*. New York: Harcourt, Brace, Jovanovich, 1975.
Miller, William, and Frances Spatz Leighton, *Fishbait*. Englewood Cliffs, New Jersey: Prentice-Hall, Inc., 1977.
Moore, William, "About Women in Washington," Chicago *Tribune* Press Service, December 24, 1960.
Moos, Malcolm, and Stephen Hess, *Hats in the Ring, The Making of Presidential Candidates*. New York: Random House, 1960.

O'Donnell, John, "Capitol Stuff," New York *Daily News*, November 8, 1948.

Pakenham, Mary, "About Women in Washington," Chicago *Tribune* Press Service, June 13, 1964.
Parks, Lillian Rogers, and Frances Spatz Leighton, *My Thirty Years Backstairs at the White House*. New York: Fleet Publishing Corp., 1961.
Peak, Mayme Ober, "Princess Alice's Baby, a Welcome Valentine," New York *World*, February 22, 1925.
———"Alice and Paulina in Hollywood," Boston *Globe*, August 30, 1936.
Pearson, Drew, and Robert S. Allen, *Washington Merry-Go-Round*. New York: Horace Liveright, Inc., 1931.
Powell, Jean, "Old Hat–New Hat," Washington *Star*, September 24, 1969.
Pringle, Henry F., *Theodore Roosevelt: A Biography*. New York: Blue Ribbon Books, Inc., 1931.

Quinn, Sally, "Alice Longworth At 90," Washington *Post*, February 12, 1974.
———, "America's Princess Alice," *The Cincinnati Enquirer Magazine*, March 17, 1974.

Randolph, Mary, *Presidents and First Ladies*. New York: D. Appleton-Century Company, Inc., 1936.
Rankin, Colonel Robert H., *Uniforms of the Marines*. New York: G. P. Putnam's Sons, 1970.
Reasoner, Harry, and Mike Wallace, *60 Minutes*. Vol. 1, No. 15, April 22, 1969.
Reston, James, *Sketches in the Sand*. New York: Alfred A. Knopf, 1967.
Robertson, Nan, "First Family," *The New York Times*, December 3, 1967.
———, "3 White House Brides Look Back to Their Weddings," *The New York Times*, January 2, 1966.
Robinson, Henry Morton, *Fantastic Interim*. New York: Harcourt, Brace & Company, 1943.

Rogers, Agnes, and Fredrick Lewis Allen, *I Remember Distinctly*. New York: Harper & Bros., 1947.

Rogers, Will, *Autobiography*, edited by Donald Day. Boston: Houghton Mifflin Company, 1949.

———, *Sanity Is Where You Find It*, selected and edited by Donald Day. Boston: Houghton Mifflin Company, 1955.

Roosevelt, Archibald B., Jr., "The Ghost of Sagamore Hill," *American Heritage*, April, 1970.

Roosevelt, Eleanor, *This I Remember*. New York: Harper & Bros., 1949.

Roosevelt, James, with Bill Libby, *My Parents, A Different View*. Chicago: Playboy Press, 1976.

Roosevelt, Nicholas, *A Front Row Seat*. Norman, Okla.: University of Oklahoma Press, 1953.

———, *Theodore Roosevelt, The Man As I Knew Him*. New York: Dodd, Mead, and Company, 1967.

Roosevelt, Theodore, *All in the Family*. New York: G. P. Putnam's Sons, 1929.

———, *An Autobiography*. New York: The Macmillan Company, 1913.

———, *Letters to His Children*. New York: Charles Scribner's Sons, 1938.

Roosevelt, Mrs. Theodore, Jr., *Day Before Yesterday*. Garden City, N.Y.: Doubleday, 1959.

Ross, Ishbel, *Power with Grace, the Life Story of Mrs. Woodrow Wilson*. New York: G. P. Putnam's Sons, 1975.

———, *Grace Coolidge and Her Era*. New York: Dodd, Mead & Company, 1962.

Sanders, Marion K., *Dorothy Thompson, a Legend in Her Time*. Boston: Houghton Mifflin Company, 1973.

Sann, Paul, *Fads, Follies, and Delusions of the American People*. New York: Crown Publishers, Inc., 1967.

Schlesinger, Arthur, Jr., *A Thousand Days*. Boston: Houghton Mifflin Company, 1965.

Schriftgiesser, Karl, *This Was Normalcy*. Boston: Little, Brown and Company, 1948.

Seligson, Marcia, *The Eternal Bliss Machine*. New York: William Morrow & Company, 1973.

Sevareid, Eric, Morley Safer and Mike Wallace, *60 Minutes*, Vol. VI, No. 6, February 17, 1974.

Sheehan, Susan, "Washington's Wittiest Woman." *McCalls*, January, 1974.

Smith, Helena Huntington, "Alice in the Looking Glass," *World's Work*, August, 1950.

Smyth, Jeanette, "Of Gifts and Criticism," Washington *Post*, February 14, 1974.

Sorensen, Theodore, *Kennedy*. New York: Harper & Row, 1965.

Steinberg, Alfred, *Mrs. R., The Life of Eleanor Roosevelt*. New York: G. P. Putnam's Sons, 1958.

Stevenson, Adlai, *Papers of Adlai Stevenson*. Walter Johnson, editor. Vols. I–VII. Boston: Little, Brown and Company, 1972–1977.

Strayer, Martha, "Paulina Lives the Simple Life," *United News*, July 14, 1927.

Sugrub, Thomas, *Starling of the White House*. New York: Simon & Schuster, 1946.

Sullivan, Mark, *Our Times*. Vols. I–VI, New York: Charles Scribner's Sons, 1926–1935.

———, "They Painted a Picture Contrary to Fact," New York *Tribune*, July 1, 1936.

Sumner, Allene, "Washington Leader and Daughter," New York *Telegram*, March 11, 1927.

Teague, Michael, "Alice in Plunderland," *Vogue*, February 1, 1972.

Tharp, Louise Hall, *Mrs. Jack: A Biography of Isabella Stewart Gardner*. Boston: Little, Brown and Company, 1965.

Thayer, William Roscoe, *Theodore Roosevelt: An Intimate Biography*. Boston: Houghton Mifflin, 1919.

Thomas, Helen, "Alice Longworth 90 Today," UPI, February 12, 1974.

Tinney, Cal, "The Political Parade," *The Saturday Evening Post*, June 3, 1936.

Tully, Grace G., *F.D.R. My Boss*. New York: Charles Scribner's Sons, 1949.

vanden Heuvel, Jean, "The Sharpest Wit in Washington," *The Saturday Evening Post*, December, 1965.

Walton, William, "Presidents She Has Known," Washington *Post*, February 12, 1969.

Watters, Susan, "Eye . . . Eye . . . Eye," *Women's Wear Daily*, August 1, 1977.

Weinraub, Bernard, "Southerners Feeling New Influence in the Capital," *The New York Times*, January 19, 1977.

Wesser, Robert F., *Charles Evans Hughes Politics and Reform in New York 1905-1910*. Ithaca, N.Y.: Cornell University Press, 1967.

Wharton, Don, editor, *The Roosevelt Omnibus*. New York: Alfred A. Knopf, 1934.

White, William Allen, *The Autobiography of William Allen White*. New York: The Macmillan Company, 1946.

———, *Calvin Coolidge, The Man Who Is President*. New York: The Macmillan Company, 1925.

———, *A Puritan In Babylon, The Story of Calvin Coolidge*. New York: The Macmillan Company, 1958.

Wicker, Tom, *JFK-LBJ: The Influence of Personality on Politics*. New York: William Morrow & Company, Inc., 1968.

Wilcox, Uthai Vincent, "Will 'Princess Alice' Return?," Brooklyn *Eagle*, February 26, 1928.

Wilhelm, Donald, *Theodore Roosevelt as an Undergraduate*. Boston: John W. Luce, 1910.

Wilson, Edith Bolling Galt, *My Memoir*. Indianapolis: The Bobbs-Merrill Company, 1938.

Wister, Owen, *Roosevelt, The Story of a Friendship*. New York: The Macmillan Company, 1930.

Wolfe, Sheila, "A Republican Roosevelt Recalls Past," Chicago *Tribune*, July 24, 1960.

Wootten, James, "Washington Journal, Where History Is Made and Repeats Itself," *The New York Times*, June 6, 1978.

□ Index